THE
Gluten-Free
VEGETARIAN KITCHEN

**Delicious and Nutritious
Wheat-Free, Gluten-Free Dishes**

DONNA KLEIN

HOME

A HOME BOOK
Published by the Penguin Group
Penguin Group (USA) Inc.
375 Hudson Street, New York, New York 10014, USA
Penguin Group (Canada), 90 Eglinton Avenue East, Suite 700, Toronto, Ontario M4P 2Y3, Canada
(a division of Pearson Penguin Canada Inc.)
Penguin Books Ltd., 80 Strand, London WC2R 0RL, England
Penguin Group Ireland, 25 St. Stephen's Green, Dublin 2, Ireland (a division of Penguin Books Ltd.)
Penguin Group (Australia), 250 Camberwell Road, Camberwell, Victoria 3124, Australia
(a division of Pearson Australia Group Pty. Ltd.)
Penguin Books India Pvt. Ltd., 11 Community Centre, Panchsheel Park, New Delhi—110 017, India
Penguin Group (NZ), 67 Apollo Drive, Mairangi Bay, Auckland 1311, New Zealand
(a division of Pearson New Zealand Ltd.)
Penguin Books (South Africa) (Pty.) Ltd., 24 Sturdee Avenue, Rosebank, Johannesburg 2196,
South Africa

Penguin Books Ltd., Registered Offices: 80 Strand, London WC2R 0RL, England

While the author has made every effort to provide accurate telephone numbers and Internet addresses at the time of publication, neither the publisher nor the author assumes any responsibility for errors, or for changes that occur after publication. Further, the publisher does not have any control over and does not assume any responsibility for author or third-party websites or their content.

First edition: April 2007

Library of Congress Cataloging-in-Publication Data

Klein, Donna (Donna M.)
    The gluten-free vegetarian kitchen : delicious and nutritious wheat-free, gluten-free dishes / Donna Klein.
        p. cm.
    Includes index.
    ISBN 978-1-55788-510-4
    1. Gluten-free diet—Recipes. 2. Wheat-free diet—Recipes. 3. Vegetarian cookery. I. Title.
    RM237.86.K64 2007
    641.5'.638—dc22

                                                                                        2006039841

PRINTED IN THE UNITED STATES OF AMERICA

10   9   8   7   6   5   4   3   2   1

PUBLISHER'S NOTE: The recipes contained in this book are to be followed exactly as written. The publisher is not responsible for your specific health or allergy needs that may require medical supervision. The publisher is not responsible for any adverse reactions to the recipes contained in this book.

Most Home Books are available at special quantity discounts for bulk purchases for sales promotions, premiums, fund-raising, or educational use. Special books, or book excerpts, can also be created to fit specific needs. For details, write: Special Markets, The Berkley Publishing Group, 375 Hudson Street, New York, New York 10014.

For Marilynn Klein,
who inspired this book

THE GLUTEN-FREE
VEGETARIAN KITCHEN

ACKNOWLEDGMENTS

As always, my sincere thanks go to the following people: To my literary agent, Linda Konner, for her ongoing encouragement and support. To John Duff, and to Jeanette Egan, for her first-rate editing skills. To my daughters, Emma and Sarah, for taking time from their busy lives to help with the huge task of recipe testing and retesting.

And to my dog, Trevor, for continuing to be my most enthusiastic taste tester and giving me cause to pause for a walk each day.

CONTENTS

The Gluten-Free Vegetarian Diet

Life without wheat can be a challenge for anyone. For vegetarians with celiac disease who must avoid all foods containing gluten—wheat, rye, barley, and usually oats, due to cross contamination—following a gluten-free diet can initially be downright daunting. No more bread, pasta, pizza, cookies, cake, pie, pancakes, muffins, biscuits—the list seems endless. But fortunately, man (or woman) does not live by bread alone. Indeed, there is a wide variety of vegetarian foods that do not contain gluten—all fresh fruits and vegetables, eggs and most dairy products, beans and legumes, nuts and seeds, rice and corn, and the list goes on. With the inclusion of breads and pastas made with special gluten-free flours, vegetarians with gluten intolerance can eat a well-balanced diet. The aim of this cookbook is to provide you with a selection of healthy, mouthwatering recipes that will leave you feeling full and satisfied.

What Is Gluten?

Gluten is a mixture of proteins found in many cereal grains. It is gluten that gives bread its elasticity and cakes their spring. For those with celiac disease, the destructive gluten is the protein found in wheat, barley, malt, and rye. Oats are gluten-free but are not recommended due to the high risk of cross contamination. There are glutens in rice and other grains such as millet, but these are not harmful.

What Is Celiac Disease?

Celiac disease is a genetic, autoimmune disease that interferes with the digestion process. When a celiac person eats foods that contain gluten, the immune system responds by damaging the villi in the small intestine. Villi are thousands of tiny hairlike protuberances that line the small intestine. Their job in the digestion process is to extract nutrients from foods that we eat. The villi in a person who has celiac disease have dropped off or have become flattened. The villi are unable to absorb the needed nutrients for the body, causing malabsorption of food and nutrients.

Wheat Allergy Versus Celiac Disease

It is generally believed that celiac disease is more common than wheat allergy, which can often mask the former. A wheat allergy occurs when the body perceives wheat as an invader and produces an allergic reaction. Symptoms of wheat allergy can include eczema, sneezing, increased acne, and abdominal bloating. It is more likely to affect young children and can be temporary. Celiac disease, on the other hand, is due to a permanent intolerance to gluten.

The main effect of celiac disease is damage to the small intestine and the resulting malabsorption of nutrients. Symptoms can include diarrhea, vomiting, cramping, nausea, weight loss, anemia, chronic tiredness, osteoporosis, thyroid problems, diabetes, stunted growth, and infertility.

GLUTEN-FREE FOODS

- Beans and lentils, dried
- Buckwheat and buckwheat groats
- Cellophane/mung bean-thread noodles
- Corn and cornmeal
- Dairy products—milk, cream, butter, plain yogurt, most cheeses
- Eggs
- Fruits and vegetables
- Herbs, fresh, and plain/individual spices without additives
- Jams, jellies, and preserves
- Millet
- Nuts and seeds (plain, without seasoning)
- Oils and shortening
- Quinoa
- Rice and wild rice
- Rice bran
- Rice noodles
- Soy and tofu
- Sugar, honey, maple syrup
- Vinegars (except malt vinegar)
- Yeast, fresh and dried

NATURALLY GLUTEN-FREE ALTERNATIVES

- Arrowroot
- Buckwheat flour
- Carob flour
- Chestnut flour
- Chickpea flour
- Cornmeal and polenta
- Cornstarch
- Linseed
- Millet flour
- Potato flour
- Potato starch flour
- Quinoa flour
- Rice flour
- Sorghum
- Soy flour
- Tapioca flour
- Xanthan gum

CEREALS AND GRAINS THAT CONTAIN GLUTEN

- Barley
- Oats (due to cross contamination)
- Rye
- Spelt
- Wheat

FOODS AND DRINKS THAT MAY CONTAIN HIDDEN GLUTEN

- Baking powder
- Beer, lager, stout, and ale (all made from grains; some gluten-free beers, made using sorghum, are available)
- Bouillon cubes and powder, canned broths and soups (especially creamed varieties)
- Breakfast beverages (such as Ovaltine)
- Cereals (including cornflakes)
- Cheese
    - Cream, cottage, and ricotta cheeses (especially reduced-fat varieties)
    - Shredded and crumbled (may contain flour to prevent clumping)
    - Veined ones such as Roquefort and blue cheese
- Cheese spreads and processed cheese foods
- Chili powder (may contain flour to prevent clumping)
- Coffees, flavored
- Corn tortillas (may also contain regular flour)
- Curry powder (may contain flour to prevent clumping)
- Dried fruits (may be dusted with flour to prevent sticking)
- French fries, frozen (flour may be present to keep them white)
- Ice cream and frozen yogurt (especially reduced-fat varieties)
- Margarine and butter spreads
- Mustard powder
- Mustard, prepared, and ketchup
- Nondairy creamers
- Nuts, dry-roasted
- Potato and tortilla chips, flavored
- Salad dressing and mayonnaise (especially reduced-fat or light varieties)
- Seasoning mixes
- Sour cream (especially reduced-fat or light varieties)
- Soy sauce
- Vanilla extract and other flavorings
- White pepper (may be bulked with flour)
- Yogurt (all reduced-fat or flavored varieties)

Note: The labels on all processed and canned foods should be checked carefully before each use. What might be safe one time might not be the next, as manufacturers tend to change their products periodically. When in doubt, contact the manufacturer directly.

FOODS OR FOOD LABELING TERMS THAT INDICATE OR SUGGEST THE PRESENCE OF GLUTEN

- Barley starch
- Binder
- Bran
- Bulgur, cracked wheat
- Caramel color
- Cereal
- Cereal protein
- Couscous
- Dextrin (unless derived from corn, potato, arrowroot, rice, or tapioca)
- Durum wheat
- Emulsifier
- Fillers
- Flour (unless made with pure rice flour, corn flour, potato flour, or soy flour)
- Hydrolyzed plant protein (HPP) (unless derived from soy or corn)
- Hydrolyzed vegetable protein (HVP) (unless derived from soy or corn)
- Kamut
- Malt or malt flavoring (unless derived from corn)
- Malted barley
- Maltodextrin (unless derived from cornstarch or potato starch)
- Maltose
- Modified food starch (unless arrowroot, corn, potato, or tapioca)
- Monoglycerides or diglycerides
- Natural flavoring
- Oat bran
- Oat germ
- Oatmeal (rolled oats)
- Pearl barley
- Rusk
- Rye starch
- Semolina
- Stabilizer
- Thickener
- Triticale (a grain crossbred from wheat and rye)
- Vegetable gum, except carob bean gum, locust bean gum, cellulose gum, guar gum, gum arabic, gum aracia, gum tragacanth, or xanthan gum
- Vegetable starch

- Wheat bran
- Wheat germ
- Wheat meal

- Wheat rusk
- Wheat starch

About the Ingredients

While most of the ingredients called for in this book's recipes are readily found in traditional supermarkets, baking without wheat requires alternative flours. For the recipes in this book, you will need the following gluten-free flours and grains, available in health food stores and some well-stocked supermarkets.

Arrowroot powder

Buckwheat flour

Chickpea flour

Cornmeal and polenta (or coarse-ground yellow cornmeal)

Cornstarch

Potato starch flour (not to be confused with potato flour, which is much heavier)

Rice flours, brown, sweet, and white

Tapioca flour

Xanthan gum, a white powder that helps these alternative flours bind together

To make the savory dishes, some of the more exotic ingredients you will need are the following, which are available in Asian markets, health food stores, and in the international section of some well-stocked supermarkets.

Arborio rice

Cellophane noodles or mung bean-thread noodles

Flat rice noodles or rice sticks

Kasha or toasted buckwheat groats

Rice paper wraps/skins

Rice vermicelli (thin rice noodles)

Sticky rice (or glutinous, sushi-style rice)

Tamari sauce, a wheat-free soy sauce essential for preparing Asian-style recipes

About the Nutritional Numbers

All the nutritional analyses in this book were compiled using MasterCook Deluxe 4.06 Software, from SierraHome. However, as certain ingredients (tapioca flour, xanthan gum) were unknown to the software at the time of compilation, substitutes of equivalent caloric and nutritional value were used in their place.

All the recipes using broth have been analyzed using low-sodium canned vegetable broth. All the recipes using rinsed and drained canned beans have been analyzed using freshly cooked dried beans. Unless salt is listed as a measured ingredient (versus to taste, with no preceding suggested measurement) in the recipe, or unless otherwise indicated, no salt has been included in the analysis; this applies to other seasonings (black pepper, cayenne, etc.) as well. None of the recipes' optional ingredients, unless otherwise indicated, have been included in the nutritional analyses. If there is a choice of two or more ingredients in a recipe (for example, light cream or whole milk), the first ingredient has been used in the analysis. Likewise, if there is a choice in the amounts of a particular ingredient in a recipe (for example, 1 to 2 tablespoons peanuts), the first amount has been used in the analysis. If there is a range in the number of servings a recipe yields (for example, 4 to 6 servings), the analysis has been based on the first amount.

What Do the Terms Mean?

Dairy-free: Contains eggs but no dairy products.

Egg-free: Contains dairy products but no eggs.

Lacto-ovo: Contains dairy products and eggs.

Vegan: No animal products, including honey, are used in the recipe, although optional ingredients may contain dairy products or eggs.

Low-carb: Contains 20 grams or less of carbohydrates per serving.

Appetizers

Appetizers offer a multitude of possibilities for vegetarians on a gluten-free diet. Crudités, plain nuts, most cheeses, olives, unflavored corn and potato chips, salsas, guacamole, and hummus are already on the approved list. Nachos made with fresh cheese (not processed cheese food) are usually another safe choice; however, be aware that if the cheese was purchased already shredded, it may have been treated with wheat flour to prevent caking.

Other popular hors d'oeuvres, such as deviled eggs and creamy dips, are generally okay if prepared with mayonnaise or sour cream free of damaging glutens in the form of stabilizers or food starches. For cracker alternatives, slices of jicama, daikon radish, or cucumber are tasty options. Artichoke bottoms, artichoke hearts, mushrooms, Belgian endive leaves, celery, and cherry tomatoes with the pulp scooped out with a melon baller are natural receptacles for fillings.

If you really want the crunch of a grain, rice crackers and mini rice cakes, available in most major supermarkets, are excellent vehicles for all sorts of spreads, dips, and assorted toppings, such as Vegetarian Paté and Wasabi Cream Cheese Spread. As always, check the labels carefully—some rice crackers, for example, are cut with wheat flour or are flavored with soy sauce, which contains wheat.

Toasted Tex-Mex Almonds

vegan|low-carb

MAKES 12 SERVINGS

The king of nuts, the almond, has the highest protein content of any nut, and is a valuable source of magnesium, potassium, phosphorous, and calcium.

3 tablespoons canola oil

3 cups whole blanched almonds

1½ teaspoons garlic salt, or to taste

1 teaspoon gluten-free chili powder

1 teaspoon ground cumin

Pinch cayenne pepper, or to taste (optional)

In a large nonstick skillet, heat the oil over medium heat. Add the almonds and cook, stirring, until golden, about 5 minutes. Remove from heat and, using a slotted spoon, immediately transfer to a heatproof bowl. Add the remaining ingredients to the nuts, tossing well to thoroughly combine. Transfer to a baking sheet and spread out in a single layer. Let cool to room temperature before serving. (Cooled nuts can be stored at room temperature in an airtight container for a few weeks.)

PER SERVING (¼ CUP)

Calories 210 | Protein 7g | Total Fat 19g |
Sat. Fat 2g | Cholesterol 0mg | Carbohydrate 7g |
Dietary Fiber 3g | Sodium 262mg

Artichoke Bottoms with Lemon-Pesto Mayonnaise

lacto-ovo|low-carb

MAKES ABOUT 12 APPETIZERS

Serve these tasty filled artichoke bottoms as finger food, or atop a bed of spinach leaves as an elegant first course.

6 tablespoons gluten-free light mayonnaise

2 tablespoons gluten-free prepared pesto sauce, or Classic Pesto Sauce (page 82)

½ teaspoon fresh lemon juice

¼ teaspoon lemon-pepper seasoning

2 (14-ounce) cans artichokes bottoms (about 12 pieces), drained

About 12 grape tomatoes (optional)

In a small bowl, mix together the mayonnaise, pesto, lemon juice, and lemon-pepper seasoning until thoroughly blended. Fill the artichoke bottoms with equal amounts (about 2 teaspoons) of the pesto mixture. Garnish each with a grape tomato (if using), and serve at room temperature. Alternatively, cover and refrigerate for a minimum of 3 hours, or up to 1 day, and serve chilled.

PER SERVING

Calories 48 | Protein 2g | Total Fat 3g |
Sat. Fat 1g | Cholesterol 3mg | Carbohydrate 5g |
Dietary Fiber 2g | Sodium 321mg

Cook's Tip

Pesto is an Italian sauce made from basil, pine nuts, Parmesan cheese, garlic, and olive oil. The refrigerated prepared variety tastes closest to homemade and is highly recommended for use in all of this book's recipes where pesto is required and you don't have time to prepare your own. Plastic containers of prepared pesto can be found in the refrigerated sections of most well-stocked supermarkets, next to the fresh pastas. Refrigerated reduced-fat pesto can be used in lieu of the regular pesto, if desired. Most of the leading brands are gluten-free, but always check labels carefully, as manufacturers tend to change ingredients periodically.

Cubed gluten-free bread, gluten-free rice crackers, and/or tortilla chips, to serve

Preheat the oven to 350F (175C). Lightly oil a shallow 2- or 2½-quart casserole and set aside.

In a medium bowl, mix all the ingredients until well combined. Spread evenly in the prepared casserole and bake for 25 to 30 minutes, or until bubbly and lightly browned. Serve at once, with the suggested foods for dipping.

PER SERVING

Calories 192 | Protein 9g | Total Fat 12g |
Sat. Fat 4g | Cholesterol 25mg | Carbohydrate 15g |
Dietary Fiber 4g | Sodium 527mg

Hot Artichoke and Spinach Dip

lacto-ovo|low-carb

MAKES 6 TO 8 SERVINGS

This is delicious served with cubed Italian-Style Herbed Cheese Bread (page 76) for dipping.

- 1 (14-ounce) can quartered artichoke hearts, drained and chopped
- ½ (10-ounce) package frozen chopped spinach, defrosted and squeezed dry
- 1 cup gluten-free light mayonnaise
- 1 cup gluten-free freshly grated Parmesan cheese

Grilled Bell Peppers with Herbed Goat Cheese

egg-free|low-carb

MAKES 8 SERVINGS

Grilling peppers brings out their natural sweetness. Plain cream cheese can replace the goat cheese, if desired.

- 2 large bell peppers (about 8 ounces each), preferably 1 green and 1 red, cored and quartered
- 1 tablespoon extra-virgin olive oil
- Salt and freshly ground black pepper, to taste

4 ounces spreadable creamy goat cheese

2 tablespoons chopped fresh basil, oregano, sage, and/or thyme leaves

Prepare a medium-hot charcoal or gas grill, or preheat a broiler. Position the grill rack or oven rack 4 to 6 inches from the heat source. If broiling, lightly oil a large baking sheet and set aside. Or place a stovetop grilling pan with grids over medium-high heat.

Rub the skins of the pepper pieces evenly with the olive oil. Sprinkle the insides with salt and pepper. Grill the peppers until browned and tender but not overly soft, 3 to 4 minutes per side. Transfer to a platter and spread evenly with the cheese. Sprinkle evenly with the herbs and serve at once.

PER SERVING

Calories 92 | Protein 5g | Total Fat 7g | Sat. Fat 4g | Cholesterol 15mg | Carbohydrate 3g | Dietary Fiber 1g | Sodium 50mg

Celery Stuffed
with Hazelnut Cream Cheese

egg-free|low-carb

MAKES 8 SERVINGS

Hazelnuts lend a touch of sophistication to the conventional combo of celery and cream cheese.

1 (8-ounce) package gluten-free Neufchâtel cream cheese, at room temperature

2 tablespoons gluten-free light sour cream

¼ cup chopped hazelnuts

1 bunch celery, separated into stalks, washed, trimmed, and strings removed, if desired

In a small bowl, mix together the cream cheese and sour cream until thoroughly blended. Stir in the hazelnuts. Spread the cream cheese mixture evenly into celery stalks. Cut into bite-size pieces. Transfer to a platter, cover, and refrigerate for 1 hour, or overnight. Serve chilled.

PER SERVING

Calories 108 | Protein 4g | Total Fat 9g | Sat. Fat 4g | Cholesterol 22mg | Carbohydrate 3g | Dietary Fiber 1g | Sodium 149mg

VARIATIONS: *To make* Celery Stuffed with Walnut-Raisin Cream Cheese: *Replace the hazelnuts with 2 tablespoons chopped walnuts and 2 tablespoons raisins.*

To make Celery Stuffed with Raisin Cream Cheese: *Replace the hazelnuts with raisins.*

Cheese Balls with Herbes de Provence, Basil, and Pine Nuts

egg-free|low-carb

MAKES 24 APPETIZERS

These petite cheese balls are the Mediterranean's answer to the giant Cheddar balls of the fifties. Herbes de Provence is a specific combination of herbs generally consisting of rosemary, thyme, basil, savory, chervil, mint, marjoram, oregano and, sometimes, lavender. If you don't have some on hand, use a combination of dried rosemary and thyme.

> 8 ounces (2 cups) gluten-free crumbled mild goat cheese, at room temperature
> 6 ounces (1½ cups) gluten-free crumbled feta cheese, at room temperature
> ½ teaspoon herbes de Provence
> Freshly ground black pepper, to taste
> ¼ cup finely chopped fresh basil
> ¼ cup finely ground pine nuts
> ¼ cup extra-virgin olive oil

In a small bowl, mix together the cheeses, herbes de Provence, and pepper until thoroughly combined. Form the mixture into about 24 small balls, about 1½ inches in diameter. (At this point, the cheese balls can be refrigerated in a covered container for a few days before continuing with the recipe.)

Place the basil and pine nuts on separate small plates. Roll the cheese balls in the basil to cover, then in the pine nuts to cover. Transfer to a serving platter, cover loosely with plastic wrap, and refrigerate for 1 to 4 hours. Drizzle evenly with the oil and serve chilled or at room temperature, accompanied by toothpicks.

PER CHEESE BALL

Calories 90 | Protein 4g | Total Fat 8g | Sat. Fat 4g | Cholesterol 16mg | Carbohydrate 1g | Dietary Fiber 0g | Sodium 112mg

Classic Cheese Fondue

egg-free|low-carb

MAKES 8 TO 12 SERVINGS

This traditional Swiss fondue is hearty enough to be enjoyed as a cold-weather supper for six. It's also delicious with cubed Italian-Style Herbed Cheese Bread (page 76) for dipping.

> ½ pound Swiss Emmentaler cheese, shredded
> ½ pound Gruyère cheese, shredded
> 1 tablespoon cornstarch
> 1 clove garlic, halved
> 1½ cups dry white wine, such as sauvignon blanc
> 2 teaspoons fresh lemon juice
> 1 tablespoon kirsch (cherry brandy)
> Steamed broccoli and/or cauliflower florets; boiled new red potatoes, halved; roasted button mushrooms; steamed asparagus spears; cherry or grape tomatoes; sliced apples; sliced pears; seedless grapes; or other dippers

ℰPlace the cheeses in a medium bowl and add the cornstarch, tossing well to combine. Set aside.

Rub the halved garlic all over the inside of a large heavy-bottomed saucepan. Add the wine and lemon juice and bring to a simmer over medium heat. Gradually add the cheese mixture, stirring constantly in a zigzag motion until smooth and melted. Add the kirsch and cook, stirring constantly, for 5 minutes. Transfer to a fondue pot and serve at once, with a selection of vegetables and fruits for dipping.

PER SERVING (WITHOUT VEGETABLES/FRUITS)

Calories 264 | Protein 17g | Total Fat 17g | Sat. Fat 10g | Cholesterol 57mg | Carbohydrate 3g | Dietary Fiber 0g | Sodium 172mg

---

Mexican Deviled Eggs

dairy-free|low-carb

MAKES 12 APPETIZERS

For a less spicy yet equally tasty appetizer, use half the amount of jalapeño chili or omit entirely, if desired.

6 eggs
3 tablespoons gluten-free light mayonnaise
1 tablespoon gluten-free chili sauce

1 tablespoon finely chopped fresh cilantro or flat-leaf parsley
1 teaspoon finely chopped jalapeño chili
1 teaspoon ground cumin
Salt and freshly ground black pepper, to taste
Sweet paprika (optional)

ℰPlace the eggs in a medium saucepan and cover with water. Bring to a boil over medium-high heat. Remove from the heat, cover, and let stand for 22 minutes. Meanwhile, prepare a bowl of ice water. Plunge the eggs into the ice water and let cool completely.

Carefully peel the shells from the eggs. Cut the eggs in half and remove the yolks from the whites. Place the yolks in a small bowl and add the remaining ingredients; mash with a fork until well blended.

Fill the egg whites with the yolk mixture. Sprinkle lightly with paprika (if using). Refrigerate, covered, for a minimum of 1 hour or up to 2 days, and serve chilled.

PER SERVING

Calories 47 | Protein 3g | Total Fat 3g | Sat. Fat 1g | Cholesterol 108mg | Carbohydrate 1g | Dietary Fiber 0g | Sodium 51mg

VARIATIONS: *To make* Chipotle Deviled Eggs: *Omit the jalapeño chili and replace the regular chili sauce with chipotle sauce, a spicy, smoky-sweet condiment made from smoked jalapeño chilies, which can be found in specialty stores and some well-stocked supermarkets.*

To make Pesto Deviled Eggs: *Replace the chili*

sauce with gluten-free prepared pesto sauce or Classic Pesto Sauce (page 82), and omit the cilantro, chili, and cumin. Garnish with a halved cherry or grape tomato (if using). For a more pronounced pesto flavor, add an extra ½ tablespoon pesto sauce to the recipe.

To make Wasabi Deviled Eggs: *Replace both the gluten-free mayonnaise and the chili sauce with gluten-free wasabi mayonnaise, made with Japanese horseradish, distinctive for its vivid green color and head-rushing heat. It can be purchased at specialty stores and many well-stocked supermarkets. Omit the cilantro, chili, and cumin. For less fiery deviled eggs, use 3 tablespoons of the wasabi mayonnaise and 1 tablespoon of the plain gluten-free mayonnaise.*

Cook's Tip

If the eggs are at room temperature before hard-cooking, let them steep for 1 minute less.

Cucumber Rounds with Pesto and Goat Cheese

egg-free|low-carb

MAKES 4 SERVINGS

Pesto and goat cheese are a delectable duo. Select a thick cucumber, about eight inches in length, for this recipe.

12 cucumber rounds, about ½ inch thick

¼ cup creamy goat cheese

2 tablespoons gluten-free prepared pesto sauce, or Classic Pesto Sauce (page 82)

6 grape tomatoes, halved

Cover each cucumber round with 1 teaspoon of the cheese, leaving cucumber edges uncovered. Spread ½ teaspoon of the pesto over the cheese, leaving the edges of the cheese exposed. Top each with a grape tomato half. Serve at once.

PER SERVING

Calories 116 | Protein 5g | Total Fat 7g |
Sat. Fat 3g | Cholesterol 10mg | Carbohydrate 11g |
Dietary Fiber 3g | Sodium 94mg

Country French Eggplant Caviar

vegan|low-carb

MAKES 8 SERVINGS

This French Provençal specialty tastes even better the next day.

2 eggplants (about 1 pound each), cut in half lengthwise

¼ cup fresh lemon juice

2 tablespoons extra-virgin olive oil

4 large cloves garlic, finely chopped

½ teaspoon sugar

½ teaspoon salt, preferably the coarse variety, or to taste

¼ teaspoon freshly ground black pepper

⅛ teaspoon cayenne pepper, or to taste (optional)

Assorted raw vegetables, for dipping

❧Preheat the oven to 400F (205C). Lightly grease a large baking sheet.

Place the eggplant halves, cut sides down, on the prepared baking sheet. Bake for 40 minutes, or until softened and collapsed. Drain on paper towels. When cool enough to handle, remove skin and cut flesh into chunks.

Transfer the eggplant to a food processor fitted with the knife blade and add the remaining ingredients, except the raw vegetables; process until smooth. Transfer to a serving bowl, cover, and refrigerate for a minimum of 2 hours, or up to 3 days. Serve chilled, with raw vegetables for dipping.

PER SERVING (WITHOUT RAW VEGETABLES)

Calories 59 | Protein 1g | Total Fat 4g |
Sat. Fat 1g | Cholesterol 0mg | Carbohydrate 7g |
Dietary Fiber 2g | Sodium 136mg

Endive Leaves
with Goat Cheese and Walnuts

egg-free|low-carb

MAKES 16 TO 18 APPETIZERS

Easy yet elegant aptly describes this delicious appetizer, perfect for the winter holidays, when Belgian endive is in season.

8 ounces creamy goat cheese

3 tablespoons gluten-free Neufchâtel cream cheese, at room temperature

1 tablespoon skim milk

Freshly ground black pepper, to taste

2 heads Belgian endive, separated into leaves (about 18)

¼ cup chopped walnuts

❧In a small bowl, mix together the goat cheese, cream cheese, milk, and pepper until almost smooth. Fill the leaves with equal amounts of the cheese mixture. Sprinkle with equal amounts of the walnuts. Serve at once.

PER SERVING

Calories 91 | Protein 6g | Total Fat 7g |
Sat. Fat 4g | Cholesterol 16mg | Carbohydrate 3g |
Dietary Fiber 2g | Sodium 69mg

Guacamole
with Spicy Jicama Chips

vegan|low-carb

MAKE 6 SERVINGS

If you are watching your carbs, this recipe is for you. Thin slices of seedless cucumber can be substituted for the jicama chips, if desired.

> 2 ripe Haas avocados, peeled, halved, and pitted
> 1 medium plum tomato (about 2 ounces), finely chopped
> 2 tablespoons finely chopped onion
> 1 tablespoon fresh lime juice
> 1 tablespoon finely chopped fresh cilantro
> ½ small jalapeño chili, finely chopped (optional)
> Salt and freshly ground black pepper, to taste
> Spicy Jicama Chips (recipe opposite)

❧ In a medium bowl, coarsely mash the avocado with a fork. Add the tomato, onion, lime juice, cilantro, jalapeño chili (if using), salt, and pepper; stir well to combine. (If not using immediately, cover with plastic wrap and refrigerate for up to 8 hours, but no longer.) Serve with the jicama chips.

PER SERVING (WITHOUT THE JICAMA CHIPS)

Calories 113 | Protein 2g | Total Fat 10g |
Sat. Fat 2g | Cholesterol 0mg | Carbohydrate 6g |
Dietary Fiber 2g | Sodium 8mg

SPICY JICAMA CHIPS

vegan|low-carb

MAKES 6 SERVINGS

Jicama, a large bulbous root vegetable often called the Mexican potato, is available in most major supermarkets. Delicious raw, its crunchy texture makes it an ideal substitute for high-carb tortilla chips as a dipper for guacamole and other dips or spreads.

> 1 large jicama (about 12 ounces), peeled, quartered, and thinly sliced
> Juice of 2 limes (about ⅓ cup)
> ½ tablespoon gluten-free chili powder
> Salt and freshly ground black pepper, to taste

❧ Place the jicama slices in a shallow nonreactive dish and add the lime juice; toss well to coat. Let marinate for 30 minutes at room temperature, tossing a few times.

To serve, drain the jicama chips and transfer to a serving platter; sprinkle with the chili powder, salt, and pepper. Serve with dips.

PER SERVING

Calories 31 | Protein 1g | Total Fat 0g |
Sat. Fat 0g | Cholesterol 0mg | Carbohydrate 7g |
Dietary Fiber 3g | Sodium 9mg

Black and Green Olive Tapenade

vegan|low-carb

MAKES 8 TO 12 SERVINGS

You can store this classic French Provençal appetizer up to three days in the refrigerator before returning it to room temperature and serving. It makes a particularly delicious topping for the Parmesan Cheese Crisps (page 20) or filling for artichoke bottoms.

- **1 cup pitted kalamata or other good-quality black olives**
- **¼ cup pitted green olives, with or without pimento**
- **¼ cup extra-virgin olive oil**
- **2 tablespoons drained capers**
- **1 tablespoon fresh lemon juice**
- **2 large cloves garlic, finely chopped**
- **Freshly ground black pepper, to taste**

❦ Place all the ingredients in a food processor fitted with the knife blade; process until a coarse-textured paste forms. Serve at room temperature.

PER SERVING

Calories 145 | Protein 0g | Total Fat 15g | Sat. Fat 1g | Cholesterol 0mg | Carbohydrate 3g | Dietary Fiber 0g | Sodium 528mg

Mushrooms Stuffed with Herbed Cream Cheese

egg-free|low-carb

MAKES 12 APPETIZERS

Everyone loves no-cook appetizers for easy entertaining, especially when they're delicious to boot. As of this writing, both Rondelé and Boursin brands of spreadable cheeses are gluten-free.

- **12 medium mushroom caps, washed and patted dry with paper towels**
- **¼ cup gluten-free spreadable herbed cream cheese, such as Rondelé or Boursin**

❦ Fill each mushroom cap with 1 teaspoon of the cheese. Cover and refrigerate for 30 minutes or overnight, and serve chilled.

PER SERVING

Calories 25 | Protein 1g | Total Fat 2g | Sat. Fat 1g | Cholesterol 5mg | Carbohydrate 2g | Dietary Fiber 0g | Sodium 15mg

Parmesan Cheese Crisps

egg-free|low-carb

MAKES ABOUT 16 PIECES

Serve these tasty gluten-free, low-carb alternatives to crackers with any number of toppings. They are especially delicious with Country French Eggplant Caviar (page 16) or Black and Green Olive Tapenade (page 19). Or serve alone, using the optional garlic salt and/or paprika, if desired.

**1 cup gluten-free freshly shredded Parmesan
  cheese (do not use grated)**
Garlic salt, to taste (optional)
Sweet paprika, to taste (optional)

Preheat oven to 325F (165C). Line a large baking sheet with parchment paper or grease a light-colored large baking sheet.

Place rounded teaspoons of the cheese on the prepared baking sheet, leaving about 2 inches between each mound. Lightly flatten with your fingertips to a circle about 1½ inches in diameter. Sprinkle lightly with garlic salt (if using), then paprika (if using). Bake for about 3 minutes, or until the cheese just begins to melt and turns a very light brown, taking care not to overcook.

When the cheese crisps are still quite warm yet cool enough to touch, using your fingers, pull off from the parchment and transfer to a wire rack to cool completely. (If a greased baking sheet was used, remove with a spatula.)

Store completely cooled cheese crisps in airtight containers for up to 2 days.

PER CHEESE CRISP

Calories 21 | Protein 2g | Total Fat 1g |
Sat. Fat 1g | Cholesterol 4mg | Carbohydrate 0g |
Dietary Fiber 0g | Sodium 85mg

Crispy Potato Skins

vegan|low-carb

MAKES 4 SERVINGS

Who says you have to give up potatoes if you are watching your carbs? At a mere ten grams of carbohydrates per serving, these crispy and golden skins taste even better and contain more fiber than French fries!

4 large russet potatoes, about 8 ounces each
2 tablespoons canola oil or butter, melted
Garlic salt, to taste
Freshly ground black pepper, to taste
**8 tablespoons (½ cup) gluten-free shredded
  cheddar or Parmesan cheese (optional)**
Sweet paprika, to taste
**Gluten-free sour cream, chives, salsa, and/or
  guacamole (optional)**

Preheat the oven to 425F (220C). Prick the potatoes with the tines of a fork and bake for 1 hour, or until tender. Remove from the oven and set aside to cool slightly. (Do not turn off oven.)

When the potatoes are cool enough to handle, cut in half lengthwise and, using a spoon, scoop out and discard most of the flesh, so that the shells are about ¼ inch in thickness. Transfer to an ungreased baking sheet and brush the insides and outsides evenly with the oil. Sprinkle the insides lightly with garlic salt and pepper. Sprinkle the insides of each shell with 1 tablespoon of the cheese (if using), and dust lightly with paprika. Bake for 10 to 12 minutes, or until shells are crisp and golden. Cut each potato skin in half and serve at once, with the optional toppings passed separately, if desired.

PER SERVING (4 PIECES)

Calories 104 | Protein 2g | Total Fat 7g | Sat. Fat 1g | Cholesterol 0g | Carbohydrate 10g | Dietary Fiber 3g | Sodium 8mg

VARIATION: *To make* Tex-Mex Potato Skins: *Omit the canola oil or butter and use the optional cheese, increasing the amount to ¾ cup. Sprinkle with the paprika, and then top with equal amounts of diced mild green chilies, drained, from 1 (4-ounce) can. Bake and serve as directed.*

Warm New Potatoes with Fresh Herb Dip
egg-free
MAKES 4 TO 6 SERVINGS

For a lower-carb, yet equally delicious version, substitute lightly steamed cauliflower florets for the potatoes.

24 to 28 tiny new potatoes, 1 to 1½ inches in diameter, scrubbed and left whole
Fresh Herb Dip (page 22)

In a medium stockpot, bring the potatoes and enough salted water to cover to a boil over high heat. Reduce the heat and boil gently until the potatoes are just tender, 10 to 15 minutes, depending on size. Drain.

To serve, place the dip in a small bowl in the center of a warmed serving platter and surround with the hot potatoes. Spear the potatoes with wooden picks and serve at once.

PER SERVING

Calories 131 | Protein 5g | Total Fat 1g | Sat. Fat 0g | Cholesterol 4mg | Carbohydrate 26g | Dietary Fiber 2g | Sodium 35mg

FRESH HERB DIP

egg-free|low-carb

MAKES ABOUT 1 CUP

Use this dip with countless raw, cooked, or lightly steamed fresh veggies.

½ cup gluten-free low-fat sour cream

½ cup gluten-free low-fat plain yogurt

2 tablespoons finely chopped fresh chives

1 tablespoon finely chopped fresh parsley

1 teaspoon finely chopped fresh thyme

½ teaspoon onion powder

Salt and freshly ground black pepper, to taste

❧ Mix all ingredients in a small bowl until thoroughly blended. Cover and refrigerate for 2 to 24 hours, and serve chilled.

PER SERVING (ABOUT ¼ CUP)

Calories 30 | Protein 2g | Total Fat 1g |
Sat. Fat 0g | Cholesterol 4mg | Carbohydrate 3g |
Dietary Fiber 0g | Sodium 28mg

Rice Paper Spring Rolls

vegan|low-carb

MAKES 15 ROLLS

Feel free to vary the filling of these popular Vietnamese-style spring rolls. I often omit the bean sprouts and replace them with additional shredded carrots, or use cashews instead of the peanuts.

About 1¼ ounces dry rice vermicelli (thin rice noodles), or enough to yield about 1 cup cooked

1 cup shredded carrots

1 cup shredded romaine or other lettuce

½ cup bean sprouts

2 scallions (white and green parts), very thinly sliced

15 leaves fresh basil, shredded

15 leaves fresh mint, shredded

2 tablespoons chopped fresh cilantro

¼ cup unsalted peanuts, crushed

1 teaspoon grated fresh ginger

1 tablespoon tamari sauce, plus additional for dipping (optional)

½ tablespoon fresh lime juice

1 teaspoon toasted (dark) sesame oil

15 (8-inch) round rice papers

Peanut Sauce (recipe opposite, optional)

❧ Bring a large pot of water to a boil over high heat. Remove from heat and stir in the rice noodles. Let stand for 10 minutes, stirring occasionally, or until soft and opaque. Drain and rinse under cold water for 30 seconds; drain well again. Cut into 1-inch lengths and transfer to a large bowl.

Add all the remaining ingredients, except the rice papers and sauce, to the noodles and mix well.

Prepare a bowl of warm water large enough to dip the rice papers. Working with one at a time, dip the rice paper in the warm water until it begins to soften, 8 to 10 seconds. Transfer to a flat work surface. Working quickly, put about ¼ cup filling on each wrapper. Fold the bottom of the wrapper up over the filling, and then fold each side toward the center. Roll from the bottom to the top of each roll, as tightly as you can without ripping the wrapper. Wrap in plastic wrap to keep from drying out. Repeat with remaining papers and filling. Serve at room temperature, with Peanut Sauce (if using). Alternatively, refrigerate for a minimum of 2 hours, or overnight, and serve chilled or return to room temperature.

PER SERVING (PER ROLL, WITHOUT PEANUT SAUCE OR ADDITIONAL TAMARI SAUCE)
Calories 56 | Protein 2g | Total Fat 2g |
Sat. Fat 0g | Cholesterol 0mg | Carbohydrate 9g |
Dietary Fiber 1g | Sodium 117mg

Cook's Tip

Rice papers, or spring roll skins, are available in Asian and gourmet markets, health food stores, and some well-stocked supermarkets. To avoid tearing as you roll them, make sure the filling ingredients are in small uniform pieces and that you only use about ¼ cup filling per each 8-inch round rice paper. Rice papers also make terrific "wraps" for sandwiches in place of flour tortillas.

PEANUT SAUCE
vegan|low-carb
MAKES ABOUT 1¼ CUPS SAUCE

This is also delicious tossed with rice noodles or cellophane noodles.

- ½ **cup warm water**
- ½ **tablespoon sugar**
- ½ **cup crunchy or smooth peanut butter**
- 1½ **tablespoons tamari sauce**
- 1 **tablespoon light coconut milk (optional)**
- 1 **tablespoon fresh lime juice**
- 1 **teaspoon Chinese chili paste (optional)**
- 1 **large clove garlic, finely chopped**

In a small bowl, combine the warm water and sugar, stirring until the sugar is dissolved. Add the remaining ingredients, whisking until smooth and well blended. Serve at room temperature.

PER SERVING (ABOUT 1 TABLESPOON)
Calories 40 | Protein 2g | Total Fat 3g |
Sat. Fat 1g | Cholesterol 0mg | Carbohydrate 2g |
Dietary Fiber 0g | Sodium 106mg

Salsa Cheesecake

lacto-ovo|low-carb

MAKES 12 APPETIZER SERVINGS

This colorful appetizer cheesecake is always a hit at parties.

3 (8-ounce) packages gluten-free Neufchâtel cream cheese, softened

3 eggs

½ cup medium salsa

¾ cup gluten-free light sour cream

½ cup chopped red bell pepper

½ cup chopped scallions (green parts only)

½ cup gluten-free shredded reduced-fat cheddar cheese

Tortilla chips, to serve (optional)

Preheat the oven to 325F (165C). Grease a 9-inch springform pan.

In a large bowl, beat the cream cheese and eggs with an electric beater on low speed until blended. Using a large spoon, stir in the salsa until thoroughly combined. Pour into prepared pan. Bake in the center of the oven for about 45 minutes, or until a knife inserted in the center comes out clean.

Let cool on a rack 10 minutes. Loosen (but do not remove) sides of pan, and let cool to room temperature. Remove sides of the pan. Cover and refrigerate for a minimum of 3 hours, or up to 2 days. Just before serving (if serving with tortilla chips, let stand at room temperature about 30 minutes to soften before proceeding), spread the top of the cheesecake with the sour cream and sprinkle evenly with the red pepper, scallions, and cheddar cheese. Cut into 12 wedges and serve with forks, or leave whole and surround with tortilla chips for scooping (if using).

PER SERVING

Calories 184 | Protein 9g | Total Fat 15g | Sat. Fat 9g | Cholesterol 99mg | Carbohydrate 3g | Dietary Fiber 0g | Sodium 303mg

Peach Salsa

vegan|low-carb

MAKES ABOUT 1½ CUPS

Serve with tortilla chips or Spicy Jicama Chips (page 18).

1 large fresh peach, peeled, pitted, and finely chopped

¼ cup finely chopped red onion

¼ cup finely chopped green bell pepper

1 tablespoon finely chopped fresh cilantro

1 tablespoon extra-virgin olive oil

1 tablespoon fresh lime juice

2 teaspoons sugar, or to taste

Pinch cayenne red pepper, or to taste

In a medium bowl, toss together all the ingredients until well combined. Cover and refrigerate for a minimum of 2 hours, or overnight, and serve chilled.

Cook's Tip

To peel peaches, bring a medium stockpot filled with water to a boil over high heat; drop in peaches and boil for 20 seconds. Drain and rinse under cold running water. Peel off the skins.

Sushi Balls
with Wasabi Dipping Sauce

vegan

MAKES 16 APPETIZERS

You don't have to be a sushi chef to master these quick and easy sushi balls, perfect for a party as they can be made up to two days before serving. Sushi-style, or glutinous rice (also known as sticky rice), is available in Asian markets and many well-stocked supermarkets. Black sesame seeds can also be purchased in Asian markets, as well as health food stores and gourmet markets.

2 cups uncooked sushi-style (glutinous or sticky) white rice

2 cups water

¼ cup hulled black or white sesame seeds

⅓ cup unseasoned rice vinegar

2 tablespoons sugar

1½ teaspoons salt

2 medium carrots (about 4 ounces each), finely chopped

5 scallions (green parts only), finely chopped

Wasabi Dipping Sauce (page 26)

Rinse the rice in a fine-meshed sieve under cold running water until the water runs clear. Drain well. Lightly oil a baking sheet with sides and set aside.

Place the rice and water in a medium saucepan and cover with a tight-fitting lid. Bring to a boil over high heat; immediately reduce the heat to medium and cook for 5 minutes. Reduce the heat to low and cook for 15 minutes. Remove from heat and let stand, covered, for 10 minutes.

Meanwhile, heat a small heavy-bottomed skillet over medium heat. Add the sesame seeds and cook without stirring for 30 seconds. Begin shaking the skillet occasionally until toasted and fragrant, about 2 minutes. Immediately transfer to a small plate and let cool.

In a large bowl, stir the rice vinegar, sugar, and salt until the sugar is dissolved. Stir in the carrots and scallions. Add the hot rice, mixing for a few minutes until the rice is barely warm. Set aside to cool to room temperature.

Fill a small bowl with cool water. Wetting your fingers in the water to prevent sticking, form the cooled rice into about 16 balls. Roll each ball after it's formed in the sesame seeds to lightly coat, then transfer to the prepared baking sheet. (At this point, the rice balls can be covered well with plastic wrap and refrigerated up to two days before returning to room temperature and serving.) Serve at room temperature, with Wasabi Dipping Sauce.

WASABI DIPPING SAUCE
vegan|low-carb

MAKES ABOUT ¾ CUP

Wasabi powder, made from green Japanese horseradish, can be found in Asian and gourmet markets, and some well-stocked supermarkets.

¼ **cup water**

3 **tablespoons unseasoned rice vinegar**

3 **tablespoons tamari sauce**

1 **tablespoon light sesame oil or peanut oil**

1 **tablespoon toasted (dark) sesame oil**

1 **inch fresh ginger, peeled and finely chopped, or**
    ½ **teaspoon ground dried ginger**

1 **to 1½ tablespoons wasabi powder**

1 **teaspoon sugar**

1 **large clove garlic, finely chopped**

In a small bowl, whisk together all the ingredients until thoroughly blended. Let stand for about 10 minutes at room temperature to allow the flavors to blend. Whisk again and serve at room temperature.

Baked Vegetable Pakoras with Raita Sauce
lacto-ovo

MAKES 5 TO 6 APPETIZER SERVINGS

Though Indian pakoras, or veggie fritters, are traditionally fried, this baked version is not only healthier to eat, but easier to prepare. For a dairy-free dish, serve with gluten-free chutney instead of the Raita Sauce.

1 **cup chickpea flour (garbanzo bean flour)**

1 **tablespoon gluten-free curry powder**

1 **teaspoon gluten-free baking powder**

½ **teaspoon salt**

½ **cup finely chopped zucchini**

½ **cup finely chopped carrot**

½ **cup finely chopped cabbage**

½ **cup finely chopped onion**

1 **egg**

2 **tablespoons canola oil**

Raita Sauce (recipe opposite)

Preheat the oven to 375F (190C). Lightly oil a baking sheet and set aside.

In a small bowl, mix together the chickpea flour, curry powder, baking powder, and salt. In a medium bowl, mix together the zucchini, carrot, cabbage, onion, egg, and oil. Add the flour mixture to the vegetable mixture, mixing until thoroughly combined.

Drop by heaping tablespoons onto prepared baking sheet, forming about 15 mounds. Bake for 20 to 25 minutes, or until golden brown. Serve warm with the sauce.

PER SERVING (WITHOUT SAUCE)

Calories 208 | Protein 5g | Total Fat 7g |
Sat. Fat 1g | Cholesterol 43mg | Carbohydrate 33g |
Dietary Fiber 4g | Sodium 317mg

RAITA SAUCE

egg-free|low-carb

MAKES ABOUT 2½ CUPS

Serve this refreshing cucumber and yogurt sauce as a dip for fresh veggies, as well.

- 1 cup gluten-free plain low-fat yogurt, drained of any visible liquids
- ½ cup chopped seeded, peeled cucumber
- ½ cup chopped seeded tomato
- ¼ cup finely chopped red onion
- 2 tablespoons finely chopped fresh mint
- ½ teaspoon ground cumin
- ¼ teaspoon salt
- Freshly ground black pepper, to taste

❦ In a small bowl, mix together all the ingredients until well combined. Cover and refrigerate for 2 hours or overnight and serve chilled, stirring well before serving.

PER SERVING (ABOUT ¼ CUP)

Calories 21 | Protein 2g | Total Fat 1g |
Sat. Fat 0g | Cholesterol 1mg | Carbohydrate 3g |
Dietary Fiber 0g | Sodium 72mg

Indonesian-Style Vegetables with **Spicy Peanut-Coconut Dipping Sauce**

vegan|low-carb

MAKES 6 SERVINGS

Known as *gado gado*, this Indonesian classic of lightly steamed or blanched vegetables, served with a spicy peanut-coconut sauce, is a vegetarian's delight.

- 1½ **cups fresh broccoli florets**
- 1½ **cups fresh cauliflower florets**
- 1½ **cups fresh whole baby carrots**
- 1½ **cups fresh snow peas**
- ½ **cup tamari sauce**
- ½ **cup light coconut milk**
- 4 **tablespoons gluten-free creamy peanut butter, at room temperature**
- ¼ **cup unseasoned rice vinegar**
- 2 **tablespoons sugar**
- 1 **tablespoon finely chopped fresh ginger**
- 1 **tablespoon Chinese chili paste**

❦ Bring a large stockpot filled with salted water to a boil. Fill a large bowl with ice water. Add the broccoli and cauliflower to the boiling water and cook for 1 minute. Add the carrots and cook for 1 minute. Add the snow peas and cook for 1 minute. Drain and immediately place the vegetables in the ice water bath to refresh for 5 minutes. Drain well.

Meanwhile, in a small bowl, whisk together the tamari sauce, coconut milk, peanut butter, rice vinegar, sugar, ginger, and chili paste until thoroughly blended. Transfer to a small serving bowl.

To serve, arrange the vegetables on a large platter and serve with the dipping sauce.

PER SERVING

Calories 163 | Protein 8g | Total Fat 8g |
Sat. Fat 3g | Cholesterol 0mg | Carbohydrate 18g |
Dietary Fiber 4g | Sodium 1,432mg

Vegetarian Paté

dairy-free|low-carb

MAKES 8 SERVINGS

This mock paté is delicious spread on rice crackers, stuffed in celery, or rolled up in lettuce leaves. It can also be served on a bed of mixed greens for an elegant first course. To hard cook the eggs, see the directions on page 15 for Mexican Deviled Eggs.

¼ **cup peanut oil**
4 **medium onions (about 6 ounces each), thinly sliced**

2 **cups frozen green peas, cooked according to package directions, drained well**
4 **hard-cooked eggs, peeled**
½ **cup walnuts**
1 **teaspoon salt**
Freshly ground black pepper, to taste

In a large, deep-sided skillet (do not use a nonstick skillet), heat the oil over medium heat. Add the onions and cook, stirring, until just softened, 3 to 5 minutes. Reduce the heat to medium-low and cook, stirring occasionally, until deep golden and caramelized, about 45 minutes.

Place the onions, peas, eggs, walnuts, salt, and pepper in a food processor fitted with the knife blade; process until smooth but still slightly chunky. Transfer to a serving bowl and refrigerate, covered, for a minimum of 6 hours, or up to 2 days. Serve chilled.

PER SERVING

Calories 204 | Protein 8g | Total Fat 14g |
Sat. Fat 2g | Cholesterol 108mg | Carbohydrate 14g |
Dietary Fiber 4g | Sodium 341mg

Wasabi Cream Cheese Spread

egg-free|low-carb

MAKES 8 SERVINGS

This Asian-style spread is delicious on gluten-free mini rice cakes or rice crackers, available in many major supermarkets. Use it as a dip or stuffing for raw veggies, as well.

1 cup gluten-free whipped cream cheese

1 tablespoon tamari sauce

1 tablespoon wasabi powder

½ teaspoon ground ginger

½ teaspoon toasted (dark) sesame oil

Gluten-free rice crackers or rice cakes, to serve

In a small bowl, mix together all the ingredients, except the crackers. Cover and refrigerate for a minimum of 1 hour, or up to a few days, and serve chilled.

PER SERVING

Calories 106 │ Protein 3g │ Total Fat 10g │
Sat. Fat 6g │ Cholesterol 31mg │ Carbohydrate 1g │
Dietary Fiber 0g │ Sodium 210mg

VARIATION: *To make* Jalapeño Cream Cheese Spread with Spicy Jicama Chips*: Omit the tamari sauce, wasabi powder, ginger, and sesame oil. Add ½ finely chopped, seeded, small jalapeño chili, 1 tablespoon chopped canned mild green chilies, 1 tablespoon finely chopped fresh cilantro, and 1 teaspoon fresh lime juice to the cream cheese. Prepare the Spicy Jicama Chips as directed on page 18 and use in lieu of the rice cakes or rice crackers.*

Soups

Of all the courses of a meal, soups wear the most hats, acting as appetizers, first courses, light lunches, quick suppers, hearty main dishes, midnight snacks, and, in certain instances, even desserts. Many soups benefit from a thickening agent, which is often a starch—fortunately for those with wheat allergy and celiac disease, cornstarch or potato starch can usually be substituted for wheat flour. Cream (heavy cream, half-and-half, crème fraîche, or sour cream) and cheeses (Parmesan, shredded cheddar) are other gluten-free thickeners, but make sure any shredded cheese isn't treated with wheat flour to prevent caking or that the sour cream (especially the light and nonfat varieties) doesn't contain gluten-based food starches. Cream cheese, Neufchâtel in particular, is a quick and easy thickener, which imparts the rich flavor of cream with a lot less fat, but read the label to make sure it's also free of suspect stabilizers. Nondairy thickeners include peanut butter, coconut milk, pureed vegetables—potatoes, winter squash, turnips, and cauliflower, to name a few—and various beans and other legumes. When a soup calls for pasta, rice can almost always be used instead, and can be boiled, pasta style, right into the soup. The starch released from a rice grain is sweeter, resulting in a richer soup without adding fat or calories. Why not make a pot of the Milanese-Style Minestrone Soup and taste-test it for yourself?

PER SERVING

Calories 164 | Protein 20g | Total Fat 7g |
Sat. Fat 4g | Cholesterol 20mg | Carbohydrate 8g |
Dietary Fiber 5g | Sodium 575mg

Broccoli and Cheddar Cheese Soup

egg-free | low-carb

MAKES 4 SERVINGS

Ready in just about fifteen minutes, this perennial favorite is perfect to serve when the urge for a warm and comforting bowl of soup strikes. Cauliflower can easily replace the broccoli, if desired.

2 cups water

1 (14-ounce) can gluten-free low-sodium vegetable broth (1¾ cups)

1 teaspoon onion powder

Salt and freshly ground black pepper, to taste

1 (16-ounce) bag frozen broccoli cuts

½ cup gluten-free Neufchâtel cream cheese

1½ cups (6 ounces) gluten-free shredded reduced-fat cheddar cheese

In a medium stockpot, bring the water, broth, onion powder, salt, and pepper to a boil over high heat. Add the broccoli and let return to a boil. Reduce the heat to medium-low and simmer, covered, until the broccoli is tender, about 8 minutes. Add the cream cheese and cook, stirring, until smooth and incorporated. Add the cheddar cheese and cook, stirring constantly, until the cheese is melted. Serve hot.

Butternut Squash Soup with Cider Cream

egg-free | with vegan option

MAKES 4 TO 6 SERVINGS

For a vegan dish, omit the Cider Cream.

2 tablespoons canola oil

1 large onion (about 8 ounces), chopped

½ cup chopped carrot

4 cups gluten-free low-sodium vegetable broth

¾ cup apple cider

1 (12-ounce) package frozen butternut squash, partially thawed

1 large Granny Smith apple (about 8 ounces), peeled, cored, and chopped

1 teaspoon dried thyme leaves

⅛ teaspoon ground sage

½ cup half-and-half, light cream, or heavy cream (optional)

Salt and freshly ground black pepper, to taste

Pinch nutmeg (optional)

Cider Cream (recipe opposite)

Chopped fresh chives (optional)

In a medium stockpot, heat the oil over medium-low heat. Add the onion and carrot; cook, stirring occasionally, until softened but not browned, 10 to 15 minutes. Add the broth, cider, squash, apple, thyme, and sage; bring to a boil over high heat. Reduce the heat to medium-low and simmer, covered, until the apple is tender, about 20 minutes, stirring occasionally.

Working in batches, puree in a blender or food processor. Return to the stockpot and stir in the half-and-half (if using). Season with salt, pepper, and nutmeg (if using); reheat over low heat as necessary. Serve warm, with each serving garnished with a dollop of Cider Cream and a sprinkle of chives (if using).

PER SERVING (WITHOUT THE CIDER CREAM)
Calories 274 | Protein 15g | Total Fat 11g | Sat. Fat 3g | Cholesterol 11mg | Carbohydrate 34g | Dietary Fiber 7g | Sodium 541mg

CIDER CREAM
egg-free|low-carb
MAKES ½ CUP

This also makes a tasty topping for baked apples, in which instance, add a pinch or two of ground cinnamon.

¼ cup apple cider
½ cup gluten-free light sour cream

In a small saucepan, bring the cider to a boil over medium-high heat. Boil until reduced to 1 tablespoon. Remove from heat and let cool to room temperature. Place the sour cream in a small bowl and whisk in the reduced cider. Serve as directed above. The cream can be stored, covered, in the refrigerator for up to 2 days before using.

PER TABLESPOON
Calories 9 | Protein 0g | Total Fat 0g | Sat. Fat 0g | Cholesterol 1mg | Carbohydrate 1g | Dietary Fiber 0g | Sodium 4mg

"Creamy" Cauliflower Soup
vegan|low-carb
MAKES 6 SERVINGS

It's hard to believe that not a pinch of flour or drop of cream is used in this thick and creamy soup, a good choice to make in the fall or winter when fresh cauliflower is abundant.

2 tablespoons canola oil
1 medium onion (about 6 ounces), chopped
3½ cups gluten-free low-sodium vegetable broth
1 large head cauliflower, cut into florets
Freshly ground black pepper, to taste
Pinch ground nutmeg (optional)
Gluten-free sour cream, shredded cheddar cheese, and/or chopped chives (optional)

In a medium stockpot, heat the oil over medium heat. Add the onion and cook, stirring, until softened, about 5 minutes. Add the broth and cauliflower; bring to a boil over high heat. Reduce the heat to medium-low and simmer, covered, until the cauliflower is tender, 8 to 10 minutes.

Working in batches, puree in a blender or food processor until smooth. Return to the stockpot and season with pepper and nutmeg (if using). Reheat over low heat as necessary, thinning with water, if needed. Serve hot, garnished with the sour cream, cheese, and/or chives (if using).

PER SERVING

Calories 84 | Protein 7g | Total Fat 5g |
Sat Fat 0g | Cholesterol 0mg | Carbohydrate 4g |
Dietary Fiber 3g | Sodium 308mg

Chilled Cream of Fennel Soup

egg-free|low-carb

MAKES 4 SERVINGS

This is an elegant first-course soup to serve during the winter holidays, when fresh fennel is in season. For a vegan variation, serve the pureed soup warm without the sour cream and half-and-half.

1 tablespoon canola oil
2 medium fennel bulbs (8 to 10 ounces each), trimmed, cored, and coarsely chopped, and about 2 tablespoons feathery fronds chopped and reserved

1 small onion (about 4 ounces), finely chopped
3 cups gluten-free low-sodium vegetable broth
½ teaspoon salt
Freshly ground black pepper, to taste
½ cup gluten-free light sour cream
¼ cup half-and-half, milk, or skim milk

In a medium stockpot, heat the oil over medium-low heat. Add the fennel and onion and cook, stirring occasionally, until softened but not browned, about 10 minutes. Add the broth, salt, and pepper; bring to a boil over medium-high heat. Reduce the heat, cover, and simmer gently until the fennel is tender, about 20 minutes, stirring occasionally.

Working in batches as necessary, transfer to a food processor fitted with the knife blade, or to a blender; process until smooth and pureed. Strain through a fine-mesh sieve into a clean bowl. Let cool to room temperature.

Cover and refrigerate for 2 to 3 hours, or until chilled. Whisk in the sour cream and half-and-half. Cover and refrigerate for 1 hour or overnight, and serve chilled, garnished with the reserved fennel fronds.

PER SERVING

Calories 124 | Protein 11g | Total Fat 4g |
Sat. Fat 0g | Cholesterol 2mg | Carbohydrate 13g |
Dietary Fiber 3g | Sodium 722mg

Instant Blender Gazpacho

vegan|low-carb

MAKES 2 SERVINGS

PER SERVING

Calories 131 | Protein 3g | Total Fat 8g |
Sat. Fat 1g | Cholesterol 0mg | Carbohydrate 16g |
Dietary Fiber 4g | Sodium 269mg

This recipe easily doubles to serve four, but make it in two batches if using a blender. If not serving immediately, omit the ice cubes and chill in the refrigerator for a minimum of two hours, or up to two days.

- 2 medium ripe tomatoes (about 6 ounces each), chopped
- ½ medium cucumber (about 4 ounces), peeled, seeded, and coarsely chopped
- ½ small onion (about 2 ounces), chopped
- ¼ medium green bell pepper (about 1½ ounces), coarsely chopped
- 1 small clove garlic, finely chopped (optional)
- ½ cup tomato juice
- 2 tablespoons gluten-free low-sodium vegetable broth
- 1 tablespoon extra-virgin olive oil
- 1 tablespoon fresh lemon juice
- 1 teaspoon sherry vinegar or red wine vinegar
- Pinch ground cumin, or more, to taste
- Salt and freshly ground black pepper, to taste
- Pinch cayenne pepper, or more, to taste (optional)
- 2 ice cubes

❦ Combine all the ingredients in a blender or a food processor fitted with the knife blade; blend until smooth and pureed. Serve at once.

Creamy Wild Mushroom Soup

egg-free

MAKES 4 SERVINGS

Serve this earthy fall or winter soup with a spinach and orange salad for a satisfying meal. For a lower-fat version, substitute skim milk for all or half of the whole milk.

- 2½ cups gluten-free low-sodium vegetable broth
- 2½ cups whole milk
- 1 tablespoon onion powder
- 2 tablespoons canola oil
- 8 ounces fresh wild or cremini mushrooms, finely chopped
- 8 ounces cultivated white mushrooms, finely chopped
- 1 large clove garlic, finely chopped
- ¼ cup potato starch flour
- Salt and freshly ground black pepper, to taste
- Chopped fresh parsley, for garnish (optional)

❦ In a medium saucepan, combine the broth, milk, and onion powder; bring to a simmer over medium-high heat. Reduce the heat to maintain a gentle simmer.

Meanwhile, in a medium stockpot, heat the oil over medium heat. Add the mushrooms and cook, stirring, until they begin to release their liquid, about 3 minutes, adding the garlic the last minute or so of cooking. Reduce the heat to low and add the potato starch flour; cook, stirring constantly, for 2 minutes.

Using a ladle, gradually add the simmering broth mixture, whisking well after each addition. Season with salt and pepper and bring to a boil over medium-high heat, whisking often. Reduce the heat to low and simmer gently, stirring occasionally, for 5 minutes. Serve hot, garnished with the parsley (if using).

PER SERVING

Calories 268 | Protein 16g | Total Fat 13g |
Sat. Fat 4g | Cholesterol 21mg | Carbohydrate 26g |
Dietary Fiber 5g | Sodium 408mg

Santa Fe–Style Pumpkin Soup

egg-free|low-carb

MAKES 4 SERVINGS

Loaded with vitamins A and C and fiber, this low-fat soup is as nutritious as it is delicious. For a vegan dish, omit the sour cream and stir all the chili-cilantro puree

into the soup while simmering. Garnish with crushed tortilla chips.

> 1 (4-ounce) can diced mild green chilies, drained
>
> ¼ cup packed fresh cilantro
>
> ¼ cup gluten-free light sour cream
>
> 2 (14-ounce) cans gluten-free low-sodium vegetable broth
>
> 1 (15-ounce) can pumpkin puree
>
> ½ cup water
>
> 1 teaspoon ground cumin
>
> ½ teaspoon onion powder
>
> ½ teaspoon gluten-free chili powder
>
> ½ teaspoon sugar
>
> ¼ teaspoon garlic powder
>
> ⅛ teaspoon cayenne pepper (optional)
>
> Salt and freshly ground black pepper, to taste

In a food processor fitted with the knife blade, process the chilies and cilantro until smooth and pureed. Transfer 2 tablespoons of the mixture to a small bowl and add the sour cream, stirring well to combine. Set both mixtures aside.

In a large saucepan or medium stockpot, combine the broth, pumpkin, water, cumin, onion powder, chili powder, sugar, garlic powder, cayenne (if using), salt, and black pepper. Bring to a boil over medium-high heat. Reduce the heat to medium and stir in the remaining chili-cilantro mixture (without sour cream). Simmer, uncovered, stirring occasionally, about 5 minutes.

To serve, divide the soup evenly among 4 soup bowls and top each with an equal dollop of the sour cream mixture. Run the tip of the spoon through each dollop to swirl and serve at once.

Easy Tomato Bisque

egg-free|low-carb

MAKES 5 TO 6 SERVINGS

Small portions of this rich soup are appropriate to begin a meal, or to serve for lunch accompanied by a tossed salad and gluten-free bread—the Italian-Style Herbed Cheese Bread (page 76) is especially delicious. Replacing the heavy cream with regular milk or even light cream is not recommended, as they both tend to curdle.

2 (8-ounce) cans tomato sauce

1 cup gluten-free low-sodium vegetable broth

1 cup heavy cream

2 teaspoons sugar

❦ In a medium saucepan, bring all the ingredients to a gentle simmer over medium heat, stirring occasionally. Serve hot.

PER SERVING

Calories 203 | Protein 3g | Total Fat 18g |

Sat. Fat 11g | Cholesterol 65mg | Carbohydrate 10g |

Dietary Fiber 1g | Sodium 578mg

Roasted Mediterranean Vegetable Potage

vegan|low-carb

MAKES 4 SERVINGS

More potage than soup, this delicious mélange of pureed roasted vegetables, garlic, and oregano will perfume your home for hours with the heady aromas of the Mediterranean.

1 small eggplant (about 8 ounces), cut into 1-inch cubes

1 medium zucchini (about 8 ounces), cut into 1-inch cubes

1 medium red bell pepper (about 6 ounces), cut into 1-inch pieces

1 medium green bell pepper (about 6 ounces), cut into 1-inch pieces

1 medium onion (about 6 ounces), cut into small chunks

3 large cloves garlic, peeled, left whole

¼ cup olive oil

½ teaspoon dried oregano

Salt, preferably the coarse variety, and freshly ground black pepper, to taste

1 cup water, plus additional as necessary

1 (14-ounce) can gluten-free low-sodium vegetable broth

❦ Preheat the oven to 450F (230C). In a 15 × 10-inch shallow glass casserole, or a large baking sheet with sides, place the eggplant, zucchini, bell peppers, onion, and garlic. Add the oil and toss well to thoroughly coat. Sprinkle with the oregano, salt, and pepper; toss again.

Bake for 15 minutes, or until the vegetables are beginning to char. Remove from the oven and stir and turn the vegetables. Bake for an additional 10 to 15 minutes, or until lightly charred.

Working in batches, if necessary, puree the vegetables with the 1 cup water in a food processor fitted with the knife blade, or in a blender. Transfer to a medium stockpot and add the vegetable broth. Bring to a simmer over medium heat, stirring occasionally. For a thinner consistency, add more water as necessary. Serve hot.

PER SERVING

Calories 202 | Protein 7g | Total Fat 14g |

Sat. Fat 2g | Cholesterol 0mg | Carbohydrate 15g |

Dietary Fiber 6g | Sodium 233mg

Chilled Tomato Soup with Mint

vegan|low-carb

MAKES 4 SERVINGS

For extra protein, garnish this refreshing soup with crumbled feta or goat cheese.

- **1 tablespoon extra-virgin olive oil**
- **1 medium onion (about 6 ounces), chopped**
- **2 cloves garlic, finely chopped**
- **1 (28-ounce) can diced tomatoes, juices included**
- **1 (14-ounce) can gluten-free low-sodium vegetable broth**

Salt and freshly ground black pepper, to taste
2 tablespoons finely chopped fresh mint

In a medium stockpot, heat the oil over medium heat. Add the onion and cook, stirring, until softened, about 3 minutes. Add the garlic and cook, stirring, for 1 minute. Add the tomatoes and their juices, the broth, salt, and pepper; bring to a boil over medium-high heat. Reduce the heat to medium and simmer, uncovered, 10 minutes, stirring occasionally.

Working in batches, if necessary, transfer the mixture to a food processor fitted with the knife blade, or to a blender; process until smooth and pureed. Transfer to a bowl and let cool to room temperature. Cover and refrigerate for a minimum of 2 hours, or up to 2 days, and served chilled, garnished with the mint.

PER SERVING

Calories 109 | Protein 7g | Total Fat 4g |

Sat. Fat 1g | Cholesterol 0mg | Carbohydrate 14g |

Dietary Fiber 4g | Sodium 631mg

Zucchini-Tomato Soup

vegan

MAKES 4 SERVINGS

Fortified with V8 juice (gluten-free as of this writing), this vitamin-rich first-course soup can become a satisfying light lunch or supper with the addition of two cups of cooked brown or white rice the last few minutes of simmering. Because V8 juice already contains a large amount of sodium, no additional salt is necessary.

2 tablespoons extra-virgin olive oil

1 medium onion (about 6 ounces), chopped

2 to 3 large cloves garlic, finely chopped

1 (28-ounce) can diced tomatoes, juices included

3 cups V8 juice

3 cups water

1 pound zucchini, preferably a mix of green and yellow, coarsely chopped

1 tablespoon sugar

½ teaspoon dried oregano

1 bay leaf

Freshly ground black pepper, to taste

Chopped fresh basil (optional)

In a large stockpot, heat the oil over medium heat. Add the onion and garlic and cook, stirring often, until softened and fragrant, about 5 minutes. Add the remaining ingredients, except the basil, and bring to a boil over high heat. Reduce the heat and simmer, uncovered, for 1 hour, stirring occasionally. Add the basil (if using) the last few minutes of cooking. Serve hot.

PER SERVING

Calories 181 | Protein 5g | Total Fat 8g |
Sat. Fat 1g | Cholesterol 0mg | Carbohydrate 28g |
Dietary Fiber 6g | Sodium 993mg

Three-Bean Summer Vegetable Ragout

vegan

MAKES 4 TO 6 MAIN-DISH OR 8 SIDE-DISH SERVINGS

This fragrant summer stew is also delicious served over rice or polenta.

2 tablespoons extra-virgin olive oil

1 medium onion (about 6 ounces), chopped

1 medium green bell pepper (about 6 ounces), chopped

3 large cloves garlic, finely chopped

1 (28-ounce) can diced tomatoes, juices included

¾ pound green beans, trimmed

1 teaspoon dried oregano

½ teaspoon dried thyme leaves

Salt, to taste

1 pound zucchini, cut into large dice

8 ounces cultivated white and/or cremini mushrooms, sliced

1 cup canned chickpeas, rinsed and drained

1 cup canned kidney beans, rinsed and drained

1 cup canned navy beans, rinsed and drained

2 tablespoons tomato paste

1 teaspoon sugar

Freshly ground black pepper, to taste

½ cup packed basil leaves, chopped

In a large deep-sided skillet with a lid, heat the oil over medium heat. Add the onion, bell pepper, and garlic; cook, stirring, until softened, about 3 minutes. Add the tomatoes with their juices, green beans, oregano, thyme, and salt, stirring well to coat the green beans. Bring to a brisk simmer over medium-high heat. Cover, reduce the heat, and simmer gently for 1 hour, stirring occasionally.

Add the zucchini, mushrooms, chickpeas, kidney beans, navy beans, tomato paste, sugar, and black pepper to the skillet; bring to a brisk simmer over medium-high heat. Cover, reduce the heat, and simmer gently for 15 minutes.

Uncover and cook over medium heat, stirring occasionally, until the zucchini and mushrooms are tender, the green beans can bend easily, and liquids are reduced and thickened, about 10 minutes, stirring in the basil the last few minutes of cooking. Serve warm.

PER SERVING

Calories 385 | Protein 19g | Total Fat 10g | Sat. Fat 1g | Cholesterol 0mg | Carbohydrate 63g | Dietary Fiber 15g | Sodium 505mg

Curried Chickpea and Potato Stew with Spinach

vegan

MAKES 4 TO 5 MAIN-DISH SERVINGS

This fragrant, Indian-style stew is one of my favorites.

2 tablespoons canola oil

1 large onion (about 8 ounces), chopped

3 large cloves garlic, finely chopped

1 teaspoon finely chopped fresh ginger

½ tablespoon cumin seed

1 pound small new potatoes, halved or quartered, depending on size

1 (19-ounce) can chickpeas, rinsed and drained

1 (14-ounce) can diced tomatoes with jalapeño chilies, juices included

½ cup gluten-free low-sodium vegetable broth

1 tablespoon tomato paste

1 teaspoon gluten-free curry powder

1 teaspoon ground cumin

Salt and freshly ground black pepper, to taste

4 ounces fresh spinach, trimmed, coarsely chopped

1 tablespoon finely chopped fresh cilantro (optional)

In a large nonstick skillet with a lid, heat the oil over medium heat. Add the onion and cook, stirring, until softened, about 3 minutes. Add the garlic, ginger, and cumin seed; cook, stirring, for 2 minutes. Add the remaining ingredients, except the spinach and cilantro; bring to a brisk simmer over medium-high heat, stirring well to combine. Reduce the heat, cover, and simmer gently until the potatoes are tender through the center, 30 to 40 minutes, stirring occasionally and adjusting the heat to maintain a simmer. Stir in the spinach and cilantro (if using); cook, uncovered, stirring occasionally, until the spinach is wilted but still bright green, about 5 minutes. Serve warm.

Polenta Chili

vegan

MAKES 4 SERVINGS

Polenta, or coarse-ground yellow cornmeal, is a wonderful gluten-free substitute for the ground meat found in most traditional chili recipes.

2 tablespoons extra-virgin olive oil

1 medium onion (about 6 ounces), chopped

1 medium green bell pepper (about 6 ounces), chopped

2 large cloves garlic, finely chopped

1 tablespoon chili powder

1 teaspoon ground cumin

1 teaspoon dried oregano

2 cups gluten-free low-sodium vegetable broth

1 (16-ounce) can pinto beans, rinsed and drained

1 (14.5-ounce) can diced tomatoes, juices included

3 tablespoons canned diced mild green chilies, drained

½ tablespoon sugar

Salt and freshly ground black pepper, to taste

½ cup polenta or coarse-ground yellow cornmeal

Gluten-free sour cream and/or shredded cheddar or Monterey Jack cheese (optional)

In a medium stockpot, heat the oil over medium-low heat. Add the onion and bell pepper and cook, stirring occasionally, until softened but not browned, about 8 minutes. Add the garlic and cook, stirring, for 1 minute. Add the chili powder, cumin, and oregano; cook, stirring, for 1 minute. Add the broth, beans, tomatoes with their juices, chilies, sugar, salt, and black pepper; bring to a boil over high heat. Gradually stir in the polenta. Reduce the heat to medium-low and cook, stirring often, until the polenta is tender and the mixture is thickened, about 20 minutes. Serve hot, with the toppings passed separately (if using).

Southwestern-Style Corn Chowder

vegan

MAKES 6 MAIN-DISH OR 8 FIRST-COURSE SERVINGS

Light coconut milk replaces the cream, and sweet potatoes replace the white variety, in this delightful southwestern variation of corn chowder. Garnish with broken tortilla chips or taco shells for a nice bit of crunch.

- 1 tablespoon canola oil
- 1 medium onion (about 6 ounces), finely chopped
- 2 cloves garlic, finely chopped
- 4 cups gluten-free low-sodium vegetable broth
- 1 (14-ounce) can diced tomatoes with jalapeño chilies, juices included
- 1 medium sweet potato (about 6 ounces), peeled and cut into small dice
- 1 large carrot (about 6 ounces), cut into small dice
- 1 (14-ounce) can light coconut milk (about 1¾ cups)
- 2 cups frozen yellow corn, thawed
- 1 (15-ounce can) pinto or kidney beans, rinsed and drained
- 1 (4-ounce) can chopped mild green chilies, drained
- ½ teaspoon sugar
- ½ teaspoon ground cumin
- ¼ teaspoon chili powder, or to taste
- Salt and freshly ground black pepper, to taste
- Chopped fresh cilantro or flat-leaf parsley (optional)

In a medium stockpot, heat the oil over medium heat. Add the onion and cook, stirring, until softened, about 3 minutes. Add the garlic and cook, stirring, for 1 minute. Add the broth, tomatoes and their juices, potato, and carrot; bring to a boil over high heat. Reduce the heat, cover, and simmer until the potato and carrot are tender, about 15 minutes.

Add the coconut milk, corn, beans, chilies, sugar, cumin, chili powder, salt, and black pep-per; bring to a gentle simmer over medium-high heat. Reduce the heat and simmer gently, un-covered, stirring occasionally, until slightly re-duced, about 15 minutes. Stir in the cilantro (if using), and serve hot.

PER SERVING

Calories 317 | Protein 17g | Total Fat 11g | Sat. Fat 7g | Cholesterol 0mg | Carbohydrate 44g | Dietary Fiber 10g | Sodium 530mg

Mediterranean-Style Eggplant and Chickpea Stew
vegan
MAKES 4 SERVINGS

This is a good choice for a buffet, as it is delicious served warm or at room temperature.

- 2 eggplants, about 1 to 1¼ pound each, cut lengthwise in half
- 4 tablespoons extra-virgin olive oil
- 1 medium onion, about 6 ounces, chopped
- 3 large cloves garlic, finely chopped
- 12 ounces plum tomatoes, chopped
- ½ teaspoon dried oregano
- ¼ teaspoon dried thyme leaves
- 1 teaspoon salt, preferably the coarse variety, or to taste
- ¼ teaspoon freshly ground black pepper, or to taste

2 tablespoons tomato paste

¼ cup water or gluten-free low sodium vegetable broth

1 (15-ounce) can chickpeas, rinsed and drained

¼ cup chopped fresh basil (optional)

❧Preheat the oven to 400F (205C). Lightly grease a large baking sheet.

Place the eggplant halves, cut sides down, on the prepared baking sheet. Bake for 40 minutes, or until softened and collapsed. Drain on paper towels. When cool enough to handle, remove the skin and cut the flesh into bite-size chunks. Set aside.

In a large nonstick skillet, heat the oil over medium heat. Add the onion and cook, stirring occasionally, until softened but not browned, about 5 minutes. Add the garlic and cook, stirring, for 1 minute. Add the tomatoes, oregano, thyme, salt, and pepper; bring to a simmer over medium-high heat. Reduce the heat to medium and cook, stirring occasionally, for 5 minutes. Add the tomato paste and water, stirring until blended. Add the reserved eggplant and the chickpeas. Cook, stirring, until heated through, about 5 minutes, adding the basil (if using) during the last minute of cooking. Serve warm or at room temperature.

PER SERVING

Calories 317 | Protein 9g | Total Fat 16g | Sat. Fat 2g | Cholesterol 0mg | Carbohydrate 39g | Dietary Fiber 9g | Sodium 617mg

Milanese-Style Minestrone Soup
vegan

MAKES 4 TO 5 SERVINGS

This is delicious accompanied with the Italian-Style Herbed Cheese Bread (page 76). You can also add about ½ cup of fresh green beans, cut into ½-inch lengths, along with the zucchini, if desired.

2 tablespoons extra-virgin olive oil

1 medium onion (about 6 ounces), chopped

1 medium carrot (about 4 ounces), chopped

1 stalk celery, finely chopped

2 cloves garlic, finely chopped

2 (14-ounce) cans gluten-free reduced-sodium vegetable broth

1 (14-ounce) can no-salt-added stewed tomatoes, juices included

1 cup water

½ teaspoon dried oregano

¼ teaspoon dried thyme leaves

Salt and freshly ground black pepper, to taste

1 (15-ounce) can red kidney beans, rinsed and drained

2 medium zucchini (about 6 ounces each), coarsely chopped

½ cup long-grain white rice

❧In a medium stockpot, heat the oil over medium heat. Add the onion, carrot, and celery; cook, stirring, until softened, about 5 minutes. Add the garlic and cook, stirring, for 1 minute. Add the broth, tomatoes and their juices, water, oregano, thyme, salt, and pepper; bring to a boil over high heat, stirring occasionally and breaking up the tomatoes with the back of a large wooden spoon. Add the beans, zucchini, and rice and return mixture to a boil. Reduce the heat to medium and simmer, uncovered, stirring occasionally, until the rice is tender yet firm to the bite, 10 to 15 minutes. Serve hot.

PER SERVING

Calories 342 | Protein 20g | Total Fat 8g | Sat. Fat 1g | Cholesterol 0mg | Carbohydrate 51g | Dietary Fiber 10g | Sodium 729mg

Tex-Mex Minestrone

vegan

MAKES 4 SERVINGS

This quick and easy soup can also be garnished with crushed tortilla chips, if desired.

- **1 cup cooked white rice (see Cook's Tip, page 145)**
- **1 cup frozen peas and carrots**
- **1 cup frozen yellow corn**
- **2 cups mild or medium salsa**
- **1 (15-ounce) can black beans, rinsed and drained**
- **1 (2.5-ounce) can sliced black olives, drained**
- **1 (14-ounce) can gluten-free low-sodium vegetable broth**
- **1 cup water**
- **1 tablespoon extra-virgin olive oil**
- **½ teaspoon gluten-free chili powder**

- **½ teaspoon ground cumin**
- **Gluten-free shredded cheddar cheese and/or sour cream, for topping (optional)**

 In a medium stockpot, combine all the ingredients, except the toppings; bring to a simmer over medium-high heat. Reduce the heat to medium-low and simmer, uncovered, stirring occasionally, until the vegetables are tender, about 10 minutes. Serve hot, with the toppings passed separately (if using).

PER SERVING

Calories 300 | Protein 15g | Total Fat 7g | Sat. Fat 1g | Cholesterol 0mg | Carbohydrate 49g | Dietary Fiber 9g | Sodium 729mg

Greek-Style Spinach, White Bean, and Feta Soup

egg-free

MAKES 4 MAIN-DISH SERVINGS

For a vegan dish, omit the feta—the soup will still be immensely satisfying.

- **2 tablespoons extra-virgin olive oil**
- **1 large onion (about 8 ounces), chopped**
- **2 large cloves garlic, finely chopped**
- **2 (14-ounce) cans gluten-free low-sodium vegetable broth**
- **½ cup water**

1 (14-ounce) can no-salt-added stewed tomatoes, juices included

½ teaspoon dried oregano

½ teaspoon dried thyme leaves

Salt and freshly ground black pepper, to taste

1 (19-ounce) can great northern, navy, or cannellini beans, rinsed and drained

8 ounces fresh spinach, tough stems removed, coarsely torn

½ cup gluten-free crumbled feta cheese

In a medium stockpot, heat the oil over medium heat. Add the onion and cook, stirring, until softened but not browned, about 5 minutes. Add the garlic and cook, stirring constantly, for 1 minute. Add the broth, water, tomatoes with their juices, oregano, thyme, salt, and pepper. Bring to a boil over high heat, breaking up the tomatoes with the back of a large wooden spoon.

Add the beans and let return to a boil. Reduce the heat to between medium and medium-low and simmer for 15 minutes, stirring occasionally, adding the spinach the last 2 minutes of cooking. Divide evenly among 4 soup bowls and sprinkle each serving with 2 tablespoons of the feta. Serve hot.

PER SERVING

Calories 342 | Protein 23g | Total Fat 12g |
Sat. Fat 4g | Cholesterol 17mg | Carbohydrate 40g |
Dietary Fiber 11g | Sodium 694mg

Taco Soup with Roasted Corn
egg-free

MAKES 6 SERVINGS

I've enriched this vegetarian version of Emeril Lagasse's taco soup with scrumptious roasted corn instead of the original chicken. Some commercial taco seasonings contain gluten, so check the label carefully.

3 cups frozen yellow corn, thawed and drained

2 tablespoons canola or other mild vegetable oil

Garlic salt, to taste

Freshly ground black pepper, to taste

2 (14.5-ounce) cans gluten-free low-sodium vegetable broth

1 (16-ounce) can kidney beans, rinsed and drained

1 (14-ounce) can hominy, rinsed and drained

1 cup medium or mild salsa

2 (4-ounce) cans no-salt-added tomato paste

1 (4-ounce) can diced mild green chilies, rinsed and drained

1 (1.25-ounce) package taco seasoning mix

8 ounces (1 cup) gluten-free reduced-fat cream cheese with chives, cut into 8 pieces

Salt, to taste

Broken taco shells or corn tortilla chips (optional)

Preheat the oven to broil.

Place the corn on a large ungreased baking sheet and toss with the oil. Season with the garlic salt and pepper and spread out in a single layer. Broil 4 to 6 inches from the heating element, stirring and turning a few times, until the corn is lightly browned, 5 to 8 minutes. Set aside.

In a medium stockpot, bring the broth, corn, beans, hominy, salsa, tomato paste, chilies, and taco seasoning to a boil over medium-high heat, stirring occasionally. Reduce the heat and simmer, uncovered, for 20 minutes, stirring occasionally. Add the cream cheese, stirring well to thoroughly blend. Simmer gently, stirring occasionally, for about 5 minutes. Season with salt. (For a thinner consistency, add water as necessary.) Serve hot, garnished with the broken taco shells (if using).

PER SERVING

Calories 394 | Protein 20g | Total Fat 13g | Sat. Fat 5g | Cholesterol 21mg | Carbohydrate 54g | Dietary Fiber 9g | Sodium 1,173mg

Tortilla Soup

vegan

MAKES 4 SERVINGS

This tasty medley of corn, beans, and fresh vegetables makes a satisfying light lunch or impressive opener for any Mexican-style meal. Kidney beans or pinto beans can replace the black variety, if desired.

1 tablespoon extra-virgin olive oil

1 large onion (about 8 ounces), chopped

1 small jalapeño chili, seeded and finely chopped

2 large cloves garlic, finely chopped

1 (14-ounce) can gluten-free low-sodium vegetable broth

1 cup water

2 medium tomatoes (about 6 ounces each), peeled, seeded, and chopped

1 small zucchini (about 4 ounces), cut into ½-inch-thick rounds

½ teaspoon dried oregano

½ teaspoon ground cumin

Salt and freshly ground black pepper, to taste

1 (15-ounce) can black beans, rinsed and drained

1 cup cooked fresh or thawed frozen yellow corn

2 tablespoons fresh lime juice

2 tablespoons chopped fresh cilantro

2 ounces gluten-free tortilla chips, broken into bite-size pieces

Tabasco sauce (optional)

In a medium stockpot, heat the oil over medium heat. Add the onion and chili and cook, stirring, until the vegetables are softened, about 5 minutes. Add the garlic and cook, stirring constantly, for 1 minute. Add the broth, water, tomatoes, zucchini, oregano, cumin, salt, and pepper; bring to a boil over medium-high heat. Add the beans and corn and reduce the heat to medium. Cook, stirring occasionally, until the zucchini is tender, about 5 minutes. Remove from the heat and stir in the lime juice and cilantro.

To serve, ladle the soup into 4 bowls and garnish with equal amounts of the tortilla chips. Serve at once, with the Tabasco sauce passed separately (if using).

Cook's Tip ✐

To peel tomatoes, bring a medium stockpot filled with water to a boil over high heat; drop in the tomatoes and boil for 20 seconds. Drain and rinse under cold-running water. Peel off the skins.

Moroccan Vegetable Stew with Rice and Mint Gremolata

vegan

MAKES 4 SERVINGS

Traditionally served over couscous, a tiny wheat pasta, this classic Moroccan vegetable stew is equally delicious with rice.

- **2 tablespoons extra-virgin olive oil**
- **6 to 8 scallions (mostly white parts), thinly sliced**
- **2 medium carrots (about 8 ounces total), coarsely chopped**
- **1 (14.5-ounce) can diced tomatoes, juices included**
- **1 cup gluten-free low-sodium vegetable broth**
- **1 tablespoon tomato paste**
- **½ teaspoon salt**
- **¼ teaspoon crushed red pepper flakes, or more to taste**
- **¼ teaspoon ground cinnamon**
- **¼ teaspoon ground ginger**
- **¼ teaspoon crushed coriander**
- **Pinch saffron threads (optional)**
- **Freshly ground black pepper, to taste**
- **1 (15-ounce) can chickpeas, rinsed and drained**
- **½ cup frozen green peas and pearl onions**
- **4 ounces fresh spinach leaves, chopped**
- **3 cups hot cooked brown or white rice (see Cook's Tip, page 145)**
- **Mint Gremolata (page 48)**

In a medium stockpot, heat the oil over medium heat. Add the scallions and carrots and cook, stirring, until softened, about 5 minutes. Add the tomatoes and their juices, broth, tomato paste, salt, red pepper flakes, cinnamon, ginger, coriander, saffron (if using), and black pepper; bring to a brisk simmer over medium-high heat. Reduce the heat and simmer gently, uncovered, for 5 minutes, stirring occasionally. Add the chickpeas and peas and onions and bring to a brisk simmer over medium-high heat. Reduce the heat and add the spinach; cook, stirring occasionally, until the spinach is just wilted, about 2 minutes.

To serve, divide the rice evenly among 4 shallow soup bowls. Top with equal amounts of the vegetable mixture, then sprinkle with Mint Gremolata. Serve at once.

MINT GREMOLATA

vegan|low-carb

MAKES ¼ CUP

Serve this tasty topping as a garnish for countless soups and stews and bean and vegetable dishes.

2 tablespoons chopped fresh mint

2 tablespoons chopped fresh parsley

1 large clove garlic, finely chopped

1 teaspoon freshly grated lemon peel

Salt and freshly ground black pepper, to taste

In a small bowl, mix together all the ingredients until well combined. If not using immediately, cover and refrigerate for up to 1 day.

PER TABLESPOON

Calories 3 | Protein 0g | Total Fat 0g |
Sat. Fat 0g | Cholesterol 0mg | Carbohydrate 1g |
Dietary Fiber 0g | Sodium 2mg

Salads

Salad is the quickest, most reliable route to healthful gluten-free eating for vegetarians and nonvegetarians alike. Whether they're first courses, side dishes, or stand-alone suppers, salads are typically based on fresh greens or quickly cooked vegetables, so the vitamins and nutrients retain their potency and the flavors don't get lost in the mix. The greens possibilities are almost endless: arugula, Belgian endive, bok choy, cabbage, curly endive, dandelion greens, escarole, mesclun, radicchio, spinach, Swiss chard, and watercress. Then, of course, there are the lettuces: iceberg, romaine, butter, green leaf, and red leaf, to name a few. The most popular salad vegetable is the tomato (technically a fruit), with bell peppers, cucumbers, carrots, radishes, mushrooms, and red onion following close behind. Marinated favorites include artichoke hearts, capers, pepperoncini, sun-dried tomatoes, and various olives. Quickly blanched asparagus and green beans are wonderful with vinaigrettes, and everyone loves potato salad. Orange slices, pear or apple wedges, chunks of mango or pineapple can all be tossed into salads. Additional protein can come from beans and other legumes, nuts, seeds, hard-cooked eggs, and cheeses. The most healthful and reliably gluten-free dressings are olive oil–based vinaigrettes, though rich and creamy dressings are acceptable if prepared with gluten-free mayonnaise. If you're concerned about fat and calories, the Ranch Dressing (page 57), made with nonfat buttermilk and light mayonnaise, contains only 17 calories and 2 grams of fat per tablespoon—it doubles as a delicious dip to boot.

Warm Beet Salad
with Parsley and Walnuts

vegan|low-carb

MAKES 4 SERVINGS

This is a pretty salad to offer on a holiday buffet, as it can be served at room temperature. Substitute balsamic vinegar for the raspberry variety, if desired.

- 1 (16-ounce) jar whole beets
- 3 tablespoons gluten-free low-sodium vegetable broth
- 1 tablespoon extra-virgin olive oil
- 1 teaspoon raspberry vinegar
- 2 shallots, thinly sliced
- 2 to 3 tablespoons chopped fresh parsley
- 2 tablespoons coarsely chopped walnuts
- Salt and freshly ground black pepper, to taste

Cook the beets according to jar directions; drain well. While still hot, transfer to a medium bowl and add the broth, oil, and vinegar, tossing well to coat. Add the remaining ingredients, tossing well to combine. Serve warm or at room temperature.

PER SERVING

Calories 99 | Protein 3g | Total Fat 6g |
Sat. Fat 1g | Cholesterol 0mg | Carbohydrate 11g |
Dietary Fiber 2g | Sodium 325mg

Asian-Style Asparagus Salad

vegan|low-carb

MAKES 4 SERVINGS

This makes a lovely first-course salad to serve in the springtime when asparagus is in season.

- 1 pound medium asparagus, tough ends snapped off, cut into 2-inch pieces
- 1 teaspoon light sesame or peanut oil
- ½ teaspoon toasted (dark) sesame oil
- 2 tablespoons sesame seeds
- 3 scallions (white and green parts), thinly sliced
- 1 medium tomato (about 6 ounces), cored, seeded, and chopped
- 2 tablespoons white wine vinegar
- 1 tablespoon extra-virgin olive oil
- 1 tablespoon water
- 1 teaspoon sugar
- 1 small clove garlic, finely chopped
- Salt and freshly ground black pepper, to taste
- 4 cups mixed baby salad greens

Bring a large stockpot of salted water to a boil. Prepare an ice-water bath. Boil the asparagus until crisp-tender, 2 to 3 minutes. Drain and immediately refresh in the ice-water bath for about 5 minutes. Drain again.

In a medium skillet, heat both sesame oils over medium heat. Add the sesame seeds and cook, stirring constantly, for 2 minutes. Add the scallions and cook, stirring constantly, for 30 seconds. Transfer to a large bowl and add the drained asparagus and remaining ingredients, except the greens. Toss well to combine. Serve at room temperature, over the greens, or cover and refrigerate for a minimum of 2 hours and serve chilled.

PER SERVING

Calories 113 | Protein 4g | Total Fat 8g | Sat. Fat 1g | Cholesterol 0mg | Carbohydrate 10g | Dietary Fiber 3g | Sodium 22mg

Russian Beet and Potato Salad

egg-free

MAKES 4 TO 6 SERVINGS

If time doesn't permit steaming the beets, substitute with well-drained and cubed, canned beets instead.

8 (about 2½ inches in diameter) beets
 (about 1½ pounds)

1 pound medium boiling potatoes, scrubbed, left whole

1 small cucumber (about 6 ounces), peeled, seeded, and chopped

4 scallions (white and green parts), thinly sliced

2 tablespoons chopped fresh dill

½ cup gluten-free plain low-fat yogurt

½ cup gluten-free light sour cream

½ to 1 tablespoon prepared horseradish, or to taste

½ tablespoon apple cider vinegar

Salt and freshly ground black pepper, to taste

2 hard-cooked eggs (see method in Mexican Deviled Eggs, page 15), peeled and chopped (optional)

Pour about 1 inch of water in a medium stockpot or saucepan large enough to accommodate a 9-inch steaming basket. Place the steaming basket in the pot and add the beets. Bring to a boil over high heat. Cover tightly, reduce the heat to medium, and steam until the beets are tender, about 30 minutes, adding water to the pot as necessary. Transfer the beets to a colander and rinse under cold-running water until cool. Slip off the skins and cut into ½-inch cubes. Transfer to a large bowl.

Meanwhile, in a large saucepan, bring the potatoes and enough salted water to cover to a boil over high heat. Reduce the heat slightly and boil until tender but not mushy, about 20 minutes, depending on size. Drain well. When cool enough to handle, peel and cut into ½-inch cubes.

Add the potatoes, cucumber, scallions, and dill to the beets; toss well to combine. Add the yogurt, sour cream, ½ tablespoon horseradish, vinegar, salt, and pepper; toss well to combine. Adjust the seasonings, adding additional horseradish if necessary. Cover and refrigerate for a minimum of 3 hours, or overnight. Serve chilled, garnished with the eggs (if using).

PER SERVING

Calories 157 | Protein 6g | Total Fat 1g | Sat. Fat 0g | Cholesterol 4mg | Carbohydrate 32g | Dietary Fiber 5g | Sodium 127mg

Broccoli, Tomato, and Cashew Salad

dairy-free|low-carb

MAKES 6 SERVINGS

This unusual side salad is always a hit at potlucks and picnics.

- 4 cups fresh broccoli florets
- 2 cups cherry or grape tomatoes, halved or quartered
- ½ cup gluten-free light mayonnaise
- ¼ cup gluten-free dry roasted cashews, chopped
- 2 teaspoons sugar
- Salt and freshly ground black pepper, to taste

In a medium bowl, toss all the ingredients until well combined. Cover and refrigerate for a minimum of 3 hours, or overnight. Serve chilled.

PER SERVING

Calories 113 | Protein 3g | Total Fat 7g | Sat. Fat 1g | Cholesterol 7mg | Carbohydrate 12g | Dietary Fiber 3g | Sodium 115mg

Southwestern-Style Coleslaw

vegan|low-carb

MAKES 6 SERVINGS

This slightly spicy slaw is an excellent accompaniment to many of the book's Mexican-style dishes.

- 1 (16-ounce) bag shredded coleslaw mix (about 8 cups)
- 2 cups cooked yellow corn, fresh or frozen
- ½ cup chopped fresh cilantro
- ¼ cup extra-virgin olive oil
- 3 tablespoons fresh lime juice
- 2 tablespoons diced canned mild green chilies, drained
- 2 tablespoons diced pimiento, drained
- 1 teaspoon sugar (optional)
- ¾ teaspoon ground cumin, or more to taste
- ½ teaspoon salt
- Freshly ground black pepper, to taste

In a large bowl, toss together all the ingredients until thoroughly combined. Cover and refrigerate for a minimum of 3 hours, or overnight, and serve chilled.

PER SERVING

Calories 152 | Protein 3g | Total Fat 10g | Sat. Fat 1g | Cholesterol 0mg | Carbohydrate 16g | Dietary Fiber 4g | Sodium 203mg

Roasted Fresh Corn and Arugula Salad with Lemon Vinaigrette

egg-free|dairy-free with vegan option|low-carb

MAKES 4 SERVINGS

For a vegan dish, substitute maple syrup or dark corn syrup for the honey.

2 ears fresh corn

3 tablespoons extra-virgin olive oil

Salt and freshly ground black pepper, to taste

2 to 3 tablespoons fresh lemon juice

½ tablespoon honey

1 teaspoon finely chopped lemon peel

8 ounces arugula or other bitter greens, washed and torn

Cherry or grape tomatoes (optional)

❧ Preheat the oven to broil.

Using a sharp knife, remove the kernels from each ear of corn. Transfer the kernels to an ungreased baking sheet and, using your fingers to evenly coat each kernel, toss with ½ tablespoon of the oil. Broil about 6 inches from the heating element until lightly browned, stirring a few times and watching carefully not to burn, 7 or 8 minutes. Season with salt and pepper and set aside to cool slightly.

In a large bowl, whisk together the remaining oil, lemon juice, honey, lemon peel, salt, and pepper. Add the arugula and toss well to combine. Divide evenly among 4 salad plates and sprinkle with equal amounts of corn. Serve at once, garnished with the cherry tomatoes (if using).

PER SERVING

Calories 174 | Protein 4g | Total Fat 11g | Sat. Fat 2g | Cholesterol 0mg | Carbohydrate 18g | Dietary Fiber 2g | Sodium 26mg

German Cucumber and Tomato Salad

egg-free|low-carb

MAKES 4 SERVINGS

This delicious cucumber salad is actually better the next day.

⅓ cup gluten-free light sour cream

1 tablespoon canola oil

1 tablespoon apple cider vinegar

1½ tablespoons chopped fresh dill, or ½ tablespoon dried

Salt and freshly ground black pepper, to taste

2 large cucumbers (about 12 ounces each), thinly sliced

4 scallions (white and green parts), thinly sliced

8 ounces plum tomatoes (about 4 medium), chopped

❧ In a large bowl, stir together the sour cream, oil, vinegar, dill, salt, and pepper until well blended. Add the cucumbers, scallions, and tomatoes; toss until thoroughly combined. Cover and refrigerate for 1 to 24 hours and serve chilled.

PER SERVING

Calories 79 | Protein 3g | Total Fat 4g |
Sat. Fat 0g | Cholesterol 2mg | Carbohydrate 10g |
Dietary Fiber 3g | Sodium 18mg

Greek Cucumber and Yogurt Salad

egg-free|low-carb

MAKES 4 SERVINGS

Tzatziki, a refreshing cucumber and yogurt salad popular in Greece and other eastern Mediterranean countries, can also be served as a chilled soup—simply stir in one cup of ice water to the prepared recipe, below. It also makes a tasty dip or filling for stuffed tomatoes—see the recipe on page 149 for Stuffed Tomatoes with Herbed Tzatziki.

1 cup gluten-free plain low-fat yogurt

¼ cup finely chopped red onion

1½ tablespoons chopped fresh mint or dill, or
   ½ tablespoon dried

2 cloves garlic, finely chopped

1 tablespoon extra-virgin olive oil

½ tablespoon red wine vinegar

Salt and freshly ground black pepper,
   to taste

1 (12-ounce) cucumber, halved lengthwise, seeded, and thinly sliced

Chopped fresh mint leaves or fresh dill, for garnish

In a medium bowl, stir together the yogurt, onion, mint, garlic, oil, vinegar, salt, and pepper until thoroughly blended. Add the cucumber and toss well to combine. Let stand for about 10 minutes to allow the flavors to blend. Toss again and serve at room temperature. Alternatively, cover and refrigerate for 1 to 24 hours and serve chilled.

PER SERVING

Calories 83 | Protein 4g | Total Fat 4g |
Sat. Fat 1g | Cholesterol 3mg | Carbohydrate 8g |
Dietary Fiber 1g | Sodium 43mg

Mexican Green Bean Salad

vegan|low-carb

MAKES 4 TO 6 SERVINGS

This is one of my favorite ways to enjoy fresh green beans.

1 pound fresh green beans, trimmed

¼ cup olive oil

1 tablespoon fresh lemon juice

½ tablespoon red wine vinegar

1 jalapeño chili, seeded and chopped

1 tablespoon finely chopped red onion

1 tablespoon finely chopped fresh parsley

1 tablespoon finely chopped fresh cilantro

Salt and freshly ground black pepper, to taste

In a large stockpot filled with boiling salted water, cook the beans until crisp-tender, 3 to 5 minutes. Prepare a large bowl of ice water. Drain the beans and immediately refresh in the ice-water bath for about 5 minutes. Drain well.

In a large bowl, stir together the remaining ingredients and let stand for about 5 minutes to allow the flavors to blend. Stir again and add the drained green beans, tossing well to combine. Let marinate at room temperature for 30 minutes before tossing again and serving. Alternatively, cover and refrigerate for 2 hours or overnight; serve chilled or return to room temperature.

PER SERVING

Calories 162 | Protein 2g | Total Fat 14g | Sat. Fat 2g | Cholesterol 0mg | Carbohydrate 10g | Dietary Fiber 4g | Sodium 8mg

Mixed Greens and Tomato Salad with Ranch Dressing

lacto-ovo|low-carb

MAKES 4 SERVINGS

You can add raw or lightly blanched vegetables for a more substantial salad—snap peas or shredded carrots are especially delicious with the dressing.

1 (10-ounce) bag mixed salad greens

4 medium plum tomatoes (about 2 ounces each), thinly sliced

Salt and freshly ground black pepper, to taste

½ cup Ranch Dressing (recipe opposite)

Divide the greens evenly among 4 salad bowls or plates. Top with equal portions of the tomatoes. Season lightly with salt and pepper. Drizzle evenly with the dressing and serve at once.

PER SERVING

Calories 95 | Protein 2g | Total Fat 7g | Sat. Fat 1g | Cholesterol 5mg | Carbohydrate 9g | Dietary Fiber 2g | Sodium 364mg

RANCH DRESSING

lacto-ovo|low-carb

MAKES ABOUT 1 CUP

Use this perennial favorite as a dip for raw veggies as well.

- ¾ cup nonfat buttermilk
- 4 tablespoons gluten-free light mayonnaise
- 1 tablespoon canola oil
- 2 teaspoons apple cider vinegar
- 1 teaspoon onion powder
- ½ teaspoon garlic powder
- ½ teaspoon sugar
- ½ teaspoon salt
- ¼ teaspoon freshly ground black pepper

❧ In a small bowl, whisk together all the ingredients until thoroughly blended. Cover and refrigerate for a minimum of 1 hour, or up to 3 days, and serve chilled.

PER SERVING (PER TABLESPOON)

Calories 17 | Protein 0g | Total Fat 2g | Sat. Fat 0g | Cholesterol 1mg | Carbohydrate 1g | Dietary Fiber 0g | Sodium 85mg

Romaine and Parmesan Salad with Balsamic Vinaigrette

egg-free|low-carb

MAKES 4 SERVINGS

This is a delicious egg-free alternative to Caesar salad. Sherry vinegar or good-quality red wine vinegar can replace the balsamic variety.

- 1½ tablespoons balsamic vinegar
- 1 clove garlic, finely chopped
- ¼ teaspoon coarse salt, or to taste
- ¼ cup extra-virgin olive oil
- 8 cups torn romaine lettuce leaves
- ½ cup gluten-free freshly shredded Parmesan cheese
- Freshly ground black pepper, to taste

❧ In a large bowl, combine the vinegar, garlic, and salt. Gradually whisk in the oil until well blended. Add the romaine and cheese, tossing gently yet thoroughly to combine. Serve at once, garnished with a grinding of pepper.

PER SERVING

Calories 181 | Protein 6g | Total Fat 17g | Sat. Fat 4g | Cholesterol 7mg | Carbohydrate 4g | Dietary Fiber 3g | Sodium 296mg

VARIATION: *For spinach salad with orange-cranberry dressing and sunflower seeds, substitute sweetened dried cranberries for the raisins.*

Spinach Salad with Orange-Raisin Dressing and Sunflower Seeds

lacto-ovo | low-carb

MAKES 4 SERVINGS

This is an especially delicious way to enjoy the iron-rich green.

- ¼ **cup plain gluten-free nonfat yogurt**
- ¼ **cup gluten-free light mayonnaise**
- ¼ **cup raisins**
- 1 **tablespoon frozen orange juice concentrate**
- 1 **tablespoon water**
- 1 **tablespoon canola oil**
- **Salt and freshly ground black pepper, to taste**
- 1 **(10-ounce) bag fresh baby spinach**
- 2 **to 4 tablespoons sunflower seeds**

In a small bowl, mix together the yogurt, mayonnaise, raisins, orange juice concentrate, water, oil, salt, and pepper. Let stand at room temperature for about 10 minutes to allow the raisins to soften.

Divide the spinach among 4 salad bowls or plates. Top with equal portions of the dressing. Sprinkle evenly with the sunflower seeds. Serve at once.

PER SERVING

Calories 148 | Protein 4g | Total Fat 9g |
Sat. Fat 1g | Cholesterol 6mg | Carbohydrate 16g |
Dietary Fiber 3g | Sodium 143mg

Mexican Tomato and Cheese Salad

egg-free | low-carb

MAKES 4 SERVINGS

I think of this as Mexico's version of Italy's *insalata caprese. Queso fresco* is a slightly salty white Mexican cheese with a texture similar to farmer cheese.

- 2 **tablespoons extra-virgin olive oil**
- 2 **tablespoons red wine vinegar**
- 1 **teaspoon dried oregano, preferably Mexican**
- 2 **cloves garlic, finely chopped**
- **Salt and freshly ground black pepper, to taste**
- 3 **medium vine-ripened tomatoes (about 5 ounces each), sliced into ¼-inch-thick rounds**
- 1 **medium red onion (about 6 ounces), thinly sliced, soaked in cold water to cover for 10 minutes, and drained well**
- 1 **jalapeño chili, seeded and thinly sliced**
- ¼ **cup** *queso fresco*, **crumbled**
- 1 **tablespoon finely chopped fresh cilantro**

In a small bowl, whisk together the oil, vinegar, oregano, garlic, salt, and pepper; set aside.

On a chilled platter, arrange the tomatoes, onion, and chili in an overlapping circular fashion. Sprinkle evenly with the cheese, then the cilantro. Drizzle evenly with the vinaigrette and serve at room temperature.

PER SERVING

Calories 115 | Protein 3g | Total Fat 8g |
Sat. Fat 1g | Cholesterol 2mg | Carbohydrate 11g |
Dietary Fiber 2g | Sodium 21mg

Stuffed Avocados and Iceberg Lettuce with Cilantro Mayonnaise

lacto-ovo|low-carb

MAKES 4 SERVINGS

These scrumptious stuffed avocados are a perfect lunch on a sultry day. The cilantro mayonnaise also makes a tasty topping for Black Bean and Brown Rice Burgers (page 84).

> **2 ripe avocados, halved, pitted, pulp removed and chopped, shells reserved**
> **2 medium plum tomatoes (about 2 ounces each), chopped**
> **2 tablespoons finely chopped red onion**
> **2 tablespoons chopped black olives**
> **3 teaspoons fresh lime juice**
> **Salt and freshly ground black pepper, to taste**
> **¼ cup gluten-free light mayonnaise**
> **¼ cup gluten-free light sour cream**
> **2 tablespoons finely chopped fresh cilantro**
> **4 cups shredded iceberg lettuce**
> **Crushed tortilla chips or taco shells, for garnish (optional)**

In a small bowl, toss the avocado pulp, tomatoes, onion, olives, 2 teaspoons of the lime juice, salt, and pepper until well combined. Fill the avocado shells with the avocado mixture.

In another small bowl, mix the mayonnaise, sour cream, remaining 1 teaspoon lime juice, cilantro, salt, and pepper until well blended. Top each avocado half with equal dollops of the mayonnaise mixture. Serve at once, over equal portions of the lettuce, garnished with the crushed tortilla chips (if using).

PER SERVING

Calories 226 | Protein 3g | Total Fat 19g | Sat. Fat 3g | Cholesterol 7mg | Carbohydrate 14g | Dietary Fiber 4g | Sodium 139mg

Tuscan-Style Bread Salad

vegan

MAKES 4 SERVINGS

Who says those with celiac disease or wheat allergies have to miss out on *panzanella*, Tuscany's famous bread salad? Share this delicious recipe for edible proof otherwise.

- 4 ounces (about 4 slices) gluten-free white bread, cut into 1-inch cubes
- 6 tablespoons extra-virgin olive oil
- Salt, preferably the coarse variety, and freshly ground black pepper, to taste
- 4 medium tomatoes (about 6 ounces each), preferably vine-ripened, cored, each cut into 8 wedges
- 2 cups loosely packed fresh basil leaves, torn in half or quarters, depending on size
- 1 (8-ounce) cucumber, sliced lengthwise, then cut crosswise into ½-inch pieces

- 1 small red onion (about 4 ounces), thinly sliced into half-rings, soaked in cold water to cover for 10 minutes, and drained well
- 4 scallions (white and green parts), thinly sliced
- 6 pitted kalamata olives, halved
- 2 tablespoons finely chopped fresh flat-leaf parsley
- 1 tablespoon fresh lemon juice
- 1 tablespoon balsamic vinegar
- 2 large cloves garlic, finely chopped

Preheat the oven to 350F (175C).

In a medium bowl, toss the bread cubes with 2 tablespoons of the oil, salt, and pepper. Place on an ungreased baking sheet in a single layer. Bake in the center of the oven for 10 to 15 minutes, or until golden, stirring and turning halfway through cooking. Remove from the oven and let cool.

Meanwhile, place the remaining ingredients in a large bowl and season with salt and pepper; toss well to combine. Let stand at room temperature for about 10 minutes to allow the flavors to blend. Add the toasted bread, tossing well to thoroughly combine. Let stand at room temperature for 30 minutes to 1 hour; toss again and serve.

PER SERVING

Calories 337 | Protein 5g | Total Fat 24g | Sat. Fat 3g | Cholesterol 0mg | Carbohydrate 29g | Dietary Fiber 5g | Sodium 263mg

Grilled Corn, Roasted Pepper, Tomato, and Fresh Mozzarella Salad

egg-free

MAKES 4 TO 6 SERVINGS

This is the quintessential summer main-course salad. For a vegan side dish, omit the fresh mozzarella.

- 4 medium vine-ripened tomatoes (about 6 ounces each), chopped
- ½ medium Vidalia or other sweet onion, sliced into very thin half-rings
- ¼ cup chopped fresh basil
- 2 large cloves garlic, finely chopped
- 2 tablespoons extra-virgin olive oil
- 2 tablespoons balsamic vinegar
- Salt and freshly ground black pepper, to taste
- 4 ears corn, in husks, soaked in water to cover for 1 hour, drained
- 1 large red bell pepper (about 8 ounces), left whole
- 8 cups mixed salad greens
- ½ pound fresh mozzarella cheese, thinly sliced

✒ Prepare a medium-hot charcoal grill or gas grill. Position the grill rack 4 to 6 inches from the heat source.

Place the tomatoes, onion, basil, garlic, oil, vinegar, salt, and pepper in a large bowl; toss well to combine. Let stand at room temperature for about 30 minutes to allow the flavors to blend.

Grill the corn in the husks until tender and slightly charred, 15 to 20 minutes, turning occasionally. Grill the bell pepper until charred, turning frequently, about 10 minutes. Place the bell pepper in a paper bag and twist to close; let cool for 15 minutes.

Remove the husks from the corn and cut the kernels from the cobs. Add the kernels to the tomato mixture. Peel the skin from the bell pepper, remove the seeds, and chop. Add the bell pepper to the tomato mixture. Toss well, taste, and season with additional salt and pepper, if needed.

To serve, divide the greens evenly among 4 serving plates. Top with equal amounts of the corn salad and dressing. Top with equal amounts of the mozzarella cheese and serve at once.

PER SERVING

Calories 440 | Protein 21g | Total Fat 23g |
Sat. Fat 10g | Cholesterol 51mg | Carbohydrate 45g |
Dietary Fiber 9g | Sodium 301mg

Classic Greek Peasant Salad

egg-free|low-carb

MAKES 4 SERVINGS

Though a classic Greek salad contains no lettuce, feel free to toss in some torn romaine, if you'd like.

3 medium tomatoes (about 6 ounces each), quartered

1 medium cucumber (about 12 ounces), peeled, sliced lengthwise in half, seeded, and thinly sliced crosswise

½ cup coarsely chopped fresh flat-leaf parsley

1 medium green bell pepper (about 6 ounces), thinly sliced

½ medium red onion (about 3 ounces), sliced into thin half-rings, soaked in cold water to cover for 10 minutes, and drained well

½ cup gluten-free crumbled feta cheese

12 pitted kalamata olives

¼ cup extra-virgin olive oil

2 tablespoons fresh lemon juice

Salt and freshly ground black pepper, to taste

Dried oregano, to taste

In a large salad bowl, toss all the ingredients together gently to combine. Serve at once.

PER SERVING

Calories 256 | Protein 5g | Total Fat 21g | Sat. Fat 5g | Cholesterol 17mg | Carbohydrate 14g | Dietary Fiber 3g | Sodium 406mg

Cook's Tip

For easy olive pitting, place each olive on its side and place the flat side of a large knife over the top; using your palm, strike the knife swiftly—the olive usually splits in half and the pit pops out.

Insalata Caprese

egg-free|low-carb

MAKES 4 TO 6 SERVINGS

You can easily make a meal out of this famous Italian tomato and fresh mozzarella salad.

¼ cup extra-virgin olive oil

2 tablespoons balsamic vinegar

Salt and freshly ground black pepper, to taste

3 medium vine-ripened tomatoes (about 5 ounces each), sliced into ¼-inch-thick rounds

About 20 fresh basil leaves

¾ pound fresh mozzarella, sliced into thin rounds

In a small bowl, whisk together the oil, vinegar, salt, and pepper; set aside.

On a chilled platter, arrange the tomatoes, basil leaves, and mozzarella in an overlapping circular fashion. Drizzle evenly with the vinaigrette and serve at room temperature.

PER SERVING

Calories 415 | Protein 20g | Total Fat 35g |
Sat. Fat 15g | Cholesterol 76mg | Carbohydrate 8g |
Dietary Fiber 1g | Sodium 363mg

Kasha Tabbouleh Salad

vegan

MAKES 3 TO 4 MAIN-DISH OR 5 TO 6 SIDE-DISH
SERVINGS

A nutlike alternative to the bulgur wheat used in traditional tabbouleh salad, kasha, or toasted buckwheat
groats, is gluten-free and has no relation to the wheat
family. Kasha can be found in the cereal aisle of most
well-stocked supermarkets.

1 cup kasha

2 cups gluten-free low-sodium vegetable
    broth

4 green onions (white and green parts), thinly
    sliced

½ cup finely chopped fresh parsley

2 tablespoons finely chopped fresh mint

3 medium plum tomatoes (about 2 ounces each),
    chopped

3 tablespoons extra-virgin olive oil

1 tablespoon fresh lemon juice

1 tablespoon red wine vinegar

Salt and freshly ground black pepper,
    to taste

Romaine lettuce leaves (optional)

Heat a medium skillet with a lid over
medium-high heat; add the kasha and cook, stirring constantly, until fragrant and toasted, 2 to 3
minutes. Transfer the kasha to a bowl and set
aside. Off the heat, carefully add the broth to
the skillet. Return to the heat and bring to a boil
over high heat; carefully stir in the reserved
kasha. Reduce the heat to medium-low and simmer, covered, until the kasha is tender and the
liquid is absorbed, 7 to 10 minutes. Remove
from the heat and let stand, covered, for 3 minutes. Fluff with a fork and transfer to a large
bowl; let cool to room temperature.

Add the remaining ingredients, except the
lettuce leaves; toss well to combine. Refrigerate,
covered, for a minimum of 2 hours or up to 2
days. Serve chilled or return to room temperature, with the lettuce leaves used as scoops (if
using).

PER SERVING

Calories 368 | Protein 15g | Total Fat 15g |
Sat Fat 2g | Cholesterol 0mg | Carbohydrate 48g |
Dietary Fiber 8g | Sodium 367mg

Lentil and Goat Cheese Salad

egg-free

MAKES 4 SERVINGS

French green lentils are preferred over the red variety as they hold their shape better during cooking. If you don't have balsamic vinegar, use sherry vinegar or red wine vinegar instead.

   1 ¼ cups lentils, preferably the French green
        variety, rinsed and picked over
   ½ teaspoon dried thyme
   ½ teaspoon salt, plus additional as necessary
   4 scallions (white and green parts), thinly sliced
   ¼ cup shredded carrot
   2 tablespoons extra-virgin olive oil
   2 tablespoons balsamic vinegar
   Freshly ground black pepper, to taste
   4 ounces gluten-free crumbled goat cheese
   8 cups mixed greens or baby spinach

In a medium stockpot, bring the lentils, thyme, ½ teaspoon salt, and enough water to cover to a boil over medium-high heat. Reduce the heat and simmer gently, partially covered, stirring occasionally, until the lentils are tender but not mushy, about 45 minutes, depending on the age of the lentils. When the lentils are done, if most of the water has not been absorbed, simmer, uncovered, stirring often, until most of the liquid has evaporated. Remove from the heat and add the scallions, tossing well to combine. Let cool to room temperature.

In a large bowl, combine the lentil mixture, carrot, oil, vinegar, salt, pepper, and all but 4 tablespoons of the goat cheese; toss gently to combine. (At this point, the lentil mixture can be refrigerated, covered, for up to 24 hours before serving chilled.)

To serve, divide the greens evenly among 4 serving plates. Top with equal amounts of the lentil mixture. Garnish with the remaining goat cheese and serve at once.

PER SERVING

Calories 402 | Protein 26g | Total Fat 18g |
Sat. Fat 8g | Cholesterol 30mg | Carbohydrate 38g |
Dietary Fiber 19g | Sodium 376mg

Mediterranean Salad with Stuffed Grape Leaves, Basil Oil, and Pine Nuts

vegan

MAKES 4 SERVINGS

Canned stuffed grape leaves (the gluten-free filling consists predominately of rice, but always check the label carefully), available in Middle Eastern markets and other specialty stores, make quick work of this refreshing Mediterranean salad.

   2 tablespoons extra-virgin olive oil
   1 cup loosely packed fresh basil leaves
   ¼ teaspoon coarse salt, plus more to taste
   2 (14-ounce) cans stuffed grape leaves, drained

1 large cucumber (about 12 ounces), peeled,
    seeded, and cut into bite-size chunks

16 cherry or grape tomatoes, halved

16 pitted kalamata or other good-quality olives

8 to 12 pepperoncini, drained

¼ cup pine nuts

Juice of 1 lemon (about 3 tablespoons)

Freshly ground black pepper

Combine the oil, basil, and ¼ teaspoon salt in a food processor fitted with the knife blade, or a blender; process until smooth. Set aside.

Divide the stuffed grape leaves, cucumber, tomatoes, olives, and pepperoncini among 4 plates. Sprinkle evenly with the pine nuts. Drizzle with the basil oil and lemon juice. Season with salt and pepper and serve.

PER SERVING

Calories 377 | Protein 7g | Total Fat 18g |
Sat. Fat 2g | Cholesterol 0mg | Carbohydrate 52g |
Dietary Fiber 6g | Sodium 578mg

Grilled Portobello Mushroom and Hearts of Romaine Salad with Goat Cheese Dressing

egg-free|low-carb

MAKES 4 SERVINGS

This makes a satisfying lunch, light supper, or elegant first course. Fresh spinach leaves can replace the romaine, if desired.

4 ounces gluten-free crumbled goat cheese

1 cup gluten-free light sour cream

¼ cup gluten-free light mayonnaise

1 tablespoon red wine vinegar

1 large clove garlic, finely chopped

Salt and freshly ground black pepper, to taste

2 romaine hearts (about 8 ounces)

4 large portobello mushroom caps (about
    2 ounces each)

2 teaspoons extra-virgin olive oil

16 cherry or grape tomatoes

In a small bowl, mash the cheese well with a fork. Stir in the sour cream, mayonnaise, vinegar, garlic, salt, and pepper until well blended. Set aside.

Cut the romaine hearts in half and divide among 4 plates. Set aside.

Meanwhile, heat a nonstick grill pan over medium-high heat. Brush each mushroom on the rounded underside and rim with ½ teaspoon of the oil; season with salt and pepper. Place the mushrooms, gill sides down, in the pan and grill for 3 minutes. Turn over and grill until nicely browned, 3 to 4 more minutes, rotating each mushroom a half turn after 2 minutes. While the tops of the mushrooms are grilling, fill gill sides with equal amounts of the reserved cheese mixture. Transfer the mushrooms to the reserved salad plates. Garnish with the cherry tomatoes and serve at once.

PER SERVING

Calories 241 | Protein 13g | Total Fat 17g |
Sat. Fat 8g | Cholesterol 40mg | Carbohydrate 12g |
Dietary Fiber 2g | Sodium 200mg

Santa Fe–Style Quinoa Salad

vegan

MAKES 4 MAIN-DISH OR 6 TO 8 SIDE-DISH SERVINGS

Quinoa (pronounced "keen-wa") is an ancient South American grain that is one of the best sources of plant protein on the planet. It is available in health food stores and some well-stocked supermarkets. Make sure to rinse the uncooked grains well under cold running water to wash away the bitter-tasting resin, or saponin.

1½ **cups water**

½ **cup mild or medium picante sauce**

1 **cup quinoa, rinsed well under cold running water**

½ **teaspoon ground cumin**

¼ **teaspoon salt**

Freshly ground black pepper, to taste

1 (15-ounce) can black beans, rinsed and drained

1½ cups fresh or frozen yellow corn, cooked, drained, and cooled

1 cup cherry or grape tomatoes, halved

4 scallions (white and green parts), thinly sliced

1 jalapeño chili, seeded and finely chopped

1 tablespoon canola oil

In a medium saucepan, combine the water, picante sauce, quinoa, cumin, salt, and pepper. Bring to a boil over high heat. Reduce the heat to medium, cover, and cook until the liquid is absorbed, 15 to 20 minutes. Remove from the heat and let stand for 5 minutes. Uncover and toss with a fork. Transfer to a large bowl and let cool slightly.

While still warm, add the remaining ingredients to the quinoa mixture, tossing well to combine. Serve slightly warm or let cool to room temperature. Alternatively, cover and refrigerate for a minimum of 3 hours, or up to 2 days, and serve chilled or return to room temperature.

PER SERVING

Calories 357 | Protein 15g | Total Fat 7g |
Sat. Fat 1g | Cholesterol 0mg | Carbohydrate 63g |
Dietary Fiber 8g | Sodium 398mg

Tex-Mex Pasta Salad

egg-free

MAKES 4 MAIN-DISH OR 6 TO 8 SIDE-DISH SERVINGS

This is an excellent choice for a picnic or potluck. Any bean can replace the pinto variety, if desired.

- 8 ounces gluten-free rice fusilli or elbow pasta, cooked according to package directions, rinsed under cold running water, and drained
- 1 (14.5-ounce) can pinto beans, rinsed and drained
- 1 cup frozen corn kernels, cooked, rinsed under cold running water, and drained
- 3 scallions (white and green parts), thinly sliced
- 1 cup gluten-free shredded reduced-fat cheddar cheese (optional)
- 1 cup medium salsa
- ½ cup gluten-free light sour cream
- 2 teaspoons ground cumin
- Salt and freshly ground black pepper, to taste

❧ In a large bowl, toss all the ingredients until well combined. Cover and refrigerate for a minimum of 2 hours or up to 3 days. Serve chilled.

PER SERVING

Calories 353 | Protein 9g | Total Fat 2g | Sat. Fat 0g | Cholesterol 2mg | Carbohydrate 78g | Dietary Fiber 6g | Sodium 187mg

Curried Rice and Cauliflower Salad with Chutney

vegan

MAKES 6 SERVINGS

Broccoli florets can easily replace the cauliflower in this delicious curried rice salad. While most commercial brands of Major Grey's mango chutney are gluten-free, always check the label carefully to be certain.

- 2 tablespoons peanut oil
- 2 cups long-grain white rice, rinsed in several changes of water until water runs clear, drained well
- 4 scallions (white and green parts), thinly sliced
- 2 cloves garlic, finely chopped
- 1 tablespoon gluten-free mild curry powder
- 1 tablespoon finely chopped fresh ginger
- 3½ cups gluten-free low-sodium vegetable broth
- ½ teaspoon salt
- 1 pound cauliflower florets, cut into bite-size pieces
- 1 cup chopped red or green bell pepper
- ¼ cup unsweetened shredded coconut
- ¾ cup gluten-free mango chutney
- ¼ cup chopped fresh mint

❧ In a medium deep-sided skillet with a lid, heat half of the oil over medium heat. Add the rice, scallions, garlic, curry powder, and ginger; cook, stirring, until the rice appears dry, about 4 minutes. Add the broth and salt and bring to a boil over high heat. Reduce the heat, cover, and simmer gently until the rice has absorbed the liquid, about 15 minutes. Uncover and fluff with a fork. Set aside to cool slightly.

Meanwhile, in a large stockpot filled with boiling salted water, cook the cauliflower for 1 minute. Drain and rinse under cold-running tap water until cool. Drain well.

In a large bowl, combine the rice mixture, cauliflower, and the remaining ingredients, tossing well to combine. Serve slightly warm or at room temperature. Alternatively, cover and refrigerate for up to 24 hours, and return to room temperature before serving.

PER SERVING

Calories 411 | Protein 13g | Total Fat 7g |
Sat. Fat 2g | Cholesterol 0mg | Carbohydrate 78g |
Dietary Fiber 7g | Sodium 521mg

Jamaican-Style Coconut Rice and Bean Salad

vegan

MAKES 6 SERVINGS

You can use any bean in this refreshing tropical salad.

2 cups long-grain white rice, rinsed in several changes of water until water runs clear, drained well
2 cups light coconut milk
2 cups water

1 (15-ounce) can red kidney beans, rinsed and drained
1 bunch scallions (white and green parts), thinly sliced
½ cup shredded carrots
1 small jalapeño chili, seeded and finely chopped
2 tablespoons chopped fresh cilantro
1 tablespoon fresh thyme leaves, or 1 teaspoon dried
2 tablespoons canola oil
2 tablespoons white wine vinegar
Salt and freshly ground black pepper, to taste

In a medium saucepan, bring the rice, coconut milk, and water to a boil over high heat. Reduce the heat, cover, and simmer gently until all the liquid is absorbed, about 15 minutes. Fluff with a fork and set aside to cool.

Transfer the cooled rice mixture to a large bowl and add the remaining ingredients, tossing well to combine. Serve at room temperature. Alternatively, cover and refrigerate for up to 24 hours, and return to room temperature before serving.

PER SERVING

Calories 403 | Protein 11g | Total Fat 10g |
Sat. Fat 5g | Cholesterol 0mg | Carbohydrate 67g |
Dietary Fiber 4g | Sodium 46mg

Thai Rice Noodle Salad
with Snow Peas

vegan

MAKES 4 TO 5 MAIN-DISH OR 6 TO 8 SIDE-DISH
SERVINGS

Rice noodles are available in Asian markets, specialty stores, and some well-stocked supermarkets.

8 ounces flat rice noodles, broken in half

2 tablespoons peanut oil

1 tablespoon toasted (dark) sesame oil

1 tablespoon finely chopped fresh ginger, or ½ teaspoon ground dried ginger

3 large cloves garlic, finely chopped

¼ teaspoon crushed red chili pepper

3 tablespoons tamari sauce

1 tablespoon unseasoned rice vinegar

1 teaspoon sugar

8 ounces fresh snow peas, trimmed, strings removed

1 bunch scallions (white and green parts), thinly sliced

½ cup unsalted peanuts, chopped

2 tablespoons diced pimiento, drained

2 tablespoons finely chopped fresh basil

In a large stockpot, soak the noodles according to package directions until al dente. (Or see Cook's Tip, below, for soaking methods.) Drain well and rinse with cold water for 30 seconds. Drain well and set aside.

Meanwhile, in a small nonstick skillet, heat the peanut oil and ½ tablespoon of the sesame oil over medium heat. Add the fresh ginger (if using), garlic, and crushed red chili pepper; cook, stirring constantly, until softened and fragrant, about 3 minutes. Remove from the heat and stir in the remaining sesame oil, tamari sauce, rice vinegar, sugar, and ground ginger (if using). Set aside to cool.

In large stockpot filled with boiling salted water, cook the snow peas for 30 seconds. Drain in a colander and rinse under cold running water to cool. Drain well. Cut in half on the diagonal and set aside.

In a large bowl, combine the noodles and reserved garlic mixture. Add the snow peas and remaining ingredients, tossing well to thoroughly combine. Serve at room temperature. Alternatively, cover and refrigerate for a minimum of 2 hours, or overnight, and serve chilled or return to room temperature.

PER SERVING

Calories 446 | Protein 9g | Total Fat 19g |
Sat. Fat 3g | Cholesterol 0mg | Carbohydrate 62g |
Dietary Fiber 4g | Sodium 770mg

Cook's Tip

There are at least two ways to soak rice noodles, for either further cooking or immediate use in a recipe. For the quicker hot-soak method, using 8 ounces of rice noodles or rice vermicelli (thin rice noodles), bring 4 to 6 cups of water to a boil in a large stockpot. Remove from heat and add the rice noodles. If noodles are to be cooked further in stir-fries, soups, or other dishes, let stand, stirring occasionally, until noodles are soft yet still quite chewy, 4 to 6 minutes for the vermicelli noodles, 6 to 8 minutes for regular noodles. If noodles require no additional cooking in the recipe, add 4 to 5 minutes to the total soaking time of either variety, or until the noodles are al dente. After noodles have soaked the appropriate amount of time, drain well and rinse under cold running water for 30 seconds. Noodles are now ready for either further cooking or immediate use in the recipe.

For a longer cold-soak method recommended mainly for noodles that are to be cooked further in recipes, soak either variety of rice noodle for about 30 minutes in like amount of cold water. Drain well and proceed to cook as directed in the recipe.

Layered Southwestern Salad

lacto-ovo|low-carb

MAKES 4 SERVINGS

Substitute broken tortilla chips for the taco shells, if desired.

1 cup gluten-free light sour cream
½ cup gluten-free light mayonnaise
1 teaspoon sugar
1 teaspoon garlic salt
½ teaspoon gluten-free chili powder
½ teaspoon onion powder
½ teaspoon ground cumin
¼ teaspoon freshly ground black pepper
⅛ teaspoon cayenne pepper (optional)
4 to 6 cups shredded iceberg lettuce
4 ounces (1 cup) gluten-free shredded reduced-fat cheddar cheese
4 ounces (1 cup) gluten-free shredded reduced-fat Monterey Jack cheese
2 medium tomatoes (about 6 ounces each), finely chopped
1 (2.25-ounce) can sliced black olives, drained
4 scallions (white and green parts), thinly sliced
2 gluten-free taco shells, broken into small pieces

In a medium bowl, stir together the sour cream, mayonnaise, sugar, garlic salt, chili powder, onion powder, cumin, black pepper, and cayenne until thoroughly blended. Spread evenly in the bottom of a 2½-quart dish. Top with the lettuce, followed with the cheeses, tomatoes, olives, and scallions. Cover and refrigerate overnight. Just before serving, sprinkle with the crushed taco shells. Toss and serve at once.

PER SERVING

Calories 291 | Protein 18g | Total Fat 15g | Sat. Fat 4g | Cholesterol 31mg | Carbohydrate 20g | Dietary Fiber 3g | Sodium 1,180mg

Stuffed Tomatoes with **Feta** and Kalamata Olives over Spinach

egg-free|low-carb

MAKES 4 SERVINGS

The best flavors of Greece are captured in these delicious stuffed tomatoes, ideal for lunch or a light supper.

1⅓ cups gluten-free crumbled feta cheese

¼ cup pitted kalamata or other good-quality black olives, chopped

2 to 3 tablespoons finely chopped fresh mint and/or flat-leaf parsley

2 large cloves garlic, finely chopped

Salt and freshly ground black pepper, to taste

4 medium tomatoes (about 6 ounces each)

4 to 8 cups baby spinach leaves

Extra-virgin olive oil and red wine vinegar, to taste

In a small bowl, mix together the cheese, olives, mint, garlic, salt, and pepper until combined. Set aside.

Cut a thin slice from the top of each tomato. Scoop out the inside of each tomato with a melon baller or small spoon. Discard the tops and pulp. Spoon equal portions of the feta mixture into each tomato. (At this point, the tomatoes can be refrigerated, covered, for a minimum of 2 hours, or overnight, and served chilled.)

To serve, divide the spinach equally among 4 serving plates. Drizzle the greens with desired amounts of oil and vinegar. Top with a stuffed tomato and serve at once, with additional oil and vinegar passed separately, if desired.

PER SERVING

Calories 221 | Protein 10g | Total Fat 15g | Sat. Fat 8g | Cholesterol 45mg | Carbohydrate 14g | Dietary Fiber 3g | Sodium 823mg

Breads, Pizzas, Tacos, Sandwiches, and Other Lighter Fare

While it's true that man doesn't live by bread alone, there's no reason why those with celiac disease and wheat allergies have to live without it. With the ever-expanding range of naturally gluten-free flours available in health food stores and many major supermarkets, once verboten sandwich breads, rolls, biscuits, muffins, scones, and pizza are not only possible, but tasty as well. That's not to say that these flours are as easily worked with as the regular varieties, but once you've familiarized yourself with the recipes, you will find yourself making them again and again. All the bread and bread-related recipes in this book (you will also find several in other chapters as well) have been formulated using natural sources of gluten-free flour. Although there are many commercial gluten-free flour mixes on the market, not all brands produce the same results, so their substitution is not recommended. When you don't feel like baking, try some of the quick and easy tacos, quesadillas, or other sandwiches. If you're watching your carbs, consider the zucchini-crusted pizza. If you don't have time to prep the zucchini, go crustless with the deep-dish "pizza." If you don't care for the suggested toppings, create your own—the possibilities are endless.

Banana Bread

lacto-ovo

MAKES 16 SLICES

This is excellent toasted. For a tasty variation, use pecans instead of walnuts.

2 cups white rice flour

2 teaspoons gluten-free baking powder

Pinch salt

½ cup (1 stick) butter, softened

1 cup sugar

2 eggs

1 teaspoon gluten-free pure vanilla extract

3 large very ripe bananas, mashed

1 cup walnuts, ground

Preheat the oven to 325F (165C). Lightly grease a 9 × 5-inch loaf pan.

In a medium bowl, using a wire whisk, mix together the rice flour, baking powder, and salt until thoroughly combined.

In a large bowl, beat the butter and sugar until creamy with an electric mixer. Beat in the eggs, vanilla, and bananas. Add the flour mixture, then the walnuts, beating on low speed until thoroughly blended. Pour the batter into the prepared pan.

Bake in the center of the oven for about 1½ hours, or until a knife inserted into the center comes out clean. (Do not underbake. After about 50 minutes, if top is browning too quickly, cover loosely with foil until done.) Cool in pan on a wire rack. Serve slightly warm or at room temperature. For optimal freshness, store completely cooled bread in an airtight container for up to 2 days, or freeze.

PER SERVING (¹⁄₁₆ OF LOAF)

Calories 248 | Protein 4g | Total Fat 11g | Sat. Fat 4g | Cholesterol 42mg | Carbohydrate 35g | Dietary Fiber 1g | Sodium 120mg

Blueberry Muffins

lacto-ovo

MAKES 12 MUFFINS

These delicious muffins are best served slightly warm. Fresh raspberries or blackberries can replace the blueberries, if desired.

1 cup white rice flour

½ cup brown rice flour or white rice flour

¾ cup superfine sugar

½ cup tapioca flour

2 teaspoons gluten-free baking powder

1 teaspoon baking soda

1¼ teaspoons xanthan gum

¼ teaspoon salt

¾ cup nonfat buttermilk

5 tablespoons canola oil

1 egg, lightly beaten

¾ cup fresh blueberries

Preheat the oven to 350F (175C). Lightly grease a 12-cup muffin pan.

In a large bowl, using a wire whisk, mix together the rice flours, sugar, tapioca flour, baking powder, baking soda, xanthan gum, and salt until thoroughly combined.

In a medium bowl, whisk together the buttermilk, oil, and egg. Make a well in the center of the dry ingredients and pour in the buttermilk mixture; stir gently with a wooden spoon to combine. Gently fold in the blueberries.

Fill the prepared muffin cups with equal portions of the batter. Bake in the center of the oven for 25 to 30 minutes, or until a knife inserted into the center of a muffin comes out clean. (If muffins are browning too quickly after about 20 minutes, cover loosely with foil until done.) Serve warm or at room temperature. For optimal freshness, store completely cooled muffins in an airtight container up to 24 hours, or refrigerate up to 3 days.

PER SERVING (PER MUFFIN)

Calories 205 | Protein 2g | Total Fat 6g |
Sat. Fat 1g | Cholesterol 18mg | Carbohydrate 36g |
Dietary Fiber 1g | Sodium 216mg

Buttermilk Biscuits

egg-free

MAKES 12 BISCUITS

If served immediately, these gluten-free biscuits are almost as light as traditional wheat flour biscuits and are equally satisfying.

1⅓ **cups rice flour**
⅔ **cup potato starch flour**
1 **teaspoon baking soda**
½ **teaspoon gluten-free baking powder**
½ **teaspoon salt**
½ **teaspoon xanthan gum**
3 **tablespoons shortening**
1 **cup buttermilk**

Preheat the oven to 400F (205C).

In a large bowl, mix together the rice flour, potato starch flour, baking soda, baking powder, salt, and xanthan gum. Add the shortening and, using your fingers, mix together until thoroughly combined and mixture resembles coarse meal. Add the buttermilk and stir until just combined. Gather into a firm ball, then divide into 12 equal balls. Place on an ungreased baking sheet and flatten slightly with your palms. Bake for 12 minutes, or until lightly browned. Serve at once.

PER SERVING

Calories 136 | Protein 3g | Total Fat 4g |
Sat Fat 1g | Cholesterol 1mg | Carbohydrate 23g |
Dietary Fiber 1g | Sodium 234mg

Italian-Style Herbed Cheese Bread

lacto-ovo

MAKES 1 LOAF

Serve this fragrant bread with just about any Italian-style entrée or soup—it's especially delicious with the Milanese-Style Minestrone Soup (page 43).

2 cups tapioca flour

1 1/2 teaspoons xanthan gum

1 teaspoon gluten-free baking powder

1/2 teaspoon baking soda

1 teaspoon dried oregano

1/2 teaspoon dried thyme

1/2 teaspoon salt

1 cup (4 ounces) gluten-free freshly shredded Parmesan or Romano cheese

1/3 cup nonfat milk

2 eggs

2 tablespoons water

1 tablespoon extra-virgin olive oil

Preheat the oven to 400F (205C). Lightly oil a 9 × 5-inch loaf pan and set aside.

In a large bowl, mix together the flour, xanthan gum, baking powder, baking soda, oregano, thyme, and salt with a large whisk until well combined. Add the cheese, mixing well to evenly distribute. In a small bowl, whisk together the milk, eggs, water, and oil until thoroughly blended; add to dry ingredients, stirring well to thoroughly combine (this is important). Transfer to prepared loaf pan and bake in the center of the oven for 15 to 18 minutes, or until lightly browned and the loaf sounds hollow when tapped.

Remove the loaf from the pan and let cool on a wire rack. For optimal freshness, store completely cooled bread in an airtight container for up to 24 hours, or freeze.

PER SERVING (1/16 OF LOAF)

Calories 110 | Protein 3g | Total Fat 3g | Sat. Fat 2g | Cholesterol 19mg | Carbohydrate 18g | Dietary Fiber 0g | Sodium 105mg

VARIATION: *To make* Italian-Style Herbed Cheese Bread with Sun-Dried Tomatoes: *Stir 1/4 cup marinated sun-dried tomatoes, well drained and finely chopped, into the liquid ingredients before adding them to the dry ingredients. Proceed as otherwise directed in the recipe.*

Cheddar Corn Bread

lacto-ovo|low-carb

MAKES 24 PIECES

Serve this savory corn bread with a steaming bowl of chili or by itself as a wholesome snack.

3 cups cornmeal

1/2 cup sugar

1 tablespoon dehydrated minced onion

1/2 teaspoon salt

2 cups boiling water

3 tablespoons canola oil

1 cup milk

2 eggs, lightly beaten

¼ cup gluten-free shredded cheddar cheese

1½ tablespoons gluten-free baking powder

1 teaspoon finely chopped jalapeño chili
    (optional)

Pinch cayenne pepper, or to taste (optional)

℘ Preheat the oven to 400F (205C). Lightly grease a 13×9-inch baking dish and set aside.

In a large bowl, combine the cornmeal, sugar, onion, and salt; stir in the water and oil. Add the milk and eggs, stirring well to combine. Add the cheese, baking powder, chili (if using), and cayenne (if using), stirring well to combine. Transfer the batter to the prepared dish. Bake for 35 to 40 minutes, or until a toothpick inserted into the center comes out clean. Cut into 24 squares and serve warm or at room temperature. For optimal freshness, store completely cooled bread in an airtight container for up to 2 days, or freeze.

PER SERVING (1 PIECE)

Calories 112 | Protein 3g | Total Fat 3g |
Sat. Fat 1g | Cholesterol 20mg | Carbohydrate 18g |
Dietary Fiber 1g | Sodium 131mg

Chickpea Flour Bread
dairy-free|low-carb
MAKES 1 LOAF

This light-textured loaf bread lends itself well to toasting, as it is more elastic and less crumbly than most gluten-free breads. Chickpea flour, or garbanzo bean flour, and tapioca flour are available in health food stores and the special dietary needs section of some major supermarkets.

1 cup plus 2 tablespoons chickpea
    flour

1 cup cornstarch

1 cup plus 1 tablespoon tapioca flour

3½ teaspoons xanthan gum

1½ teaspoons salt

3 tablespoons light brown sugar

3 eggs, lightly beaten

1 cup plus 2 tablespoons warm water
    (105F to 115F; 40C to 45C)

3 tablespoons canola oil

1 (¼-ounce) package gluten-free active
    dry yeast (about 1 tablespoon)

℘ Lightly oil a 9×5-inch loaf pan and set aside.

In a large bowl, mix together the chickpea flour, cornstarch, tapioca flour, xanthan gum, salt, and sugar with a large whisk until combined. In a medium bowl, mix together the eggs, water, oil, and yeast; add to the flour mixture, stirring until smooth and thoroughly combined. Transfer to prepared pan. Cover with plastic wrap and let rise at room temperature to the top of the pan, 1 to 1½ hours.

Preheat the oven to 375F (190C).

Remove the plastic wrap and bake in the center of the oven for 30 to 35 minutes, or until the loaf sounds hollow when tapped. Remove from the pan and let cool on a wire rack. For optimal freshness, store completely cooled bread in an airtight container for up to 24 hours, or freeze.

PER SERVING (¹⁄₂₄ OF LOAF)

Calories 104 | Protein 2g | Total Fat 3g |

Sat. Fat 0g | Cholesterol 27mg | Carbohydrate 18g |

Dietary Fiber 1g | Sodium 145mg

Cook's Tip

Xanthan gum is a white powder that helps bind together the flours in gluten-free baking and keeps breads and cakes from crumbling. It is available in health food stores and many major supermarkets in the special dietary needs section.

Irish Potato Bread
lacto-ovo|low-carb

MAKES 10 PIECES

Typically pan-fried, this lower-fat version of Celtic potato bread—also known as "boxty" bread—is a fine accompaniment to egg dishes. It makes a tasty snack on its own.

1¼ pounds boiling potatoes, peeled, cut into
　　halves or quarters, depending on size
2 tablespoons butter
½ teaspoon onion powder
½ teaspoon salt, or to taste
Salt and freshly ground black pepper, to taste
1 egg, lightly beaten
¼ cup potato starch flour

Preheat the oven to 350F (175C). Lightly oil a large baking sheet and set aside.

In a large saucepan or medium stockpot, place the potatoes in enough salted water to cover by a few inches. Bring to a boil over high heat. Reduce the heat to medium-high and cook until the potatoes are very tender, about 20 minutes. Drain well in a colander.

Transfer the potatoes to a large bowl or return to the saucepan and add the butter, onion powder, salt, and pepper; mash briefly with a potato masher or fork. Let cool for a few minutes, then add the egg, mashing until thoroughly blended. Add the potato starch flour, mashing until the mixture is smooth and well combined.

Divide the potato mixture into 10 pieces and pat into 4-inch squares. Transfer to prepared baking sheet. Using a table knife, make a diagonal slash across each piece, taking care not to cut all the way through. Bake for 20 to 25 minutes, or until golden. Serve warm or at room temperature.

PER SERVING (1 PIECE)

Calories 77 | Protein 2g | Total Fat 3g | Sat. Fat 2g | Cholesterol 27mg | Carbohydrate 11g | Dietary Fiber 1g | Sodium 140mg

Bell Pepper, Black Olive, and Onion Pizza with Zucchini Crust

lacto-ovo|low-carb

MAKES 6 SERVINGS

Many of the best flavors of the Mediterranean are captured in this low-carb pizza, but if you are not an olive fan, leave them out—the results will still be delicious.

> ¾ **cup gluten-free pizza sauce**
> 1 **Zucchini Pizza Crust (page 80)**
> ½ **small red bell pepper (about 2 ounces), cut into very thin strips**
> ½ **small green bell pepper (about 2 ounces), cut into very thin strips**
> ½ **small onion (about 2 ounces), cut into very thin half-rings**
> ¼ **cup pitted kalamata or other good-quality black olives, halved**
> 1 **cup gluten-free shredded part-skim mozzarella cheese**
> ½ **cup gluten-free freshly grated Parmesan cheese**
> **Dried oregano, to taste**
> 1 **tablespoon extra-virgin olive oil**

Preheat the oven to 375F (190C).

Spread the pizza sauce over the top of the zucchini crust. Arrange the bell peppers, onion, and olives evenly over the top. Sprinkle evenly with the mozzarella, then the Parmesan cheese. Sprinkle with oregano, then drizzle with the oil.

Bake for 10 minutes. Cut into wedges and serve warm.

PER SERVING

Calories 241 | Protein 16g | Total Fat 16g |
Sat. Fat 6g | Cholesterol 96mg | Carbohydrate 9g |
Dietary Fiber 1g | Sodium 689mg

ZUCCHINI PIZZA CRUST

lacto-ovo|low-carb

MAKES 1 STANDARD-SIZE RECTANGULAR PIZZA CRUST

Use this fabulous grain-free crust as a base for all your favorite pizza toppings—just take care not to overbake it the second time in the oven.

2 to 2½ cups grated raw zucchini (about ¾ pound)
Salt
2 eggs
1 cup shredded gluten-free part-skim mozzarella cheese
Freshly ground black pepper, to taste

Preheat the oven to 375F (190C). Lightly grease a standard-size nonstick baking sheet with sides.

Place the zucchini in a colander set in the sink and sprinkle liberally with salt; let drain for about 15 minutes. Rinse under cold-running water and drain well. Transfer to several layers of paper towels and squeeze to thoroughly dry. Transfer to a large bowl and add the eggs, mozzarella, and pepper; toss well to thoroughly combine. Transfer to the prepared baking sheet, pressing mixture evenly into the sheet with your fingers. Bake in the center of the oven until light brown and crisp, 12 to 15 minutes. Use as directed in recipe.

PER ⅙ OF RECIPE

Calories 86 | Protein 8g | Total Fat 5g |
Sat. Fat 3g | Cholesterol 81mg | Carbohydrate 2g |
Dietary Fiber 1g | Sodium 122 mg

Deep-Dish "Pizza"

lacto-ovo|low-carb

MAKES 8 SERVINGS

After one bite of this pizza, most won't believe it's crustless unless you tell them. Feel free to substitute the cheeses and vegetables with your favorites.

4 ounces gluten-free Neufchâtel cream cheese, softened
4 eggs
⅓ cup gluten-free light sour cream
¼ cup gluten-free grated Parmesan cheese
½ teaspoon dried oregano, plus additional, if desired
½ teaspoon onion powder
¼ teaspoon garlic powder
2 cups gluten-free shredded part-skim mozzarella cheese

- 1 cup gluten-free shredded reduced-fat cheddar cheese
- ½ cup gluten-free pizza sauce
- 2 ounces green bell pepper (about ½ small), chopped (optional)
- 2 ounces onion (about ½ small), chopped (optional)

Preheat the oven to 375F (190C). Lightly oil a 13 × 9-inch nonstick baking dish and set aside.

In a medium bowl, beat together the cream cheese and eggs until smooth. Add the sour cream, Parmesan cheese, ½ teaspoon oregano, onion powder, and garlic powder, beating until just blended.

In a small bowl, combine 1 cup of mozzarella cheese with the cheddar cheese. Arrange the cheese mixture in the prepared baking dish and pour the egg mixture over it. Bake for 25 minutes, or until the center is set. Remove from the oven and spread the pizza sauce evenly over the top. Sprinkle with the remaining mozzarella, followed by the bell pepper and onion (if using). Sprinkle with additional oregano, if desired. Bake for about 10 minutes, or until the cheese is melted and toppings (if used) are beginning to brown. Let stand for 5 minutes before cutting into wedges and serving.

PER SERVING

Calories 221 | Protein 17g | Total Fat 15g |
Sat. Fat 8g | Cholesterol 144mg | Carbohydrate 5g |
Dietary Fiber 0g | Sodium 457mg

Pesto Pizza

egg-free

MAKES 8 SERVINGS

This pesto pizza can also be made with 6 ounces of well-drained fresh mozzarella, thinly sliced or in tiny balls.

- 1 cup gluten-free pizza sauce
- 1 Rice Flour Pizza Crust (page 82)
- ½ recipe Classic Pesto Sauce (page 82), or ⅓ cup gluten-free refrigerated prepared pesto
- 1½ cups (6 ounces) gluten-free shredded part-skim mozzarella cheese
- Shredded fresh basil leaves (optional)

Preheat the oven to 400F (205C).

Spread the pizza sauce evenly over the baked pizza crust. Using a teaspoon, arrange mounds of pesto evenly over the sauce. Using a fork, swirl the pesto into the pizza sauce. Sprinkle evenly with the cheese. Bake in the center of the oven for 10 to 15 minutes, or until the cheese is melted and the crust is crisp and browned. Garnish with the fresh basil (if using), and serve at once.

PER SERVING

Calories 367 | Protein 11g | Total Fat 16g |
Sat. Fat 4g | Cholesterol 13mg | Carbohydrate 46g |
Dietary Fiber 3g | Sodium 665mg

RICE FLOUR PIZZA CRUST

vegan

MAKES 1 (12-INCH) PIZZA CRUST

Prebaking the crust ensures that it will be cooked through and crispy after it is baked with the toppings of your choice. While you can use all regular white rice flour in the recipe, the resulting crust will not be as chewy.

Cornmeal (optional)

1¾ cups white rice flour

¾ cup sweet rice flour

1 (¼-ounce) package gluten-free rapid rise yeast (about 1 tablespoon)

½ tablespoon sugar

1 teaspoon table salt or garlic salt

½ teaspoon xanthan gum

1 to 1¼ cups very warm water (120 to 130F; 50 to 55C)

3 tablespoons extra-virgin olive oil

Preheat the oven to 400F (205C). Lightly grease a 12- to 14-inch nonstick pizza pan. Sprinkle with cornmeal (if using).

In a large bowl, mix together the flours, yeast, sugar, salt, and xanthan gum. Stir in 1 cup water and the oil. Using your hands to work the dough, add enough of the remaining water to hold the mixture together. Knead the dough in the bowl for 5 minutes. Cover with a kitchen towel and let rest for 10 minutes.

Flatten the dough into a round disk and press into prepared pan. Bake in the center of the oven for 10 minutes. Remove and proceed as directed in recipe.

PER ⅛ OF CRUST

Calories 234 | Protein 4g | Total Fat 6g | Sat. Fat 1g | Cholesterol 0mg | Carbohydrate 41g | Dietary Fiber 2g | Sodium 267mg

Classic Pesto Sauce

egg-free|low-carb

MAKES ABOUT ⅔ CUP

This famous Ligurian sauce is delicious tossed with rice, rice noodles, potatoes, and countless vegetables, spread over pizza and breads, or stirred into soups and dips. Chopped walnuts can replace some or all of the pine nuts, if desired.

2 cups loosely packed fresh basil leaves

¼ cup extra-virgin olive oil

¼ cup gluten-free freshly grated Parmesan and/ or pecorino Romano cheese

3 tablespoons pine nuts

2 cloves garlic, finely chopped

½ teaspoon coarse salt, or to taste

Process all the ingredients in a food processor fitted with the knife blade, or in a blender, until smooth. Serve at room temperature. The sauce can be stored, covered, in the refrigerator for 2 to 3 days.

PER ABOUT 1 TABLESPOON

Calories 84 | Protein 3g | Total Fat 8g | Sat. Fat 2g | Cholesterol 2mg | Carbohydrate 2g | Dietary Fiber 0g | Sodium 142mg

Three-Cheese Pizza with Cornmeal Crust

lacto-ovo

MAKES 8 MAIN-DISH OR 12 APPETIZER SERVINGS

Use this recipe as a model and experiment with your favorite toppings.

1 cup gluten-free pizza sauce

1 Cornmeal Pizza Crust (recipe opposite)

¾ cup gluten-free shredded part-skim mozzarella cheese

¾ cup gluten-free shredded provolone cheese

½ cup gluten-free shredded Parmesan cheese

1 tablespoon extra-virgin olive oil

Dried oregano (optional)

Preheat the oven to 350F (175C).

Spread the pizza sauce evenly on the pizza crust. Sprinkle evenly with the cheeses. Drizzle evenly with the oil, then sprinkle lightly with oregano (if using). Bake in the center of the oven for 10 to 15 minutes, or until the cheese is melted and the crust is lightly browned. Cut into squares and serve warm.

PER SERVING

Calories 328 | Protein 17g | Total Fat 13g | Sat. Fat 6g | Cholesterol 77mg | Carbohydrate 36g | Dietary Fiber 5g | Sodium 778mg

CORNMEAL PIZZA CRUST

lacto-ovo

MAKES 1 LARGE RECTANGULAR PIZZA CRUST

You can add dried herbs—oregano is always a good choice—along with the garlic salt and pepper, if desired.

2 cups polenta or coarse-ground yellow cornmeal

1 cup cold water

1 cup boiling water

2 eggs, lightly beaten

1 cup gluten-free shredded part-skim mozzarella cheese

1 teaspoon garlic salt

Freshly ground black pepper, to taste

Preheat the oven to 450F (230C). Lightly oil a large nonstick baking sheet with sides.

In a large bowl, combine the polenta with the cold water. Slowly stir in the boiling water. Stir a few minutes until the mixture cools and some of the water is absorbed by the polenta. Stir in the eggs, mozzarella cheese, garlic salt, and pepper. Pour the mixture onto the prepared baking sheet, spreading with a spatula and raking with a fork to evenly distribute. Bake in the center of the oven for about 10 minutes, or until lightly browned. Use in the recipe as directed.

PER ⅛ OF RECIPE

Calories 204 | Protein 9g | Total Fat 4g | Sat. Fat 2g | Cholesterol 61mg | Carbohydrate 32g | Dietary Fiber 5g | Sodium 347mg

❧

Stuffed Avocados with Tomato Salsa and Tortilla Chips

vegan

MAKES 4 MAIN-DISH SERVINGS

This quick and delicious lunch or light dinner just doesn't get any easier. Add a couple tablespoons of cooked yellow corn to the salsa for a southwestern variation.

2 ripe avocados, halved and pitted

½ cup mild or medium salsa, plus additional, to taste

Gluten-free sour cream and/or shredded cheddar cheese (optional)

4 ounces gluten-free tortilla chips

❧ Fill each avocado cavity with 2 tablespoons of the salsa. Top with a dollop of sour cream and sprinkle with the cheese (if using). Serve at once, surrounded by equal portions of tortilla chips, with additional salsa passed separately.

PER SERVING

Calories 311 | Protein 4g | Total Fat 23g |

Sat. Fat 4g | Cholesterol 0mg | Carbohydrate 27g |

Dietary Fiber 5g | Sodium 244mg

Black Bean and Brown Rice Burgers with Salsa Mayonnaise

dairy-free

MAKES 4 SERVINGS

You can use refried vegetarian pinto beans in lieu of the black variety, if desired. For a vegan dish, omit the rolls (most commercially prepared gluten-free rolls such as Trader Joe's, contain egg products) and place inside heated taco shells; top with plain salsa instead of the Salsa Mayonnaise.

1 cup cooked brown or white rice (see Cook's Tip, page 145)

1 cup vegetarian refried black beans

2 tablespoons mild or medium salsa

1 teaspoon onion powder

1 tablespoon canola oil

4 gluten-free rolls

Salsa Mayonnaise (recipe opposite)

Lettuce leaves (optional)

❧ In a small bowl, combine the rice, beans, salsa, and onion powder until thoroughly blended. Form into 4 patties.

In a large nonstick skillet, heat the oil over medium heat. Add the patties and, with a spatula, flatten to ½-inch thickness. Cook until brown, 5 minutes per side.

To serve, place a burger on the bottom half of each roll. Spread with equal amounts (1½ tablespoons) of the mayonnaise. Top with lettuce (if using). Cover with the roll tops and serve at once.

SALSA MAYONNAISE
dairy-free|low-carb
MAKES ABOUT ⅓ CUP

This also makes a quick and delicious dressing for salads.

4 tablespoons gluten-free light mayonnaise
2 to 3 tablespoons medium salsa

✂ Combine the mayonnaise and salsa in a small bowl. If not using immediately, cover and refrigerate for a few days.

Basmati Rice Burgers with Pistachio Mayonnaise
dairy-free|low-carb
MAKES 6 SERVINGS

Most commercially prepared vegetarian burgers contain wheat or other damaging glutens. These fragrant rice patties hit the spot when a craving for a veggie burger strikes.

2 cups cooked basmati rice (see Cook's Tip, page 145)
½ cup finely chopped carrot
½ cup finely chopped onion
1 egg
½ teaspoon salt
¼ teaspoon freshly ground black pepper, or to taste
¼ teaspoon gluten-free mild curry powder
¼ teaspoon ground cumin
2 tablespoons canola oil
6 gluten-free rolls
Pistachio Mayonnaise (page 86)
Romaine lettuce or spinach leaves (optional)

✂ In a medium bowl, mix the rice, carrot, onion, egg, salt, pepper, curry powder, and cumin until thoroughly combined. Cover and refrigerate for 1 hour, or overnight.

In a large nonstick skillet, heat the oil over medium heat. Shape the rice mixture into 6 balls and flatten slightly with your palms. Add the patties to the skillet and cook until golden brown, 4 to 5 minutes per side.

To serve, place a burger on the bottom half of each roll. Spread with equal amounts (about 4 teaspoons) of the mayonnaise. Top with lettuce (if using). Cover with the roll tops and serve at once.

PER BURGER (WITHOUT ROLL AND MAYONNAISE)

Calories 135 | Protein 3g | Total Fat 6g |
Sat. Fat 1g | Cholesterol 35mg | Carbohydrate 18g |
Dietary Fiber 1g | Sodium 192mg

PISTACHIO MAYONNAISE
dairy-free|low-carb
MAKES ABOUT ½ CUP

Serve this tasty mayonnaise with grilled portobello mushrooms and steamed asparagus, as well.

6 tablespoons gluten-free light mayonnaise
2 tablespoons ground pistachios
½ teaspoon gluten-free mild curry powder
¼ teaspoon ground turmeric
Salt and freshly ground black pepper, to taste
Pinch cayenne pepper (optional)

In a small bowl, mix all the ingredients until well combined. Serve at room temperature, or cover and refrigerate and serve chilled.

PER TABLESPOON

Calories 44 | Protein 1g | Total Fat 4g |
Sat. Fat 1g | Cholesterol 4mg | Carbohydrate 3g |
Dietary Fiber 0g | Sodium 56mg

Green Chili and Black Olive Quesadillas
egg-free
MAKES 2 SERVINGS

This quick-and-easy favorite easily doubles to serve four, but cook in two separate batches.

1 tablespoon extra-virgin olive oil
4 (6-inch) gluten-free corn tortillas
3 ounces (¾ cup) gluten-free shredded reduced-fat cheddar cheese
2 tablespoons chopped canned mild green chilies
2 tablespoons chopped black olives
Salsa, gluten-free sour cream, and/or guacamole, for topping (optional)

In a large nonstick skillet, heat the oil over medium-high heat. Add 2 tortillas and, working quickly, layer with equal amounts of the cheese, then the chilies, then the olives. Top each with another tortilla and press down with a spatula. Cook until lightly browned, about 2 minutes; carefully flip over with a wide spatula and cook until golden, 1 to 2 minutes. Remove from the skillet and serve at once, with the toppings (if using).

PER SERVING

Calories 259 | Protein 13g | Total Fat 12g |
Sat. Fat 3g | Cholesterol 9mg | Carbohydrate 26g |
Dietary Fiber 3g | Sodium 427mg

Spinach and Cheddar Quesadillas

egg-free

MAKES 2 SERVINGS

Quesadillas are the ultimate grilled cheese sandwich in my house. This recipe easily doubles to serve four, but cook in two separate batches.

- 1 tablespoon extra-virgin olive oil
- 4 (6-inch) gluten-free corn tortillas
- ½ cup fresh baby spinach leaves
- 6 grape or cherry tomatoes, halved
- 2 ounces (½ cup) gluten-free shredded cheddar cheese
- 2 tablespoons chopped canned mild green chilies
- Salsa, gluten-free sour cream, and/or guacamole, for topping (optional)

❦ In a large nonstick skillet, heat the oil over medium-high heat. Add 2 tortillas and, working quickly, layer with equal amounts of the spinach, then the tomatoes, cheese, and chilies. Top each with another tortilla and press down with a spatula. Cook until lightly browned, about 2 minutes; carefully flip over with a wide spatula and cook until golden, 1 to 2 minutes. Remove from the skillet and serve at once, with the toppings (if using).

PER SERVING

Calories 237 | Protein 11g | Total Fat 10g | Sat. Fat 2g | Cholesterol 6mg | Carbohydrate 28g | Dietary Fiber 4g | Sodium 270mg

Grilled Portobello Mushroom Sandwiches with Red Pepper Sauce

lacto-ovo

MAKES 4 SERVINGS

I use Trader Joe's gluten-free French rolls for this recipe. If desired, omit the rolls and serve over a bed of spinach or romaine.

- 4 large portobello mushroom caps (about 2 ounces each)
- 2 teaspoons extra-virgin olive oil
- Salt and freshly ground black pepper, to taste
- 4 gluten-free sandwich rolls
- ½ cup Red Pepper Sauce (page 88)
- Spinach leaves (optional)

❦ Heat a nonstick grill pan over medium-high heat. Brush each mushroom on rounded side and rim with ½ teaspoon of the oil; season with salt and pepper. Place the mushrooms, gill sides down, in pan and grill for 3 minutes. Turn and grill until nicely browned, 3 to 4 minutes, rotating each mushroom a half turn after 2 minutes. Place a mushroom, gill sides up, on the bottom half of each roll. Fill each cap with about 2 tablespoons of Red Pepper Sauce, then top with the spinach leaves (if using). Cover with roll tops and serve at once.

PER SERVING

Calories 200 | Protein 5g | Total Fat 8g | Sat. Fat 1g | Cholesterol 6mg | Carbohydrate 28g | Dietary Fiber 1g | Sodium 319mg

RED PEPPER SAUCE

lacto-ovo|low-carb

MAKES ABOUT 1 CUP

This versatile sauce is also delightful as a topping for grilled eggplant or zucchini.

1 (7.25-ounce) jar roasted red bell peppers, drained

½ cup gluten-free light mayonnaise

2 tablespoons gluten-free light sour cream

1 large clove garlic, finely chopped

Salt and freshly ground black pepper, to taste

❧ In a food processor fitted with the knife blade, or in a blender, process all the ingredients until smooth and pureed. Serve chilled or at room temperature.

PER TABLESPOON

Calories 43 | Protein 0g | Total Fat 3g |
Sat. Fat 1g | Cholesterol 6mg | Carbohydrate 4g |
Dietary Fiber 1g | Sodium 76mg

Marinated Lentil and Spinach Roll-Ups

vegan|low-carb

MAKES 4 SERVINGS

Cooked canned lentils make quick work of these tasty spinach roll-ups, perfect for a light lunch or healthy snack. As with all canned products, check the label carefully for harmful added glutens.

1 (16-ounce) can gluten-free lentils

½ teaspoon onion powder

¼ teaspoon dried thyme leaves

1 bay leaf

1 tablespoon extra-virgin olive oil

1 tablespoon red wine vinegar

½ tablespoon gluten-free Dijon mustard

Salt and freshly ground black pepper, to taste

4 large fresh spinach leaves

❧ In a small saucepan, combine the lentils, onion powder, thyme, and bay leaf. Bring to a simmer over medium heat, stirring occasionally. Remove from the heat and let cool to room temperature. Discard the bay leaf.

Transfer the lentils to a small bowl and add the oil, vinegar, mustard, salt, and pepper; stir well to combine. Cover and refrigerate for a minimum of 3 hours or up to 2 days. To serve, place equal amounts of the lentil mixture in the center of each spinach leaf. Roll up and serve at once.

PER SERVING

Calories 123 | Protein 7g | Total Fat 4g |
Sat. Fat 1g | Cholesterol 0mg | Carbohydrate 16g |
Dietary Fiber 4g | Sodium 33mg

Easy Refried Bean Tacos

vegan|low-carb

MAKES 8 TACOS

These economical tacos are proof that cheap eats often taste the best of all.

8 taco shells

½ tablespoon extra-virgin olive oil

¼ cup finely chopped onion

1 (16-ounce) can vegetarian refried beans

1 (4-ounce) can chopped mild green chilies

Shredded lettuce, chopped tomatoes, gluten-free shredded cheddar cheese, gluten-free sour cream, and/or taco sauce, for topping (optional)

✀ Preheat the oven to 350F (175C). Arrange the taco shells on an ungreased baking sheet. Bake in the center of the oven for 3 to 5 minutes, or until heated through and crisp.

Meanwhile, in a medium saucepan, heat the oil over medium heat. Add the onion and cook, stirring, until softened, about 3 minutes. Add the refried beans and chilies; cook, stirring, until heated through, about 5 minutes.

Divide the refried bean mixture evenly among the taco shells (about ¼ cup per taco). Garnish with the toppings (if using) and serve at once.

PER SERVING

Calories 116 | Protein 4g | Total Fat 4g | Sat. Fat 1g | Cholesterol 0mg | Carbohydrate 17g | Dietary Fiber 4g | Sodium 242mg

Three-Bean Tacos

vegan|low-carb

MAKES 12 TACOS

You can use any combination of beans here—the results will invariably be delicious.

1 tablespoon extra-virgin olive oil

1 small onion (about 4 ounces), finely chopped

1 small green bell pepper (about 4 ounces), finely chopped

2 cloves garlic, finely chopped

1 (8-ounce) can tomato sauce

½ cup water

1 cup canned chickpeas, rinsed and drained

½ cup canned black beans, rinsed and drained

½ cup canned pinto beans, rinsed and drained

1 (1.25-ounce) package gluten-free taco seasoning mix

12 taco shells, heated according to package directions

Shredded lettuce, chopped tomato, gluten-free sour cream, olives, gluten-free shredded cheddar cheese, taco sauce, for topping (optional)

✀ In a medium nonstick skillet, heat the oil over medium heat. Add the onion and bell pepper and cook, stirring, until softened, about 3 minutes. Add the garlic and cook, stirring, for 1 minute. Add the tomato sauce, water, chickpeas, black beans, pinto beans, and taco seasoning mix; bring to a boil over medium-high heat. Reduce the heat and simmer, uncovered, stirring occasionally, until reduced and thickened, about 15 minutes.

To serve, fill each taco shell with about ¼ cup of the bean mixture. Garnish with the toppings (if using) and serve at once.

PER SERVING

Calories 124 | Protein 4g | Total Fat 4g |
Sat. Fat 1g | Cholesterol 0mg | Carbohydrate 19g |
Dietary Fiber 3g | Sodium 350mg

Mexican Egg Salad Tacos

lacto-ovo|low-carb

MAKES 5 TACOS

You can also serve this tasty egg salad on a bed of lettuce and garnish with crushed tortilla chips, if desired. Though optional, the use of taco sauce or salsa is highly recommended for flavor. To hard-cook eggs, see the method in Mexican Deviled Eggs (page 15).

4 large hard-cooked eggs, peeled and chopped

3 tablespoons gluten-free light mayonnaise

1 tablespoon gluten-free light sour cream

1 tablespoon chopped red bell pepper or pimiento, drained

1 tablespoon canned chopped mild green chilies, drained

1 tablespoon finely chopped fresh cilantro (optional)

1 scallion (white and green parts), thinly sliced

¼ teaspoon gluten-free chili powder

¼ teaspoon ground cumin

Pinch cayenne pepper, or to taste (optional)

5 taco shells, heated according to package directions

Taco sauce or salsa, shredded lettuce, for topping (optional)

In a medium bowl, mix together the eggs, mayonnaise, sour cream, bell pepper, chilies, cilantro (if using), scallion, chili powder, cumin, and cayenne (if using) until well combined. Fill the taco shells with equal amounts of the egg salad (about ¼ cup) and serve, garnished with the toppings (if using).

PER SERVING

Calories 136 | Protein 6g | Total Fat 8g |
Sat. Fat 2g | Cholesterol 173mg | Carbohydrate 10g |
Dietary Fiber 1g | Sodium 138mg

Smoky Black Bean and Cheese Tostadas

egg-free

MAKES 4 SERVINGS

These tasty tostadas make a quick-and-easy weeknight supper accompanied by a tossed green salad. Chipotle sauce, a spicy, smoky-sweet condiment made from smoked jalapeño chilies, can be found in specialty stores and some well-stocked supermarkets.

2 tablespoons canola oil

4 (6-inch) gluten-free corn tortillas

Salt, preferably the coarse variety, to taste (optional)

1 (15-ounce) can black beans, rinsed and drained

1 cup diced canned tomatoes with jalapeño chilies, drained

1 to 2 teaspoons chipotle sauce, or to taste

½ teaspoon ground cumin

Salt and freshly ground black pepper, to taste

1 cup gluten-free shredded reduced-fat cheddar or Monterey Jack cheese

Sliced black olives, gluten-free sour cream, and/or guacamole, for topping (optional)

❧ Preheat the oven to 225F (105C). Line a baking sheet with several layers of paper towels and set aside. In a 7- or 8-inch skillet, heat the oil over medium-high heat. Working with 1 tortilla at a time, fry the tortillas until light golden, 20 to 30 seconds per side. Transfer the tortillas to the prepared baking sheet and blot between paper towels. Remove the paper towels and sprinkle the tortillas lightly with coarse salt (if using).

Meanwhile, in a medium saucepan, bring the beans, tomatoes, chipotle sauce, cumin, salt, and pepper to a gentle simmer over medium heat, stirring occasionally. Spread equal amounts of the bean mixture over the tortillas. Sprinkle each with ¼ cup of the cheese. Place in the oven and heat for about 5 minutes, or until the cheese has melted. Serve at once, with the toppings passed separately (if using).

PER SERVING

Calories 263 | Protein 15g | Total Fat 10g | Sat. Fat 2g | Cholesterol 6mg | Carbohydrate 30g | Dietary Fiber 5g | Sodium 342mg

Taco Bowls

egg-free|low-carb

MAKES 4 TO 6 MAIN-DISH OR 12 SNACK-SIZE OR APPETIZER SERVINGS

For a tasty vegan variation, omit the cheese and mix about ¾ cup cooked white or brown rice with the refried bean mixture.

1½ cups gluten-free vegetarian refried beans

⅓ cup mild or medium salsa

12 (6-inch) gluten-free corn tortillas

1½ cups gluten-free shredded reduced-fat cheddar and Monterey Jack cheese, with or without jalapeño chilies

Gluten-free chili powder (optional)

Gluten-free sour cream and/or taco sauce, for topping (optional)

❧ Preheat the oven to 350F (175C). In a small bowl, mix the refried beans and salsa until thoroughly combined.

Arrange the tortillas on a large ungreased baking sheet (overlapping is okay) and place in the oven for about 5 minutes, or until just warmed and softened. Trim about ½ inch from the edge of each tortilla. Using a 12-cup nonstick muffin pan, fit the tortillas in the cups, making a few 1-inch slits in the tops for easy fitting. Return to the oven and bake for 10 minutes.

Remove the muffin pan from the oven and fill each tortilla bowl with equal portions (about 2 tablespoons) of the refried bean mixture. Top each with 2 tablespoons of the cheese. Sprinkle very lightly with chili powder (if using). Return to the oven and bake for 10 to 12 minutes, or until the cheese is melted and the cups are lightly browned. Serve at once, garnished with the toppings (if used).

PER SERVING (1 TACO BOWL)

Calories 140 | Protein 9g | Total Fat 3g |
Sat. Fat 1g | Cholesterol 7mg | Carbohydrate 19g |
Dietary Fiber 3g | Sodium 313mg

Cook's Tip

After trimming the corn tortillas, save the scraps and cut into small pieces. Place on an ungreased baking sheet and season lightly with garlic salt, if desired. Toast in a 350F (175C) oven for 5 to 10 minutes, or until lightly browned. Use as a topping for soups and salads.

Entrées

This chapter is proof positive that main dishes don't have to be intimidating for vegetarians with celiac disease or wheat allergies. Indeed, gluten-free dinners prepared without meat can be as easy—or as complicated—as those with meat. Furthermore, meat substitutes in the form of tofu and other soy-derived foods don't have to be included in each meal for proper nutrition. While those vegetarians and vegans who have celiac disease, in particular, need to take extra care to include protein and iron-rich foods in their already restrictive diets, like everyone else, they need to eat lots of fresh fruits, vegetables, beans, and other legumes to maintain optimal health. Happily, beans and other legumes are natural sources of protein and iron—in combination with gluten-free grains such as rice and corn, they form complete proteins. Best of all, gluten-free vegetarian main courses don't have to be boring. Many of the world's most enticing cuisines—Asian, Eastern Indian, Mexican, Caribbean, Mediterranean, American Southwestern, to name a few—offer some of the tastiest gluten-free meatless entrées on the planet, several of which can be found in the following chapter, as well as in the Soups and Salads chapters.

Refried Bean Enchiladas
with Mexican Fresh Cheese and Chipotle Salsa

egg-free

MAKES 4 SERVINGS

White, spongy, and moist, Mexican *queso fresco*, or "fresh cheese," is used in authentic enchiladas as it softens when it's heated, but doesn't melt. While common substitutes like Monterey Jack or cheddar are considered too runny by most Mexican cooks, you can certainly use them if you'd prefer, but add the cheese topping the last five or ten minutes of baking. Regular tomato salsa can stand in for the chipotle variety, if desired.

1¾ cups prepared chipotle salsa

8 (6-inch) gluten-free corn tortillas

1 (15-ounce) can gluten-free vegetarian refried beans

1½ cups crumbled *queso fresco* or other fresh Mexican cheese

1 large tomato (about 8 ounces), seeded and chopped

1 bunch scallions (white and green parts), thinly sliced

2 teaspoons ground cumin

Gluten-free light sour cream (optional)

Preheat oven to 350F (175C). Lightly oil an 11×7-inch baking dish and line with ¼ cup of the salsa; set aside.

Arrange the tortillas on a large ungreased baking sheet (some overlap is okay) and place in the center of the oven for about 5 minutes, or until just warmed and softened.

In a large bowl, combine the beans, ½ cup of the salsa, ½ cup of the cheese, half the tomato, half the scallions, and the cumin. Spoon equal portions of the bean mixture (about ⅓ cup) along the center of each tortilla and roll up; snugly arrange tortillas, seams side down, in the prepared baking dish.

In a small bowl, mix together the remaining salsa, tomato, and scallions. Spread the salsa mixture evenly over the enchiladas, then sprinkle evenly with the remaining cheese. Bake for 20 minutes, or until the sauce is beginning to bubble and the enchiladas are heated through. Serve at once, with the sour cream (if using).

PER SERVING

Calories 323 | Protein 16g | Total Fat 7g | Sat. Fat 3g | Cholesterol 14mg | Carbohydrate 54g | Dietary Fiber 11g | Sodium 843mg

Black Bean Enchiladas

vegan

MAKES 4 SERVINGS

This quick and easy dinner is perfect for busy week-nights.

1 tablespoon extra-virgin olive oil

1 small onion (about 4 ounces), chopped

3 large cloves garlic, finely chopped

1 teaspoon ground cumin

2 (15-ounce) cans black beans, rinsed and drained

1 (4-ounce) can chopped mild green chilies, drained

1 to 2 tablespoons fresh lime juice

1 to 2 tablespoons chopped fresh cilantro

Salt and freshly ground black pepper, to taste

8 (6-inch) gluten-free corn tortillas

Quick Enchilada Sauce (recipe opposite)

Gluten-free shredded cheddar cheese (optional)

Gluten-free light sour cream (optional)

Preheat the oven to 350F (175C). Lightly oil an 11 × 7-inch baking dish and set aside.

In a large nonstick skillet, heat the oil over medium heat. Add the onion and cook, stirring, until softened, 3 to 5 minutes. Add the garlic and cumin and cook, stirring constantly, for 1 minute. Add the beans, chilies, lime juice, cilantro, salt, and pepper; stir until thoroughly combined and remove from the heat.

Meanwhile, arrange the tortillas on a large ungreased baking sheet (some overlap is okay) and place in the oven until just warmed and softened, about 5 minutes.

Spread about ⅓ cup of Quick Enchilada Sauce along the bottom of the prepared baking dish. Spoon equal portions of the black bean mixture (about ½ cup) along the center of each tortilla and roll up; snugly arrange tortillas, seams side down, in the baking dish. Pour the remaining Quick Enchilada Sauce evenly over the tortillas. Bake for 20 minutes, or until the sauce is bubbling and the enchiladas are heated through, sprinkling with the cheese (if using) the last 5 minutes or so of cooking. Serve at once, with the sour cream (if using).

PER SERVING

Calories 388 | Protein 22g | Total Fat 7g | Sat. Fat 1g | Cholesterol 0mg | Carbohydrate 66g | Dietary Fiber 12g | Sodium 402mg

QUICK ENCHILADA SAUCE

vegan|low-carb

MAKES ABOUT 2⅓ CUPS

You simply can't beat the convenience of this straight-from-the-pantry enchilada sauce. For a slightly less spicy version, use ½ tablespoon less of chili powder.

2 cups gluten-free low-sodium vegetable broth

3 tablespoons gluten-free chili powder

½ teaspoon ground cumin

½ teaspoon onion powder

⅛ teaspoon garlic powder

1½ tablespoons cornstarch, dissolved in 3 tablespoons water

In a small saucepan, bring all the ingredients, except the cornstarch mixture, to a boil over medium heat. Whisk in the cornstarch mixture and boil for 1 minute, whisking constantly. Remove from the heat and serve warm.

PER SERVING (ABOUT ⅓ CUP)

Calories 30 | Protein 4g | Total Fat 1g |
Sat. Fat 0g | Cholesterol 0mg | Carbohydrate 3g |
Dietary Fiber 2g | Sodium 181mg

Curried Cauliflower and Chickpeas with Golden Raisins

vegan

MAKES 4 TO 6 SERVINGS

This delicious Indian curry can be stretched to serve up to eight if served over steamed basmati rice. Dark raisins can replace the golden variety, if desired.

- 2 tablespoons canola oil
- 1 medium onion (about 6 ounces), chopped
- 1 head cauliflower (about 2 pounds), cut into bite-size pieces
- 3 cloves garlic, finely chopped
- 1 tablespoon gluten-free mild curry powder, or to taste
- 1 teaspoon ground cumin
- ¼ teaspoon ground ginger
- 1 (14.5-ounce) can sliced stewed tomatoes, juices included
- ½ cup water
- 2 (15.5-ounce) cans chickpeas, rinsed and drained
- 6 tablespoons gluten-free golden raisins
- Salt and freshly ground black pepper, to taste
- ½ cup chopped fresh basil, parsley, or cilantro (optional)

In a large nonstick skillet with a lid, heat the oil over medium heat. Add the onion and cook, stirring, until softened, 3 to 5 minutes. Add the cauliflower and increase the heat to medium-high; cook, stirring often, until the cauliflower and onion are lightly browned, about 8 minutes. Add the garlic, curry powder, cumin, and ginger; cook, stirring constantly, for 1 minute.

Add the tomatoes and their juices, water, chickpeas, raisins, salt, and pepper; bring to a boil over high heat, stirring to combine. Reduce the heat to medium-low, cover, and simmer until cauliflower is tender, about 15 minutes, stirring a few times. Stir in the basil (if using); cook, stirring, for 1 minute. Serve warm or at room temperature.

PER SERVING

Calories 419 | Protein 18g | Total Fat 11g |
Sat. Fat 1g | Cholesterol 0mg | Carbohydrate 70g |
Dietary Fiber 13g | Sodium 343mg

Cellophane Noodle Casserole with Mushrooms, Ginger, and Peanuts

vegan

MAKES 6 TO 8 SERVINGS

Cellophane noodles, or bean thread noodles, are a popular Chinese pasta made from gluten-free mung bean starch. When cooked, they become clear and slippery and easily absorb the flavors of this delicious casserole.

3 (3.75-ounce) packages bean thread noodles

1 tablespoon peanut oil or light sesame oil

1 bunch scallions (white and green parts divided), thinly sliced

1 pound cultivated white mushrooms, quartered

1 tablespoon chopped fresh ginger

4 large cloves garlic, finely chopped

1 ounce dried shiitake or oyster mushrooms, soaked in warm water to cover for 15 minutes, drained, rinsed, and chopped

4 cups gluten-free low-sodium vegetable broth

¼ cup low-sodium tamari sauce

2 tablespoons toasted (dark) sesame oil

1 tablespoon Chinese chili paste, or to taste (optional)

Salt and freshly ground black pepper, to taste

½ cup unsalted chopped peanuts

Preheat the oven to 350F (175C). Lightly oil a 13 × 9-inch casserole and set aside.

In a medium stockpot, soak the noodles in boiling water to cover until soft and transparent, about 10 minutes. Drain well and rinse briefly under cold running water, discarding any white bits. Return the noodles to the stockpot, pulling them into long bunches and tearing into 6-inch clumps with your fingers as you go.

Meanwhile, in a large nonstick skillet, heat the peanut oil over medium heat. Add the white parts of the scallions and cook, stirring, until softened, 2 to 3 minutes. Add the white mushrooms, ginger, and garlic; cook, stirring often, until the mushrooms begin to release their liquids, 4 to 5 minutes. Add the shiitake mushrooms and the green parts of the scallions; cook, stirring, for 1 minute. Remove from the heat and add the broth, tamari sauce, sesame oil, chili paste (if using), salt, and pepper, stirring well to combine. Add to the stockpot with the cellophane noodles and toss well to thoroughly combine. Transfer to prepared casserole and bake for 20 minutes. Serve at once, in deep-sided plates or soup bowls, garnished with the peanuts.

PER SERVING

Calories 401 | Protein 20g | Total Fat 14g | Sat. Fat 2g | Cholesterol 0mg | Carbohydrate 53g | Dietary Fiber 8g | Sodium 1,731mg

Cheese and Cherry Tomato Pie with Rice Crust

lacto-ovo

MAKES 4 TO 6 SERVINGS

This silken savory pie is one of my favorites. You can easily use the rice crust as a base to create your own versions.

1½ cups hot cooked white or brown rice (see Cook's Tip, page 145)

4 scallions (white and green parts), finely chopped, 1 tablespoon reserved

1 egg white

½ teaspoon salt

Freshly ground black pepper, to taste

3 eggs

1 egg yolk

1 (12-ounce) can evaporated nonfat milk

½ cup (2 ounces) gluten-free shredded reduced-fat cheddar or Monterey Jack cheese

12 cherry or grape tomatoes, halved

2 tablespoons gluten-free freshly shredded Parmesan cheese

Preheat the oven to 350F (175C). Lightly grease a 9-inch pie plate.

In a medium bowl, mix together the rice, 1 tablespoon reserved scallions, egg white, ¼ teaspoon salt, and pepper. Using a rubber spatula or back of a spoon, spread evenly along the bottom and halfway up the sides of the prepared pie plate. Bake in the center of the oven for 5 minutes. Let cool slightly.

In a large bowl, whisk together the eggs, egg yolk, milk, remaining ¼ teaspoon salt, and pepper until thoroughly blended. Stir in the cheddar cheese and remaining scallions. Pour carefully into crust. Top with the cherry tomato halves, cut sides down.

Bake for 35 to 40 minutes, or until a knife inserted in the center comes out clean, sprinkling with the Parmesan cheese the last couple minutes of baking. Immediately run the tip of a sharp knife around the edge to loosen the crust. Let stand for 10 minutes before cutting into wedges and serving. Serve warm.

PER SERVING

Calories 283 | Protein 20g | Total Fat 7g |
Sat. Fat 3g | Cholesterol 220mg | Carbohydrate 34g |
Dietary Fiber 1g | Sodium 565mg

Chili–Brown Rice Casserole

egg-free

MAKES 4 SERVINGS

Serve a simple tossed green salad with this quick and easy Tex-Mex casserole. White rice can replace the brown variety, if desired.

2 cups cooked brown rice (see Cook's Tip, page 145)

1 (16-ounce) can gluten-free vegetarian chili

4 ounces (1 cup) gluten-free shredded reduced-fat cheddar cheese

6 grape or cherry tomatoes, halved (optional)

2 tablespoons chopped fresh cilantro or flat-leaf parsley (optional)

❦ Preheat the oven to 350F (175C). Lightly oil an 8-inch-square baking dish or casserole.

Arrange the rice on the bottom of the prepared baking dish. Top evenly with the chili. Bake for 30 minutes, or until hot and bubbly, sprinkling evenly with the cheese the last 10 minutes or so of cooking. Garnish with the tomato halves and cilantro (if using), and serve warm.

PER SERVING

Calories 313 | Protein 29g | Total Fat 5g | Sat. Fat 2g | Cholesterol 6mg | Carbohydrate 41g | Dietary Fiber 6g | Sodium 735mg

Mexican Cornmeal Pie

lacto-ovo

MAKES 4 SERVINGS

Serve this hearty cornmeal pie with a tossed green salad for a complete meal. Black beans or kidney beans can replace the pinto variety, if desired.

¾ cup coarse-ground yellow cornmeal or polenta

2 cups gluten-free low-sodium vegetable broth

¼ teaspoon salt

1 egg, lightly beaten

1 (15-ounce) can pinto beans, rinsed and drained

½ cup mild or medium salsa

3 ounces (¾ cup) gluten-free shredded reduced-fat Monterey Jack cheese with or without jalapeño chilies

1 ounce gluten-free tortilla chips, crushed

Gluten-free sour cream, guacamole, and/or sliced black olives (optional)

❦ Preheat the oven to 375F (190C). Lightly grease an 8½- or 9-inch pie plate and set aside.

In a medium stockpot, combine the cornmeal, broth, and salt; bring to a boil over high heat, stirring constantly with a long-handled wooden spoon (mixture will sputter). Reduce the heat to medium and cook, stirring often, until the mixture is very thick but still creamy, 3 to 5 minutes. Remove from the heat and let stand for 5 minutes. Quickly stir in the egg. Immediately transfer to the prepared pie plate, spreading evenly and building up the sides with the back of a spoon or spatula. (At this point, the mixture can be cooled and refrigerated, covered, for up to 24 hours before continuing with the recipe.) Bake uncovered for 15 minutes (add a couple minutes if refrigerated). Remove from the oven and set aside.

Meanwhile, in a small bowl, combine the beans and salsa. Spread evenly over the top of the cornmeal mixture. Sprinkle evenly with the cheese, followed by the tortilla chips. Return to oven and bake, uncovered, about 20 minutes, or until the cheese is melted and the center is heated through. Let stand for 5 minutes before cutting into wedges and serving with the optional toppings, if desired.

PER SERVING

Calories 321 | Protein 21g | Total Fat 6g |
Sat. Fat 2g | Cholesterol 61mg | Carbohydrate 44g |
Dietary Fiber 10g | Sodium 645mg

Mini Eggplant Lasagnas

egg-free|low-carb

MAKES 4 SERVINGS

Serve these scrumptious eggplant stackers with a mixed green salad for a delightful Italian-style meal. If desired, substitute one pound of fresh mozzarella cheese, cut into 16 slices, for the ricotta.

1 eggplant (about 1½ pounds), at least 12 inches in length after trimming

2 tablespoons extra-virgin olive oil
Salt and freshly ground black pepper, to taste
12 tablespoons prepared marinara sauce or other favorite pasta sauce
16 tablespoons gluten-free reduced-fat ricotta cheese
Dried oregano
4 tablespoons gluten-free freshly grated Parmesan cheese

Preheat the oven to 475F (245C). Lightly oil 2 baking sheets and set aside.

Slice the eggplant in 24 (½-inch-thick) slices. Arrange in a single layer on each baking sheet. Evenly brush with the oil and season with salt and pepper. Cover tightly with foil and bake for 30 minutes. Remove from the oven and reduce the oven temperature to 425F (220C).

Assemble in 8 stacks on one of the baking sheets in the following manner: 1 eggplant slice, ½ tablespoon marinara sauce, 1 tablespoon ricotta cheese, a light sprinkling of oregano and pepper, 1 eggplant slice, ½ tablespoon marinara sauce, 1 tablespoon ricotta cheese, a light sprinkling of oregano and pepper, 1 eggplant slice, ½ tablespoon marinara sauce, ending with ½ tablespoon Parmesan cheese. Bake for 7 to 10 minutes, or until heated through and the Parmesan cheese is melted. Serve warm.

PER SERVING

Calories 235 | Protein 11g | Total Fat 15g |
Sat. Fat 5g | Cholesterol 23mg | Carbohydrate 17g |
Dietary Fiber 4g | Sodium 469mg

Grilled Eggplant Sesame Steaks with Peanut Sauce

vegan|low-carb

MAKES 4 SERVINGS

Meaty center-cut eggplant slices are satisfying substitutes for the beef steaks of tradition. If you don't have garlic-flavored olive oil, use the regular variety and season with garlic salt.

4 center-cut, crosswise slices eggplant, each about ¾ inch thick

2 tablespoons garlic-flavored olive oil

2 teaspoons toasted (dark) sesame oil

Salt, preferably the coarse variety, and freshly ground black pepper, to taste

4 teaspoons sesame seeds

½ recipe Peanut Sauce (page 23)

❦ Prepare a medium-hot charcoal or gas grill, or preheat a broiler. Position the grill or oven rack 4 to 6 inches from heat source. Or heat a large nonstick stovetop grill pan with ridges over medium-high heat.

Bring a large pot of liberally salted water (use about 2 tablespoons salt) to a boil over high heat; add the eggplant slices and return to a boil. Reduce the heat to medium and simmer until the eggplant is tender but still firm, about 5 minutes, turning the slices occasionally in the water. Remove with a slotted spatula and dry well between paper towels.

Brush the eggplant cutlets evenly on both sides with the olive oil, then the sesame oil. Season both sides with salt and pepper, then sprinkle each side evenly with the sesame seeds. Grill about 2 minutes per side, or until nicely browned. Serve at once, topped with equal portions of the peanut sauce.

PER SERVING (INCLUDES SAUCE)

Calories 210 | Protein 5g | Total Fat 19g | Sat. Fat 3g | Cholesterol 0mg | Carbohydrate 8g | Dietary Fiber 2g | Sodium 267mg

Poached Eggs on Grilled Eggplant

dairy-free|low-carb

MAKES 4 SERVINGS

I think of this delicious entrée as a low-carb, Italian-style alternative to eggs Benedict.

1 small eggplant (about 8 ounces), at least 4 inches in length after trimming

Salt

2 tablespoons extra-virgin olive oil

Freshly ground black pepper, to taste

1½ to 2 cups gluten-free prepared pasta sauce

8 eggs

Gluten-free freshly grated Parmesan cheese (optional)

❦ Cut the eggplant into 8 (½-inch-thick) rounds and sprinkle with salt. Place in a colander for 30 minutes. Rinse under cold-running water and drain well; pat dry with paper towels.

Preheat the oven to 170F (75C). Preheat a grill pan over medium-high heat.

Brush both sides of the eggplant evenly with the oil. Season both sides with salt and pepper. Working in batches, if necessary, grill the eggplant until nicely browned, about 3 minutes per side. Transfer to a baking sheet and place in the warm oven until needed.

Meanwhile, in a small saucepan, bring the pasta sauce to a simmer over medium heat. Cover and keep warm over low heat until needed.

Fill a deep-sided skillet with 4 inches of water and bring to a brisk simmer over medium-high heat. Crack the eggs into individual cups or small bowls and slip carefully into the water. Reduce the heat and simmer gently until the yolks are soft-set, 4 minutes. Remove with a slotted spoon and transfer to a holding plate.

To assemble the dish, divide the sauce evenly among 4 serving plates and top with 2 eggplant slices. Top each eggplant slice with an egg and serve at once, garnished with the Parmesan cheese (if using).

PER SERVING

Calories 323 | Protein 15g | Total Fat 21g | Sat. Fat 5g | Cholesterol 425mg | Carbohydrate 19g | Dietary Fiber 4g | Sodium 591mg

Szechwan Eggplant

vegan

MAKES 4 MAIN-DISH OR 6 SIDE-DISH SERVINGS

This spicy eggplant dish is also good over rice noodles. For a milder taste, use the lesser amount of Chinese chili paste. Cultivated white mushrooms can replace the shiitake variety, if desired.

- **1 eggplant (about 1 pound), cut into 1-inch cubes, sprinkled with salt, and set in a colander to drain for 30 minutes (salting is optional)**
- **1 tablespoon peanut oil**
- **2 large cloves garlic, finely chopped**
- **½ cup gluten-free low-sodium vegetable broth, plus additional, if necessary**
- **12 fresh shiitake mushrooms, stemmed and chopped**
- **4 scallions (white and green parts), thinly sliced**
- **1 to 1½ tablespoons Chinese chili paste, or less to taste**
- **2 tablespoons tamari sauce**
- **1 tablespoon dry sherry**
- **½ tablespoon toasted (dark) sesame oil**
- **½ teaspoon ground ginger**
- **Salt and freshly ground black pepper, to taste**
- **3 cups hot cooked brown or white rice (see Cook's Tip, page 145)**

If salted, rinse the eggplant under cold-running water. Dry between paper towels.

In a large nonstick skillet with a lid, heat the oil over medium-high heat. Add the eggplant and cook, stirring and tossing constantly, until softened, about 4 minutes. Add the garlic and cook, stirring constantly, for 1 minute. Remove from the heat and add the remaining ingredients, except the rice. Return to the heat and let come to a brisk simmer. Reduce the heat to medium-low and cook, covered, until the eggplant is tender, about 15 minutes, stirring occasionally. Serve warm, over the rice.

PER SERVING

Calories 307 | Protein 9g | Total Fat 6g | Sat. Fat 1g | Cholesterol 0mg | Carbohydrate 56g | Dietary Fiber 5g | Sodium 580mg

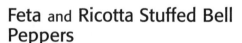

Feta and Ricotta Stuffed Bell Peppers

egg-free|low-carb

MAKES 4 SERVINGS

This Greek-inspired dish is also terrific served on a bed of rice.

- 2 large red or green bell peppers (about 8 ounces each), halved lengthwise, seeds and ribs removed
- 4 ounces (1 cup) gluten-free crumbled feta
- 1 cup (about 10 ounces) gluten-free nonfat ricotta cheese
- 2 tablespoons chopped fresh parsley
- 1 tablespoon chopped fresh dill
- 3 large cloves garlic, finely chopped

- ½ teaspoon lemon-pepper seasoning
- Salt, to taste
- ¼ cup fresh lemon juice (the juice from 1 large lemon)
- 2 tablespoons extra-virgin olive oil
- 4 cups baby spinach leaves (optional)

Preheat the oven to 375F (190C). Lightly oil a baking dish just large enough to accommodate the pepper halves in a single layer.

In a medium bowl, mash together the feta and ricotta until well-combined. Add the parsley, dill, garlic, lemon-pepper seasoning, and salt, stirring well to combine. Fill the pepper halves evenly with the feta mixture. Transfer to the prepared dish and drizzle with the lemon juice and oil. Cover and bake for about 45 minutes, or until the peppers are tender. Serve warm, over the spinach leaves (if using).

PER SERVING.

Calories 226 | Protein 16g | Total Fat 13g | Sat. Fat 5g | Cholesterol 35mg | Carbohydrate 14g | Dietary Fiber 3g | Sodium 527mg

Pesto–Green Bean Pie

lacto-ovo|low-carb

MAKES 6 SERVINGS

This rustic dish from Liguria, which gave the world pesto, is delicious accompanied by a tossed green salad.

1¼ pounds fresh green beans, trimmed, cut into
   1-inch lengths

4 eggs, lightly beaten

¾ cup gluten-free freshly shredded Parmesan
   cheese

½ cup gluten-free nonfat ricotta cheese

⅓ cup gluten-free prepared pesto sauce, or
   Classic Pesto Sauce (page 82)

Salt and freshly ground black pepper, to taste

2 tablespoons pine nuts

1½ to 2 cups favorite gluten-free prepared pasta
   sauce, heated

Preheat the oven to 350F (175C). Lightly grease an 8½- or 9-inch deep-dish pie dish and set aside.

In a large stockpot filled with boiling salted water, cook the beans until tender but not mushy, about 5 minutes. Drain and rinse under cold-running water. Drain well.

In a large bowl, whisk together the eggs, ½ cup of the Parmesan cheese, the ricotta cheese, pesto, salt, and pepper until well blended. Add the beans, stirring well to combine. Transfer to the prepared pie dish and bake in the center of the oven for 30 to 35 minutes, or until just set and lightly browned. Sprinkle with the remaining Parmesan cheese, then top with the pine nuts; bake for an additional 5 minutes, or until the cheese is melted and nuts are lightly toasted.

Let stand for 10 minutes before cutting into wedges and serving warm, with the pasta sauce.

PER SERVING

Calories 292 | Protein 17g | Total Fat 17g |
Sat. Fat 5g | Cholesterol 157mg | Carbohydrate 20g |
Dietary Fiber 6g | Sodium 674mg

Kasha Pilaf with Eggplant, Tomatoes, Basil, and Olives

vegan

MAKES 4 MAIN-DISH OR 6 SIDE-DISH SERVINGS

This is a higher-fiber alternative to the usual rice pilaf, and equally as tasty.

1 small eggplant (8 to 10 ounces), peeled and cut
   into 1-inch cubes, sprinkled with salt, and set
   in a colander to drain for 30 minutes (salting is
   optional)

1 cup whole kasha

3 tablespoons extra-virgin olive oil

1 medium onion (about 6 ounces), chopped

2 large cloves garlic, finely chopped

2 cups gluten-free low-sodium vegetable broth

½ teaspoon dried thyme leaves

Salt and freshly ground black pepper, to taste

1 cup cherry or grape tomatoes, halved

½ cup torn basil leaves

¼ cup pitted kalamata olives, halved lengthwise

If salted, rinse the eggplant under cold-running water. Dry between paper towels.

Heat a large nonstick skillet with a lid over

medium-high heat; add the kasha and cook, stirring, until fragrant and toasted, 2 to 3 minutes. Transfer the kasha to a bowl and set aside. Reduce the heat to medium and add 2 tablespoons of the oil to the skillet. Add the eggplant and onion and cook, stirring, until softened, about 5 minutes. Add the remaining oil and the garlic; cook, stirring, for 1 minute.

Add the broth, thyme, salt, and pepper. Bring to a boil over high heat; stir in the reserved kasha. Cover and reduce the heat to medium-low; simmer until the kasha is tender and the liquid is absorbed, about 7 minutes. Remove from the heat and stir in the tomatoes, basil, and olives. Let stand, covered, for 3 minutes. Serve warm or at room temperature.

PER SERVING

Calories 343 | Protein 12g | Total Fat 16g |
Sat. Fat 2g | Cholesterol 0mg | Carbohydrate 43g |
Dietary Fiber 7g | Sodium 507mg

Mexican Lasagna

egg-free

MAKES 6 TO 8 SERVINGS

Serve this delicious lasagna at your next fiesta. For a milder dish, omit the chili.

1 tablespoon extra-virgin olive oil

1 medium onion (about 6 ounces), chopped

1 jalapeño chili, seeded and finely chopped

4 cloves garlic, finely chopped

1 (15-ounce) can pinto beans, rinsed and drained

1 (15-ounce) can black beans, rinsed and drained

2 cups mild or medium salsa

1 tablespoon gluten-free chili powder

½ tablespoon ground cumin

2 tablespoons fresh lime juice

½ teaspoon salt

8 (6-inch) gluten-free corn tortillas

8 ounces (2 cups) gluten-free reduced-fat shredded cheddar and Monterey Jack cheese, with or without jalapeño chilies

8 ounces gluten-free Neufchâtel cream cheese, in 8 pieces

¼ cup skim milk

1 tablespoon chipotle chili sauce

Chopped tomatoes, sliced green parts of scallions, crushed tortilla chips, for topping (optional)

Preheat the oven to 350F (175C). Lightly grease a 13×9-inch casserole and set aside.

In a large nonstick skillet, heat the oil over medium heat. Add the onion and chili and cook, stirring, until softened, about 3 minutes. Add the garlic and cook, stirring, for 1 minute. Add the beans, salsa, chili powder, cumin, lime juice, and salt; bring to a simmer over medium-high heat. Reduce the heat and simmer gently, stirring occasionally, about 5 minutes.

Arrange 4 of the tortillas along the bottom of the prepared casserole. Spread half of the bean mixture over the tortillas. Sprinkle half of the shredded cheese over the beans. Repeat to make another layer, ending with the cheese. Cover with lightly oiled aluminum foil and bake for 25 minutes.

Meanwhile, in a small saucepan, combine the cream cheese, milk, and chipotle sauce; cook, stirring, over low heat, until smooth and thoroughly blended. Remove the lasagna from the oven and spread the cream cheese mixture over the top. Garnish with the toppings (if using), and serve warm.

PER SERVING

Calories 448 | Protein 26g | Total Fat 17g | Sat. Fat 8g | Cholesterol 42mg | Carbohydrate 49g | Dietary Fiber 10g | Sodium 831mg

Lentil Moussaka

lacto-ovo

MAKES 8 SERVINGS

This delicious iron-rich vegetarian variation of the famous Greek eggplant casserole is a good choice to serve company, as it can be assembled and refrigerated a day before topping with the sauce and baking.

2 cups lentils, picked over, rinsed, and drained

2 medium eggplants (about ¾ pound each), sliced into ⅜-inch-thick rounds

4 tablespoons extra-virgin olive oil

Salt, to taste, plus 1 teaspoon

Freshly ground black pepper, to taste

1 large onion (about 8 ounces), finely chopped

¼ pound cultivated white mushrooms, coarsely chopped

3 large cloves garlic, finely chopped

2 teaspoons dried oregano

¼ teaspoon dried thyme

1 (8-ounce) can tomato sauce

6 large plum tomatoes (about 3 ounces each), sliced into ¼-inch-thick rounds

1½ cups skim milk

2 tablespoons cornstarch

2 tablespoons canola oil

1 teaspoon onion powder

Pinch grated nutmeg

2 egg yolks, lightly beaten

¼ cup gluten-free freshly grated Parmesan cheese (optional)

Preheat the oven to 475F (245C). Lightly oil 2 baking sheets and set aside.

In a medium stockpot, combine the lentils and enough water to cover. Bring to a boil over medium-high heat. Reduce the heat and simmer gently, partially covered, until the lentils are tender but not mushy, stirring occasionally. This should take about 45 minutes, depending on the age of the lentils. When the lentils are done, if most of the water is not absorbed, simmer, uncovered, stirring often, until most of the liquid evaporates.

Arrange the eggplant slices in a single layer on each baking sheet. Brush the tops evenly with 2 tablespoons of the olive oil and season with salt and pepper. Cover tightly with foil and bake for 20 minutes. Remove from the oven, uncover, and let cool.

Reduce the oven temperature to 350F (175C). Lightly grease a 13×9-inch baking dish and set aside.

In a large deep-sided nonstick skillet, heat the remaining olive oil over medium heat. Add the onion and cook, stirring, until softened, about 3 minutes. Add the mushrooms, garlic, oregano, and thyme; cook, stirring, until the mushrooms begin to release their liquid, about 3 minutes. Stir in the tomato sauce, 1 teaspoon salt, and pepper; let come to a simmer. Add the lentils, stirring well to combine. Remove from the heat and set aside.

To assemble the casserole: Arrange half the lentil mixture in the prepared baking dish. Top with half of the eggplant slices, followed by half of the tomato slices. Repeat layers. (At this point, the casserole can be refrigerated, covered, for up to 24 hours; heat in a 350F (175C) oven about 10 minutes before proceeding with the recipe.)

To make the sauce: Place ½ cup of the milk and the cornstarch in a covered container; shake well to thoroughly blend. In a medium saucepan, combine remaining milk, canola oil, onion powder, salt, and pepper; bring to a gentle simmer over medium heat. Gradually add cornstarch mixture, whisking constantly until thickened, about 2 minutes. Remove from heat and whisk in the nutmeg; let cool for 2 minutes. Gradually add the egg yolks, whisking until thoroughly blended.

Slowly pour the sauce evenly over top of the assembled casserole. Bake for 30 minutes, or until the top is lightly golden, sprinkling with the cheese (if using) the last 5 minutes or so of cooking. Let stand for 10 minutes before cutting into wedges and serving.

PER SERVING

Calories 348 | Protein 18g | Total Fat 13g | Sat. Fat 2g | Cholesterol 54mg | Carbohydrate 45g | Dietary Fiber 18g | Sodium 478mg

Mushroom, Pea, and Pearl Onion Pot Pie with Herbed Potato Topping

lacto-ovo

MAKES 6 TO 8 SERVINGS

The ultimate comfort food, this pot pie is a complete meal when served with a tossed green salad.

1½ tablespoons canola oil

1 medium onion (about 6 ounces), finely chopped

16 ounces medium cultivated white mushrooms, stemmed and quartered

1 (16-ounce) bag frozen green peas and pearl onions

½ cup gluten-free low-sodium vegetable broth

Salt and freshly ground black pepper, to taste

½ cup skim milk

8 ounces gluten-free Neufchâtel cream cheese, in 8 pieces

2 tablespoons finely chopped fresh basil

Herbed Potato Topping (recipe opposite)

Preheat oven to 350F (175C). Lightly grease a deep-dish 10-inch quiche dish and set aside.

In a large nonstick skillet, heat the oil over

medium heat. Add the onion and cook, stirring, until softened, about 3 minutes. Add the mushrooms and cook, stirring, until they begin to release their liquid, about 4 minutes. Add the peas and pearl onions, broth, salt, and pepper; bring to a brisk simmer over medium-high heat. Reduce the heat to medium and stir in the milk and cream cheese, stirring until smooth and incorporated. Simmer gently until slightly thickened, about 5 minutes, stirring occasionally. Remove from the heat and stir in the basil. Let cool slightly.

Place the prepared quiche dish on a baking sheet and fill with the mushroom mixture. Using a spatula, spread the potato topping lightly yet evenly over the top. Bake for 30 to 40 minutes, or until the top is golden brown and the filling is hot. Serve warm.

PER SERVING

Calories 332 | Protein 14g | Total Fat 17g |

Sat. Fat 8g | Cholesterol 73mg | Carbohydrate 34 g |

Dietary Fiber 6g | Sodium 329mg

HERBED POTATO TOPPING

lacto-ovo

MAKES ABOUT 6 SERVINGS

Use this topping for your other favorite pot pie fillings, as well.

1½ pounds medium boiling potatoes, peeled and quartered

½ cup skim milk, or more as needed

1½ tablespoons butter

Salt and freshly ground black pepper, to taste

1 egg

1 to 2 tablespoons finely chopped fresh herbs

In a large saucepan or medium stockpot, bring the potatoes and enough salted water to cover to a boil over high heat. Reduce the heat slightly and boil gently until tender, 15 to 20 minutes. Drain well and return to the pan. Using an electric mixer, beat in the ½ cup milk, butter, salt, and pepper. Let cool for a few minutes, then beat in the egg, adding more milk if needed to create a fluffy consistency. Stir in the herbs. Proceed as directed in recipe.

PER SERVING (⅙ OF RECIPE)

Calories 112 | Protein 4g | Total Fat 4g |

Sat. Fat 2g | Cholesterol 43mg | Carbohydrate 17g |

Dietary Fiber 1g | Sodium 55mg

Baked Stuffed Portobello Mushrooms with Parmesan and Pine Nuts

egg-free

MAKES 4 MAIN-DISH OR 8 FIRST-COURSE OR SIDE-DISH SERVINGS

Giant portobello mushrooms are ideal receptacles for this tasty gluten-free stuffing, which can also serve as a filling for large globe artichokes.

4 ounces gluten-free bread, lightly toasted

1½ tablespoons extra-virgin olive oil

2 medium onions (about 6 ounces each), finely chopped

4 large cloves garlic, finely chopped

½ cup finely chopped fresh basil

¼ cup pine nuts, slivered almonds, or walnut pieces

Salt and freshly ground black pepper, to taste

1 egg, lightly beaten (optional)

½ cup gluten-free freshly grated Parmesan cheese

8 large portobello mushroom caps (about 2 ounces each)

Fresh spinach leaves (optional)

❧ Preheat the oven to 400F (205C). Lightly oil a shallow casserole large enough to hold the mushrooms in a single layer and set aside.

Place the bread in a food processor fitted with the knife blade; process until about 2 cups of coarse crumbs form. Set aside.

In a large nonstick skillet, heat the oil over medium heat. Add the onions and cook, stir-ring, until softened, about 3 minutes. Add the garlic and cook, stirring, for 1 minute. Remove from the heat and stir in the bread crumbs, basil, pine nuts, salt, and pepper; toss well to thoroughly combine. Let cool for a few minutes. Add the egg (if using) and cheese, tossing well to thoroughly combine.

Fill the mushrooms with equal portions of the bread crumb mixture. Transfer to prepared casserole and cover tightly with foil. Bake for 40 minutes. Uncover and bake for 5 to 10 minutes, or until lightly browned. Serve warm, over the spinach leaves (if using).

PER SERVING

Calories 295 | Protein 14g | Total Fat 16g | Sat. Fat 4g | Cholesterol 10mg | Carbohydrate 30g | Dietary Fiber 4g | Sodium 395mg

Portobello Mushroom and White Bean Cassoulet

vegan

MAKES 4 SERVINGS

Serve this tasty vegetarian version of the popular French peasant dish with a simple green salad for a complete meal.

2 tablespoons extra-virgin olive oil

½ pound portobello mushrooms, stemmed, cut into bite-size pieces

1 medium onion (about 6 ounces), chopped

3 large cloves garlic, chopped

1 (14-ounce) can diced tomatoes, juices included

2 tablespoons dry red wine (optional)

2 tablespoons chopped fresh parsley

1 teaspoon dried thyme leaves

1/4 teaspoon dried rosemary leaves

1 bay leaf

Salt and freshly ground black pepper, to taste

2 (15-ounce) cans navy, great northern, or
   cannellini beans, rinsed and drained

In a large nonstick skillet with a lid, heat the oil over medium heat. Add the mushrooms and onion and cook, stirring, until the onion is softened and the mushrooms begin to release their juice, about 5 minutes. Add the garlic and cook, stirring, for 1 minute. Add the tomatoes and their juices, wine (if using), parsley, thyme, rosemary, bay leaf, salt, and pepper; bring to a boil over medium-high heat. Reduce the heat, cover, and simmer gently for 15 minutes, stirring occasionally. Add the beans and cook, uncovered, stirring occasionally, until the mixture is slightly thickened, about 10 minutes. Remove and discard the bay leaf. Serve warm.

PER SERVING

Calories 308 | Protein 15g | Total Fat 8g |
Sat. Fat 1g | Cholesterol 0mg | Carbohydrate 47g |
Dietary Fiber 10g | Sodium 217mg

Quick Brown Rice Paella
vegan

MAKES 6 SERVINGS

The use of quick-cooking brown rice ensures that this delicious Spanish-style dinner will be ready in just about 30 minutes.

3 tablespoons extra-virgin olive oil

1 medium onion (about 6 ounces), chopped

1 medium green bell pepper (about 6 ounces),
   chopped

4 ounces cultivated white mushrooms, sliced

3 large cloves garlic, finely chopped

3 1/4 cups gluten-free low-sodium vegetable broth

2 cups quick-cooking brown rice

1 teaspoon salt

1/2 teaspoon saffron threads, crushed, or ground
   turmeric

1/2 teaspoon dried thyme

Freshly ground black pepper, to taste

1 1/2 cups frozen green peas and pearl onions,
   thawed

1 (14-ounce) can artichoke hearts, drained and
   coarsely chopped

2 to 3 tablespoons chopped pimiento

In a large deep-sided nonstick skillet with a lid, heat the oil over medium heat. Add the onion, bell pepper, and mushrooms; cook, stirring, until softened, about 5 minutes. Add the garlic and cook, stirring, for 1 minute. Add the broth, rice, salt, saffron, thyme, and black pepper; bring to a boil over high heat. Cover, reduce the heat to medium-low, and simmer for 10 minutes. Stir in the peas and pearl onions, artichokes, and pimiento. Cook, uncovered, stirring occasionally, until the rice is tender and the mixture is heated through, 3 to 5 minutes. Serve at once.

PER SERVING

Calories 288 | Protein 13g | Total Fat 7g | Sat. Fat 1g | Cholesterol 0mg | Carbohydrate 45g | Dietary Fiber 8g | Sodium 731mg

Roasted Vegetable Paella

vegan

MAKES 4 MAIN-DISH OR 6 TO 8 SIDE-DISH SERVINGS

This paella is an excellent choice for a buffet or picnic, as it can be served warm or at room temperature. Unlike regular long-grain white rice, the plumper, starchier arborio variety will not harden as it cools.

3 cups gluten-free low-sodium vegetable broth

¼ teaspoon saffron threads

1 head garlic, cloves separated, unpeeled

1 large red bell pepper (about 8 ounces), cut into bite-size chunks

1 large yellow bell pepper (about 8 ounces), cut into bite-size chunks

1 large green bell pepper (about 8 ounces), cut into bite-size chunks

2 small zucchini (about 4 ounces each), cut into ½-inch-thick rounds

3 tablespoons extra-virgin olive oil

Salt, preferably the coarse variety, and freshly ground black pepper, to taste

1 large onion (about 8 ounces), finely chopped

3 medium plum tomatoes (about 2 ounces each), chopped

1 teaspoon dried oregano

1 teaspoon dried thyme

1¼ cups arborio rice

2 tablespoons chopped fresh flat-leaf parsley

In a medium saucepan, combine the broth and saffron; bring to a boil over high heat. Reduce the heat to low and simmer, covered, for 20 minutes.

Meanwhile, in another saucepan, combine the garlic and enough water to cover. Bring to a boil, reduce the heat to low, and simmer, uncovered, for 5 minutes. Drain and let cool. Peel the garlic and set aside.

Preheat the oven to 400F (205C). Place the bell peppers, zucchini, and garlic cloves on a large baking sheet with sides. Drizzle with 2 tablespoons of the oil and sprinkle with salt and pepper; toss well to combine. Bake for 25 to 30 minutes, or until tender and beginning to char.

Meanwhile, in a large deep-sided nonstick skillet with a lid, heat the remaining oil over medium heat. Add the onion and cook, stirring, until light golden, about 8 minutes. Add the tomatoes, oregano, thyme, salt, and pepper. Cook, stirring, until the liquids have almost completely evaporated, 3 to 5 minutes. Add the rice and broth mixture; bring to a boil over high heat. Reduce the heat, cover, and simmer gently until the rice is tender yet firm to the bite and has absorbed most of the liquid, about 25 minutes. Stir in the roasted vegetables and parsley and cook, stirring, until heated through. Serve warm or at room temperature.

PER SERVING

Calories 432 | Protein 16g | Total Fat 11g |
Sat. Fat 2g | Cholesterol 0mg | Carbohydrate 69g |
Dietary Fiber 7g | Sodium 412mg

VARIATION: *To make* Mexican-Style Roasted Vegetable Paella: *Add 2 teaspoons finely chopped jalapeño chili along with the onion. Substitute ground cumin for the thyme and cilantro for the flat-leaf parsley.*

Peppers Stuffed with Pesto Rice

egg-free

MAKES 4 SERVINGS

This is a great company dish as the assembled stuffed peppers can be stored, covered, in the refrigerator overnight before baking. The use of arborio rice ensures that the grains will not harden in the refrigerator like regular long-grain white rice tends to do.

1½ tablespoons extra-virgin olive oil

1 medium onion (about 6 ounces), finely chopped

3 large cloves garlic, finely chopped

1 cup arborio rice, slightly undercooked according to package directions (see Cook's Tip, page 145)

1 cup grape or cherry tomatoes, halved or quartered, depending on size

¼ cup gluten-free prepared pesto sauce, or Classic Pesto Sauce (page 82)

Salt and freshly ground black pepper, to taste

4 large bell peppers (8 to 10 ounces each)

Preheat the oven to 400F (205C).

In a large nonstick skillet, heat 1 tablespoon of the oil over medium heat. Add the onion and cook, stirring, until softened but not browned, 3 to 5 minutes. Add the garlic and cook, stirring, for 1 minute.

Remove the skillet from the heat and add the rice, tomatoes, pesto, salt, and pepper, stirring well to thoroughly combine. Set aside.

Cut the top off the stem end of each bell pepper and reserve. Remove the seeds and white membranes from each pepper shell. Brush the outsides of the shells with the remaining ½ tablespoon of oil. Stuff each pepper shell lightly (do not pack) with equal amounts of the rice mixture and top with the corresponding lid (lids will not close).

Place the stuffed peppers upright in a baking dish just large enough to accommodate their size. Add enough water to the dish to measure ½ inch. Cover tightly with foil and bake for 50 minutes. Uncover and bake for 10 minutes, or until the tops are lightly browned and peppers are tender when pierced with the tip of a sharp knife. Serve warm.

PER SERVING

Calories 368 | Protein 9g | Total Fat 13g |
Sat. Fat 3g | Cholesterol 4mg | Carbohydrate 57g |
Dietary Fiber 5g | Sodium 122mg

Italian-Style Polenta-Stuffed Peppers with Sun-Dried Tomatoes

egg-free

MAKES 4 SERVINGS

For a vegan dish, omit the Parmesan cheese; the stuffed peppers will still be delicious but not quite as creamy.

1 tablespoon extra-virgin olive oil

½ cup chopped onion

2 large cloves garlic, finely chopped

¼ cup marinated sun-dried tomatoes, drained, ½ tablespoon marinade reserved, finely chopped

Salt and freshly ground black pepper, to taste

¾ cup regular or instant polenta

1 (14-ounce) can gluten-free low-sodium vegetable broth (1¾ cups)

1 cup water

½ cup gluten-free freshly grated Parmesan cheese plus additional, if desired

4 large green bell peppers (about 8 ounces each), tops cut off, seeds and membranes removed

Preheat oven to 375F (190C).

In a small nonstick skillet, heat the oil over medium heat. Add the onion and cook, stirring, until softened, about 3 minutes. Add the garlic and cook, stirring, for 1 minute. Stir in the sun-dried tomatoes and reserved marinade and remove from heat. Season with salt and pepper and set aside.

Meanwhile, *if using regular polenta*: In a medium stockpot, bring the broth and water to a boil over high heat. Slowly add the polenta, stirring constantly with a long-handled wooden spoon. Reduce the heat to low and add the reserved tomato mixture, stirring well to combine. Cover and cook, stirring occasionally, until the polenta is tender, about 15 minutes. Remove from the heat and immediately add the cheese, stirring well to thoroughly combine. Cover and let stand for 5 minutes.

If using instant polenta: In a medium stockpot, bring the broth and water to a boil over high heat. Slowly add the polenta, stirring constantly with a long-handled spoon. Reduce the heat to medium and add the reserved tomato mixture; cook, stirring constantly, until the mixture is the consistency of porridge, about 5 minutes. Remove from the heat and immediately add the cheese, stirring well to thoroughly combine.

Working quickly (the polenta will harden as it cools), lightly pack the bell peppers with equal amounts of the polenta mixture. Place in a shallow baking dish just large enough to accommodate the peppers in a single layer. Add enough water to the dish to measure ½ inch. Bake, uncovered, for 30 to 35 minutes, or until set and heated through, sprinkling with additional cheese (if using) the last 5 minutes of cooking. Serve immediately.

PER SERVING

Calories 320 | Protein 15g | Total Fat 12g | Sat. Fat 4g | Cholesterol 10mg | Carbohydrate 42g | Dietary Fiber 9g | Sodium 481mg

VARIATION: *To make* Southwestern-Style Polenta-Stuffed Bell Peppers with Chilies: *Omit the sundried tomatoes and reserved marinade and replace with 2 tablespoons drained canned chopped mild green chilies and an additional ½ tablespoon of olive oil. Substitute the Parmesan cheese with shredded Monterey Jack, cheddar, and/or Mexican-blend cheese.*

Polenta Loaf with Pesto and Sun-Dried Tomatoes

egg-free

MAKES 4 TO 6 MAIN-DISH OR 8 SIDE-DISH SERVINGS

Commercially prepared reduced-fat pesto can be used in lieu of the regular variety, but check the label carefully for any damaging glutens.

3½ cups gluten-free low-sodium vegetable broth

1 cup polenta

¼ cup sun-dried tomato bits

1 tablespoon extra-virgin olive oil

2 large cloves garlic, finely chopped

Salt and freshly ground black pepper, to taste

1 cup gluten-free freshly grated Parmesan cheese

4 to 6 tablespoons gluten-free prepared pesto
    sauce, or Classic Pesto Sauce (page 82)

Sprigs of fresh basil and/or sun-dried tomato
    strips, packed in oil, drained (optional)

Preheat the oven to 170F (75C). Lightly oil a 9 × 5-inch loaf pan and set aside.

In a large stockpot, bring the broth to a boil over high heat. Slowly add the polenta, stirring constantly with a long-handled wooden spoon. Reduce the heat to low and add the tomato bits, oil, garlic, salt, and pepper, stirring well to combine. Cover and cook, stirring occasionally, until the polenta is tender, about 15 minutes. Remove from the heat and add the cheese, stirring well to thoroughly combine. Cover and let stand for 5 minutes.

Spread one-third of the polenta mixture in the bottom of the prepared pan. Let stand for 1 minute. Spread with half the pesto. Repeat, ending with the polenta. Place in the warm oven for 20 minutes, or until set. Unmold onto a serving platter and garnish with the fresh basil and/or sun-dried tomato strips (if using). Slice and serve warm or at room temperature.

PER SERVING

Calories 420 | Protein 27g | Total Fat 19g |
Sat. Fat 7g | Cholesterol 24mg | Carbohydrate 37g |
Dietary Fiber 8g | Sodium 1,096mg

Five-Ingredient Potato Lasagna

egg-free

MAKES 6 SERVINGS

Preparing lasagna just doesn't get any easier than the following recipe, ready in less than one hour from start to finish. For stress-free entertaining, the casserole can be assembled and refrigerated, covered, for up to twenty-four hours before baking. If refrigerated, add about ten minutes to the initial baking time.

2½ cups gluten-free prepared spaghetti sauce

2 (15-ounce) cans sliced potatoes, drained

2 cups gluten-free low-fat cottage cheese

2 cups (8-ounces) gluten-free shredded mozzarella cheese

4 tablespoons gluten-free freshly shredded Parmesan cheese

❧ Preheat the oven to 425F (220C). Lightly oil an 11×7-inch baking dish and spread with ½ cup of the spaghetti sauce. Layer with half of the potatoes, 1 cup of the sauce, 1 cup of the cottage cheese, and 1 cup of the mozzarella cheese. Repeat layers, starting with potatoes and ending with the Parmesan cheese. Cover with foil (lightly oil the underside, if desired) and bake for 35 to 40 minutes. Uncover and bake for 5 minutes, or until bubbly. Let stand for 10 minutes before cutting into wedges and serving.

PER SERVING

Calories 387 | Protein 23g | Total Fat 16g | Sat. Fat 8g | Cholesterol 40mg | Carbohydrate 39g | Dietary Fiber 5g | Sodium 1,046mg

Mexican-Style Baked Potatoes

egg-free

MAKES 4 MAIN-DISH OR 8 SIDE-DISH SERVINGS

If you prebake and stuff the potatoes a day in advance, these tasty spuds make a perfect quick weeknight supper with a tossed green salad. For a vegan dish, omit the cheese.

4 large russet potatoes (about 8 ounces each), washed and scrubbed

¾ cup vegetarian refried beans

2 scallions (white and green parts), thinly sliced

1 teaspoon cumin seed

Salt and freshly ground black pepper, to taste

¾ cup mild or medium salsa

2 tablespoons gluten-free ketchup

1 cup gluten-free reduced-fat shredded cheddar cheese

Gluten-free sour cream and/or guacamole (optional)

❧ Preheat the oven to 450F (230C). Prick the potatoes with a fork and bake in the center of the oven for 1 hour, or until tender. Reduce the heat to 375F (190C) and let the potatoes cool at room temperature for about 15 minutes before handling.

When the potatoes are cool enough to handle, cut in half lengthwise and scoop out the potato pulp, transferring to a small bowl and leaving a shell about ¼ inch thick. Add the refried beans, scallions, cumin seed, salt, and pepper to the potato pulp; mash well to thoroughly blend. Stuff the mixture back into the potato halves and transfer to an ungreased baking sheet. (At this point, the potatoes can be covered with plastic wrap and refrigerated for up to 24 hours before continuing with the recipe.)

In a small bowl, mix together the salsa, ketchup, salt, and pepper until well combined. Top each potato half with equal amounts (about 1½ tablespoons) of the salsa mixture. Bake in the center of the oven, about 15 minutes (about 20 minutes if they've been refrigerated), or until heated through. Sprinkle each half with 2 tablespoons of the cheese. Return to the oven and bake until the cheese is melted, about 5 minutes. Serve at once, with the toppings (if using).

PER SERVING

Calories 257 | Protein 14g | Total Fat 3g |
Sat. Fat 2g | Cholesterol 6mg | Carbohydrate 45g |
Dietary Fiber 7g | Sodium 601mg

Curried Pumpkin Risotto

vegan

MAKES 3 TO 4 MAIN-DISH OR 6 SIDE-DISH SERVINGS

Though this exotic risotto requires about thirty minutes of almost constant stirring, after one mouthful, you'll agree that it was well worth your time and attention.

4 cups gluten-free low-sodium vegetable broth

1 cup canned pumpkin puree

2 tablespoons canola oil

¼ cup finely chopped onion

½ cup finely chopped red bell pepper

1 cup arborio rice

2 large cloves garlic, finely chopped

½ cup dry white wine

2 teaspoons gluten-free mild curry powder

1 teaspoon ground cumin

½ teaspoon salt

⅛ teaspoon freshly ground black pepper

3 tablespoons light coconut milk

¼ cup pine nuts, toasted, if desired (optional; see Cook's Tip, page 118)

In a medium saucepan, combine the broth and pumpkin and bring to a gentle simmer over medium heat. Reduce the heat to low and partially cover to maintain a simmer.

In a large deep-sided nonstick skillet, heat the oil over medium heat. Add the onion and bell pepper and cook, stirring, until softened but not browned, 2 to 3 minutes. Add the rice and garlic and cook, stirring, for 2 minutes.

Add the wine and cook, stirring constantly, until almost all the wine has been absorbed. Add the curry powder, cumin, salt, and pepper and stir until well blended. Add ½ cup of the simmering broth mixture and cook, stirring constantly, until almost all the liquid has been absorbed. Continue adding the simmering broth mixture by half-cupfuls, cooking and stirring after each addition, until the mixture is creamy, the rice is tender yet firm to the bite, and almost all the liquid has been absorbed.

When just a small amount of the last addition of the broth mixture is left in the skillet, add the coconut milk; cook, stirring constantly, until almost all the liquids are absorbed, about 3 minutes. Remove from the heat and stir in the pine nuts (if using). Serve at once.

PER SERVING

Calories 459 | Protein 21g | Total Fat 11g |
Sat. Fat 2g | Cholesterol 0mg | Carbohydrate 63g |
Dietary Fiber 8g | Sodium 1,071mg

Cook's Tip

To toast chopped walnuts, slivered almonds, pine nuts, or other small nuts or nut pieces in the oven: Preheat the oven to 350F (175C). Spread the nuts in a single layer on an ungreased light-colored baking sheet. Bake until lightly golden, about 5 minutes, stirring halfway through the cooking time. Immediately remove from the baking sheet and set aside briefly to cool.

To toast on the stovetop: Heat a small skillet over medium heat. Add the nuts and cook, stirring constantly, until lightly golden, 3 to 5 minutes. Immediately remove from the skillet and set aside briefly to cool. For larger whole nuts and nut pieces, increase the cooking time by a few minutes.

Garden Ratatouille Casserole
egg-free|low-carb
MAKES 6 MAIN-DISH SERVINGS

Enjoy this delicious baked variation of the famous Provençal stewed dish with a tossed green salad for a satisfying meal. If you are short on time, skip salting the eggplant, as the other flavors will typically mask any bitterness.

1 eggplant (1 to 1¼ pounds), peeled and cut into 1-inch cubes, sprinkled with salt, and set in a colander to drain for 30 minutes (salting is optional)
2 tablespoons extra-virgin olive oil
1 medium onion (about 6 ounces), chopped
1 medium green bell pepper (about 6 ounces), thinly sliced
1 medium red bell pepper (about 6 ounces), thinly sliced
3 to 4 large cloves garlic, finely chopped
2 medium zucchini (about 6 ounces each), sliced into thin rounds
1 cup gluten-free prepared pasta sauce, preferably the tomato-basil variety
¼ cup pitted kalamata olives, chopped (optional)
3 tablespoons finely chopped basil
Salt and freshly ground black pepper, to taste
6 ounces sliced provolone cheese
¼ cup gluten-free freshly grated Parmesan cheese

Preheat the oven to 400F (205C). Lightly grease a 12×8-inch baking dish and set aside.

If salted, rinse the eggplant under cold-running water. Dry between paper towels and set aside.

In a large nonstick skillet, heat the oil over medium heat. Add the onion and cook, stirring, until softened, about 3 minutes. Add the bell peppers and garlic and cook, stirring often, for 2 to 3 minutes. Add the eggplant and cook, stirring often, for 2 to 3 minutes. Add the zucchini and cook, stirring often, until the zucchini is just tender, 4 to 5 minutes. Add ¼ cup of the pasta sauce, olives (if using), basil, salt, and black pepper; cook, stirring, for 2 minutes. Transfer to prepared baking dish and top with the provolone cheese. Top with the remaining sauce and cover with foil (if sauce will touch foil, cover with a sheet of waxed paper first).

Bake for 30 minutes. Uncover, sprinkle with the Parmesan cheese, and bake, uncovered, until the cheese is melted and mixture is bubbly, 5 to 8 minutes. Let stand for 10 minutes before cutting into wedges and serving.

PER SERVING

Calories 255 | Protein 12g | Total Fat 16g |
Sat. Fat 7g | Cholesterol 23mg | Carbohydrate 19g |
Dietary Fiber 5g | Sodium 538mg

Arborio Rice with Tomatoes and Fresh Mozzarella

egg-free

MAKES 4 SERVINGS

This delicious rice dish can be made using regular short-grain white rice, but serve it warm as the grains will harden as it cools to room temperature.

1½ **cups arborio rice**

2 **tablespoons extra-virgin olive oil**

2 **large cloves garlic, finely chopped**

¼ **cup chopped fresh basil**

1 **tablespoon balsamic vinegar**

½ **teaspoon salt, preferably the coarse variety, or more to taste**

Freshly ground black pepper, to taste

3 **medium tomatoes (about 6 ounces each), preferably vine-ripened, cut into bite-size pieces**

4 **ounces small fresh mozzarella balls, drained**

Fresh basil leaves, for garnish (optional)

Bring a large stockpot of salted water to a boil over high heat. Add the rice and boil until al dente, 12 to 15 minutes, stirring a few times. Drain in a colander.

Meanwhile, in a large nonstick skillet, heat the oil over medium-low heat. Add the garlic and chopped basil and cook, stirring constantly, for 2 minutes. Add the vinegar, salt, and pepper and cook, stirring constantly, for 30 seconds. Add the tomatoes and rice and toss until just heated through. Remove from heat and let stand until barely warm. Add the cheese, tossing gently yet thoroughly to combine. Serve slightly warm or at room temperature. Garnish with basil leaves (if using).

PER SERVING

Calories 428 | Protein 12g | Total Fat 14g |
Sat. Fat 5g | Cholesterol 25mg | Carbohydrate 62g |
Dietary Fiber 1g | Sodium 407mg

Spiced Basmati Rice Pilaf
with **Peas**

vegan

MAKES 4 MAIN-DISH OR 6 TO 8 SIDE-DISH SERVINGS

This Indian-inspired pilaf is also excellent prepared with fresh or frozen cauliflower or broccoli.

2 tablespoons canola or other mild vegetable oil

1 medium onion (about 6 ounces), chopped

1 large clove garlic, finely chopped

1½ cups basmati rice

2 teaspoons cumin seed

1 teaspoon turmeric

¼ teaspoon gluten-free chili powder

2 cups gluten-free low-sodium vegetable broth

1½ cups frozen green peas

Salt and freshly ground black pepper, to taste

In a large nonstick deep-sided skillet with a lid, heat the oil over medium heat. Add the

onion and cook, stirring, for 3 minutes. Add the garlic and cook, stirring constantly, for 1 minute. Add the rice, cumin, turmeric, and chili powder; cook, stirring constantly, for 1 minute. Add the broth, peas, salt, and pepper; bring to a boil over high heat. Reduce the heat and simmer, covered, 15 minutes, or until the rice has absorbed all the liquid. Fluff with a fork and serve at once.

PER SERVING

Calories 382 | Protein 15g | Total Fat 9g |
Sat. Fat 1g | Cholesterol 0mg | Carbohydrate 61g |
Dietary Fiber 5g | Sodium 369mg

Santa Fe–Style Rice-and-Cheddar Bake with **Corn** and **Chilies**

lacto-ovo

MAKES 4 SERVINGS

For a milder dish, omit the chilies and replace with minced pimiento, if desired.

3 eggs, separated

1½ cups cooked white or brown rice (see Cook's Tip, page 145)

1 cup frozen yellow corn, thawed

1 cup gluten-free shredded reduced-fat cheddar cheese

½ cup skim milk

2 tablespoons chopped mild green chilies

1 teaspoon ground cumin

1 teaspoon salt, or to taste

Freshly ground black pepper, to taste

❦ Preheat the oven to 350F (175C). Lightly grease an 8-inch-square baking dish.

In a large bowl, mix together the egg yolks, rice, corn, cheese, milk, chilies, cumin, salt, and pepper.

In a medium bowl, beat the egg whites with an electric mixer on medium speed until stiff peaks form. Gently fold into the rice mixture. Pour into the prepared baking dish. Bake, uncovered, in the center of the oven for about 40 minutes, or until a knife inserted in the center comes out clean. Serve at once.

PER SERVING

Calories 245 | Protein 16g | Total Fat 6g | Sat. Fat 3g | Cholesterol 166mg | Carbohydrate 31g | Dietary Fiber 1g | Sodium 773mg

Glazed Snow Peas
with Rice

vegan

MAKES 3 TO 4 MAIN-DISH SERVINGS

Though optional, peanuts lend protein and crunch to this tasty entrée. For a side dish to serve six, simply omit the rice.

4 cups snow peas, trimmed, strings removed

3 tablespoons water

⅓ cup balsamic vinegar

1 tablespoon light brown sugar

1 tablespoon peanut oil

2 large cloves garlic, finely chopped

½ tablespoon toasted (dark) sesame oil

Salt and freshly ground black pepper, to taste

3 cups hot cooked rice

¼ cup chopped unsalted peanuts (optional)

❦ Place the snow peas and water in a large nonstick skillet with a lid. Cover and bring to a boil over high heat. Reduce the heat to medium and steam until crisp-tender, about 2 minutes. Drain well and dry skillet with a paper towel.

Meanwhile, in a small saucepan, combine the vinegar and sugar and bring to a boil over medium heat. Boil until reduced to 2 tablespoons.

Heat the peanut oil in the dried nonstick skillet over medium heat. Add the garlic and cook, stirring, for 1 minute. Add the snow peas, vinegar mixture, and sesame oil; cook, tossing until the snow peas are heated through and glazed, 2 to 3 minutes. Season with salt and pepper. Serve at once, over the rice, garnished with the peanuts (if using).

PER SERVING

Calories 379 | Protein 9g | Total Fat 8g | Sat. Fat 1g | Cholesterol 0mg | Carbohydrate 69g | Dietary Fiber 4g | Sodium 11mg

Southwestern-Style Corn Spaghetti with Chili Beans

vegan

MAKES 4 SERVINGS

This spicy bean sauce lends pizzazz to any gluten-free pasta.

1 tablespoon extra-virgin olive oil

½ cup finely chopped onion

1 (16-ounce) can gluten-free chili beans in mild sauce

1 (14.5-ounce) can stewed tomatoes, juices included

½ cup medium salsa

¼ cup canned chopped green chilies

1 tablespoon gluten-free chili powder

½ teaspoon ground cumin

8 ounces corn spaghetti

Gluten-free shredded cheddar cheese and/or gluten-free light sour cream (optional)

In a large saucepan, heat the oil over medium heat. Add the onion and cook, stirring, until softened, about 3 minutes. Add the beans, tomatoes with their juices, salsa, chilies, chili powder, and cumin; bring to a simmer over medium-high heat. Cover, reduce the heat, and simmer gently for 10 minutes, stirring occasionally.

Meanwhile, cook the spaghetti in boiling salted water according to package directions until al dente. Drain well and return to the pot. Add the bean mixture and stir well to combine.

Serve at once, with the toppings passed separately (if using).

PER SERVING

Calories 373 | Protein 11g | Total Fat 6g | Sat. Fat 1g | Cholesterol 0mg | Carbohydrate 77g | Dietary Fiber 17g | Sodium 745mg

Spaghetti Squash with Pesto

egg-free | low-carb

MAKES 4 TO 6 SERVINGS

Spaghetti squash is nature's gift to those in search of both a gluten-free and low-carb noodle alternative—each time I twist out the long, squiggly strands of cooked flesh, I am amazed by the likeness to its namesake. Like spaghetti, the squash is naturally bland and lends itself well to most pasta sauces. For an Asian-style vegan alternative, see the variation below, which uses Japanese tamari sauce in lieu of soy sauce, which typically contains wheat.

1 (4-pound) spaghetti squash

½ cup gluten-free prepared pesto sauce, or Classic Pesto Sauce (page 82)

Preheat the oven to 375F (190C). Prick the squash in several places with a large fork. Place on an ungreased baking sheet and bake for 1 hour, or until softened and easily pierced through the center, turning over halfway through cooking time. Cut in half and, while still hot, scoop out the seeds. Using a fork, twist out the flesh, transferring to a large bowl. If necessary, separate any thick strands of flesh into thinner strands with your fingers. Add the pesto, tossing well to thoroughly coat. Serve at once.

PER SERVING

Calories 219 | Protein 6g | Total Fat 15g |
Sat. Fat 4g | Cholesterol 9mg | Carbohydrate 16g |
Dietary Fiber 2g | Sodium 241mg

VARIATION: *To make* Sesame Spaghetti Squash: *Bake and prepare the squash as directed. Omit the pesto and toss with ¼ cup thinly sliced scallions (mostly green parts), ¼ cup tamari sauce, 2 tablespoons toasted (dark) sesame oil, 1 tablespoon peanut oil, and 1 teaspoon onion powder. Serve warm, at room temperature, or chilled.*

Spaghetti Squash Primavera

egg-free

MAKES 5 TO 6 SERVINGS

Use this recipe as a model for showcasing your favorite fresh veggies.

1 (4-pound) spaghetti squash

1½ cups sugar snap peas

6 medium-thick asparagus spears, trimmed, cut into 2-inch lengths

1 medium zucchini (about 6 ounces), quartered lengthwise, thinly sliced crosswise

4 ounces baby carrots, cut lengthwise in half if thick

10 medium cultivated white mushrooms, quartered

1 cup bite-size broccoli florets

1 tablespoon extra-virgin olive oil

¼ cup pine nuts or walnut pieces

2 large cloves garlic, finely chopped

¼ cup skim milk

8 ounces gluten-free light cream cheese with chives, in 4 pieces, at room temperature

2 medium plum tomatoes (about 3 ounces each), coarsely chopped

¼ cup finely chopped fresh basil

¼ cup finely chopped fresh flat-leaf parsley

Salt and freshly ground black pepper, to taste

¼ cup gluten-free freshly grated Parmesan cheese

Preheat the oven to 375F (190C). Prick the squash in several places with a large fork. Place on an ungreased baking sheet and bake for 1 hour, or until softened and easily pierced through the center, turning over halfway through cooking time. Cut in half and, while still hot, scoop out the seeds. Using a fork, twist out the flesh, transferring to a large bowl. If necessary, separate any thick strands of flesh into thinner strands with your fingers. Set aside.

In a medium stockpot, put about 1 inch of water. Place a 9-inch steaming basket in the pot and add the peas, asparagus, zucchini, carrots, mushrooms, and broccoli; bring to a boil over high heat. Cover tightly, reduce the heat to medium, and steam until barely tender, about 3 minutes. Transfer to a colander and rinse under cold running water until cool. Drain well.

Meanwhile, in a large deep-sided nonstick skillet, heat the oil over medium heat. Add the pine nuts and garlic and cook, stirring constantly, until they begin to turn golden, 1 to 2 minutes. Reduce the heat to medium-low and add the milk and cream cheese; cook, stirring, until smooth. Add the spaghetti squash, steamed vegetables, tomatoes, basil, parsley, salt, and pepper; cook, stirring occasionally, until heated through, about 5 minutes. Serve at once, sprinkled with the Parmesan cheese.

PER SERVING

Calories 368 | Protein 15g | Total Fat 19g |
Sat. Fat 8g | Cholesterol 30mg | Carbohydrate 41g |
Dietary Fiber 8g | Sodium 437mg

Greek Spinach and Feta Pie
lacto-ovo|low-carb
MAKES 6 SERVINGS

Of course, there's no phyllo dough here, just lots of healthy spinach, tangy feta, and creamy ricotta cheese, the stuff of traditional Greek spanakopita.

2 tablespoons extra-virgin olive oil
1 bunch scallions (white and green parts), thinly sliced
2 (10-ounce) packages chopped frozen spinach, cooked according to package directions, drained well, and squeezed dry between paper towels
Salt and freshly ground black pepper, to taste
6 eggs, lightly beaten
1 (15-ounce) container gluten-free reduced-fat ricotta cheese
8 ounces (2 cups) gluten-free crumbled feta cheese
¼ cup chopped fresh flat-leaf parsley
1 tablespoon chopped fresh dill
Pinch nutmeg (optional)

Preheat the oven to 350F (175C). Lightly oil a 13×9-inch baking dish and set aside.

In a large nonstick skillet, heat the oil over medium heat. Add the scallions and cook, stirring, until softened but not browned, about 3 minutes. Add the spinach, salt, and pepper and cook, stirring often, until the spinach is heated through, about 3 minutes.

In a large bowl, whisk together the eggs and ricotta. Add the spinach mixture and remaining ingredients, stirring well to thoroughly combine. Transfer to prepared dish and bake for 30 to 40 minutes, or until set through the center and lightly browned. Remove from the oven and let stand for 10 minutes before cutting into wedges and serving.

PER SERVING

Calories 278 | Protein 25g | Total Fat 16g |
Sat. Fat 8g | Cholesterol 258mg | Carbohydrate 11g |
Dietary Fiber 4g | Sodium 700mg

Spinach-Pesto Pie

lacto-ovo|low-carb

MAKES 6 SERVINGS

If you like pesto sauce, you'll love this scrumptious pie.

5 eggs

½ cup skim milk

⅓ cup gluten-free prepared pesto sauce, or Classic Pesto Sauce (page 82)

1 (10-ounce) package frozen chopped spinach, cooked according to package directions, well drained, and squeezed dry between paper towels

2 cups (8 ounces) gluten-free shredded part-skim mozzarella cheese

Salt and freshly ground black pepper, to taste

1 or more cups pasta sauce, heated, to serve (optional)

❧Preheat the oven to 375F (190C). Lightly grease an 8½- or 9-inch pie plate.

In a large bowl, whisk together the eggs, milk, and pesto sauce. Stir in the spinach, 1½ cups of the cheese, salt, and pepper. Pour into prepared pie plate. Bake about 30 minutes, or until a knife inserted in the center comes out clean, sprinkling with remaining cheese the last few minutes of cooking. Let stand for 10 minutes before cutting into wedges and serving warm, with the pasta sauce (if using).

PER SERVING

Calories 254 | Protein 20g | Total Fat 17g | Sat. Fat 7g | Cholesterol 202mg | Carbohydrate 6g | Dietary Fiber 2g | Sodium 389mg

Caribbean-Style Sweet Potatoes and Black Beans over Brown Rice

vegan

MAKES 4 SERVINGS

High in vitamins A and C and other important nutrients, sweet potatoes are good for you. To serve as a side dish, omit the rice.

3 medium sweet potatoes (about 6 ounces each), peeled and cut into bite-size pieces

¾ cup orange juice

2 teaspoons cornstarch

1 teaspoon jerk seasoning

1 teaspoon ground cinnamon

¼ teaspoon ground cumin

1 (15-ounce) can black beans, rinsed and drained

Salt and freshly ground black pepper, to taste

3 cups hot cooked brown rice

❧In a large saucepan, bring the potatoes and enough salted water to cover to a boil over high heat. Reduce the heat to low, cover, and simmer until tender but not falling apart, 10 to 12 minutes. Drain and set aside.

In the same saucepan, whisk together the orange juice, cornstarch, jerk seasoning, cinnamon, and cumin. Bring to a boil over medium heat. Boil until thickened, whisking constantly, about 1 minute. Stir in the sweet potatoes, beans, salt, and pepper. Cook, stirring, until heated through, about 3 minutes. Serve warm, over the rice.

PER SERVING

Calories 366 | Protein 11g | Total Fat 2g |
Sat. Fat 0g | Cholesterol 0mg | Carbohydrate 77g |
Dietary Fiber 8g | Sodium 14mg

Jamaican Jerk Tofu with Rice

vegan

MAKES 4 SERVINGS

For a New Orleans–style dish, use Cajun spice in lieu of the jerk seasoning.

1 pound extra-firm tofu, drained and rinsed

2 teaspoons jerk seasoning

2 tablespoons canola or other mild vegetable oil

3 cups hot cooked rice

Place the tofu on a deep-sided plate or shallow bowl. Top with a second plate and weight with a heavy can. Let stand for a minimum of 15 minutes (preferably 1 hour). Drain off the excess water. Slice the tofu lengthwise into quarters.

Sprinkle the bottom of a shallow dish just large enough to hold the tofu slices in a single layer with half of the jerk seasoning. Arrange the tofu slices over the seasoning and rub the tops evenly with the remaining seasoning. Cover with plastic wrap and refrigerate for 8 hours, or overnight.

Just before cooking, scrape off most of the jerk seasoning from the tofu slices. In a large nonstick skillet, heat the oil over medium-high heat. Add the tofu and cook until browned, about 4 minutes per side. Serve at once, over the rice.

PER SERVING

Calories 331 | Protein 13g | Total Fat 13g |
Sat. Fat 1g | Cholesterol 0mg | Carbohydrate 42g |
Dietary Fiber 2g | Sodium 18mg

Teriyaki Tofu with Sugar Snap Peas and Rice

vegan

MAKES 4 SERVINGS

Mirin is a Japanese sweet rice wine available in Asian markets, specialty stores, and well-stocked supermarkets; a medium-dry or sweet sherry can be substituted. Brown rice syrup is a natural sweetener available in health food stores, but sometimes it contains barley malt. If necessary, use 1/4 cup honey instead. Snow peas can replace the snap peas, if desired, but cook for slightly less time.

1 pound firm tofu, drained and rinsed

⅓ cup gluten-free brown rice syrup

¼ cup tamari sauce

¼ cup mirin

¼ cup apple or white grape juice

1 tablespoon toasted (dark) sesame oil

1 tablespoon light sesame or peanut oil

½ pound fresh sugar snap peas, trimmed and strings removed

3 large cloves garlic, finely chopped

3 cups hot cooked rice

Place the tofu on a deep-sided plate or shallow bowl. Top with a second plate and weight with a heavy can. Let stand for a minimum of 15 minutes (preferably 1 hour). Drain off the excess water. Cut the tofu into 1½-inch cubes.

Meanwhile, in a small bowl, whisk together the rice syrup, tamari, mirin, apple juice, and toasted sesame oil. Set aside.

In a large nonstick skillet, heat the light sesame oil over medium-high heat. Add the tofu and cook for 2 minutes, turning frequently with a wide spatula. Add the reserved sauce and cook, uncovered, turning often, until the liquids are reduced and syrupy and coat the tofu, 10 to 15 minutes, adding the snap peas and garlic the last few minutes of cooking. Serve at once, over the rice.

PER SERVING

Calories 463 | Protein 16g | Total Fat 13g |
Sat. Fat 2g | Cholesterol 0mg | Carbohydrate 71g |
Dietary Fiber 4g | Sodium 1,040mg

Stuffed Tomatoes with Avocado and Fresh Mozzarella

egg-free|low-carb

MAKES 4 MAIN-DISH SERVINGS

Though relatively high in total fat, avocados are low in saturated fat and loaded with essential vitamins and minerals, namely potassium, vitamin E, B vitamins, and folic acid. For a vegan alternative, replace the mozzarella cheese with a mixture of chopped cucumber and red onion.

1 ripe avocado, peeled, pitted, and cut in ½-inch cubes

4 ounces tiny fresh mozzarella cheese balls, well-drained, quartered

4 large cloves garlic, finely chopped

1 tablespoon finely chopped fresh basil

2 tablespoons extra-virgin olive oil

2 tablespoons balsamic vinegar

1 teaspoon gluten-free Dijon mustard

Salt, preferably the coarse variety, and freshly ground black pepper, to taste

4 large tomatoes (about 8 ounces each), preferably vine-ripened

Lettuce leaves, for garnish

In a small bowl, mix together the avocado, cheese, garlic, basil, oil, vinegar, mustard, salt, and pepper. Set aside.

Cut a thin slice from the top of each tomato and discard. Gently squeeze out the seeds from each tomato. Using a small sharp knife or a melon batter, scoop out the pulp and reserve, discarding any white core. Chop the pulp and add to the avocado mixture, tossing well to combine.

Spoon equal portions of the avocado mixture into each tomato. To serve, arrange equal amounts of lettuce leaves on 4 serving plates. Top with a stuffed tomato and serve at once.

PER SERVING

Calories 281 | Protein 9g | Total Fat 22g |
Sat. Fat 7g | Cholesterol 25mg | Carbohydrate 16g |
Dietary Fiber 4g | Sodium 158mg

Stir-Fried Vegetables and Crispy Marinated Tofu

vegan

MAKES 4 TO 6 MAIN-DISH SERVINGS

Feel free to substitute your favorite fresh veggies for those suggested in the recipe.

12 ounces extra-firm tofu

¼ cup tamari sauce

1 tablespoon unseasoned rice vinegar

1 tablespoon toasted (dark) sesame oil

1 tablespoon plus 1 teaspoon peanut oil

1 medium red or green bell pepper (about 6 ounces), cut into thin strips

1 medium onion (about 6 ounces), thinly sliced

16 ounces fresh broccoli florets

8 ounces cultivated white and/or wild mushrooms, sliced

1 tablespoon chopped fresh ginger

2 large cloves garlic, finely chopped

¼ cup water

1½ tablespoons creamy peanut butter

4 cups hot cooked white or brown rice

Place the tofu on a deep-sided plate or shallow bowl. Top with a second plate and weight with a heavy can. Let stand for a minimum of 15 minutes (preferably 1 hour). Drain off the excess water. Cut the tofu into 1½-inch cubes.

In a medium bowl, combine the tofu, tamari sauce, vinegar, and sesame oil. Marinate for 30 minutes at room temperature, or cover and refrigerate 1 hour or overnight.

In a wok or large nonstick skillet, heat 1 tablespoon of the peanut oil over medium-high heat. Using a slotted spoon, remove the tofu from the marinade (reserve the marinade) and add to the wok; cook, stirring often, until crispy, 5 to 7 minutes. Transfer the tofu to a holding plate and add the remaining peanut oil, bell pepper, and onion; cook, stirring often, for 2 minutes. Add the broccoli, mushrooms, ginger, and garlic; cook, stirring often, for 5 minutes. Stir in the water and reserved marinade; let come to a simmer. Reduce the heat to low and add the peanut butter, stirring until thoroughly blended. Stir in the reserved tofu and cook until heated through. Serve at once, over the rice.

PER SERVING

Calories 483 | Protein 20g | Total Fat 16g |
Sat. Fat 3g | Cholesterol 0mg | Carbohydrate 68g |
Dietary Fiber 7g | Sodium 1,067mg

Mexican-Style Stuffed Zucchini

egg-free|low-carb

MAKES 3 MAIN-DISH OR 6 SIDE-DISH SERVINGS

For a milder dish, replace the fresh jalapeño chili with a few tablespoons of canned diced mild green chilies, or omit altogether, if desired.

- **3 large zucchini (about 8 ounces each), trimmed and halved lengthwise**
- **1 tablespoon extra-virgin olive oil**
- **1 medium red bell pepper (about 6 ounces), chopped**
- **3 scallions (white and green parts), thinly sliced**
- **2 cloves garlic, finely chopped**
- **1 cup gluten-free shredded reduced-fat Monterey Jack or cheddar cheese (4 ounces)**
- **2 tablespoons finely chopped fresh cilantro**
- **½ to 1 small jalapeño chili, seeded and finely chopped**
- **Salt and freshly ground black pepper, to taste**

Preheat the oven to 350F (175C). Prepare a large bowl of ice water. Lightly oil a baking sheet or shallow baking dish and set aside.

In a large stockpot filled with boiling salted water, cook the zucchini until just fork-tender in the center, 2 to 3 minutes. Immediately plunge in the ice-water bath and let rest for about 5 minutes, or until cooled. Drain well and pat dry with paper towels. Scoop out the pulp, leaving a ⅜-inch-thick shell. Coarsely chop the pulp and blot lightly with paper towels. Transfer to a medium bowl and set aside.

In a medium nonstick skillet, heat the oil over medium heat. Add the bell pepper, scallions, and garlic; cook, stirring often, until fragrant and softened, about 5 minutes. Remove from the heat and let cool a few minutes.

Add the bell pepper mixture to the bowl containing the zucchini pulp, along with half of the cheese, the cilantro, chili, salt, and pepper; toss well to combine. Stuff the cheese mixture into the zucchini shells and transfer to the prepared baking sheet. (At this point, the mixture can be covered and refrigerated up to 24 hours before continuing with the recipe.) Bake for about 20 minutes, or until very lightly browned, sprinkling evenly with the remaining cheese the last few minutes of cooking. Serve warm.

PER SERVING

Calories 294 | Protein 26g | Total Fat 13g | Sat. Fat 4g | Cholesterol 28mg | Carbohydrate 16g | Dietary Fiber 5g | Sodium 434mg

Zucchini Fettucine with Herbed Chevre Sauce

egg-free|low-carb

MAKES 2 TO 3 MAIN-DISH OR 4 TO 6 SIDE-DISH SERVINGS

This scrumptious goat cheese sauce is also excellent tossed with fresh asparagus and green beans, or as a topping for baked potatoes. As of this writing, both

Rondelé and Boursin spreadable cheeses are gluten-free.

- **4 medium zucchini (about 6 ounces each)**
- **½ (5.3-ounce) container mild spreadable goat cheese (about ⅓ cup)**
- **⅓ cup reduced-fat garlic-and-herb spreadable cheese, such as Rondelé or Boursin**
- **2 tablespoons skim milk, plus additional as necessary**
- **Salt and freshly ground black pepper, to taste**

Bring a large stockpot of salted water to a boil over high heat.

With a vegetable peeler, working on a flat surface, slice the zucchini lengthwise into thin strips, turning each time you peel it (if center is difficult to cut with the peeler, cut into thin strips with a knife). Add the zucchini to the stockpot and let return to a boil. Drain and re-fresh under cold running water. Drain well.

Add the cheeses and milk to the stockpot. Heat over medium-low heat, stirring until smooth. Add the zucchini, salt, and pepper; toss well to combine, adding additional milk as necessary for a thinner sauce. Serve at once.

PER SERVING
Calories 226 | Protein 14g | Total Fat 14g | Sat. Fat 9g | Cholesterol 41mg | Carbohydrate 14g | Dietary Fiber 4g | Sodium 296mg

Zucchini Lasagna
egg-free
MAKES 6 SERVINGS

This tasty protein-packed lasagna is ideal to make in late summer when garden-fresh zucchini are plentiful. It can be assembled and refrigerated twenty-four hours before baking, but add about fifteen minutes to the covered cooking time.

- **4 large zucchini (7 to 8 ounces each), trimmed, unpeeled, sliced lengthwise into ⅛-inch-thick slices**
- **1 cup gluten-free nonfat ricotta cheese**
- **1 cup gluten-free low-fat cottage cheese**
- **1 tablespoon finely chopped fresh parsley (optional)**
- **Salt and freshly ground black pepper, to taste**
- **26 ounces gluten-free prepared pasta sauce, preferably the tomato-basil variety**
- **8 ounces (2 cups) gluten-free shredded part-skim mozzarella cheese**
- **½ cup (2 ounces) gluten-free freshly shredded Parmesan cheese**

Preheat the oven to 375F (190C). Fill a large stockpot with salted water and bring to a boil over high heat. Lightly oil a 13×9-inch baking dish and set aside.

Add the zucchini to the boiling water and cook until just tender, about 2 to 3 minutes. Drain well in a colander. Transfer to a cutting board lined with paper towels to further drain.

In a medium bowl, mix together the ricotta

cheese, cottage cheese, parsley (if using), salt, and pepper until well combined.

Make layers in the prepared baking dish in the following order: ⅓ of the zucchini, half of the pasta sauce, ⅓ of the zucchini, all the ricotta mixture, half of the mozzarella and Parmesan cheeses, the remaining ⅓ of the zucchini, the remaining pasta sauce, ending with the remaining mozzarella and Parmesan cheeses. Cover with oiled foil (if sauce will touch foil, cover with a sheet of waxed paper first) and bake for 35 minutes. Uncover and bake for 7 to 10 minutes, or until the cheeses are melted and just beginning to brown. Let stand for 10 minutes before cutting and serving.

PER SERVING

Calories 325 | Protein 26g | Total Fat 15g |
Sat. Fat 6g | Cholesterol 34mg | Carbohydrate 24g |
Dietary Fiber 4g | Sodium 1,155 mg

Zucchini Risotto Pie with Rosemary and Marinara Sauce

lacto-ovo

MAKES 6 MAIN-DISH OR 8 SIDE-DISH SERVINGS

You can use regular long-grain white rice here, but the texture of the pie will be slightly less creamy. Basil can replace the rosemary, if desired, but only use the fresh herb.

1½ cups arborio rice

2 tablespoons extra-virgin olive oil

2 large onions (about 8 ounces each), finely chopped

3 medium zucchini (about 6 ounces each), chopped

3 tablespoons chopped fresh rosemary or 1 tablespoon dried

2 large cloves garlic, finely chopped

Salt and freshly ground black pepper, to taste

3 eggs, lightly beaten

¾ cup gluten-free freshly shredded Parmesan cheese

¼ cup skim milk

3 cups favorite gluten-free prepared marinara sauce

Fresh rosemary sprigs, for garnish (optional)

Preheat the oven to 350F (175C). Lightly grease a 10-inch quiche dish or pie plate.

In a large stockpot filled with boiling salted water, boil the rice for 8 minutes; drain well.

Meanwhile, in a large nonstick skillet, heat the oil over medium heat. Add the onions and cook, stirring, until softened, about 3 minutes. Add the zucchini, 2 tablespoons of the rosemary, garlic, salt, and pepper; cook, stirring, for 5 minutes. Remove from heat and let cool.

Add the rice, eggs, ½ cup of the cheese, and the milk to the skillet; mix well to thoroughly combine. Transfer to the prepared quiche dish. Bake, uncovered, for about 35 minutes, or until set and beginning to brown. Sprinkle with the remaining cheese and bake for 5 minutes, or until the cheese is melted.

Meanwhile, in a medium saucepan, bring the

marinara sauce and remaining rosemary to a simmer over medium heat, stirring occasionally. Cover, remove from heat, and let stand for 10 minutes to allow the flavors to blend.

To serve, cut the pie into 6 equal pieces. Ladle equal portions of the marinara sauce on each of 6 serving plates and top with a piece of pie. Serve at once, garnished with fresh rosemary sprigs (if using).

PER SERVING

Calories 424 | Protein 15g | Total Fat 15g |
Sat. Fat 4g | Cholesterol 115mg | Carbohydrate 60g |
Dietary Fiber 3g | Sodium 1,022mg

Side Dishes

Many traditional side dishes are naturally gluten-free, whether they consist of vegetables from A to Z, or starches—save for wheat noodles, of course—in the form of potatoes, rice, corn, beans, and other legumes. Problems arise for those with celiac disease and wheat allergies when these vegetables and starches are tossed with sauces and gravies thickened by wheat flour. Fortunately, cornstarch is a good substitute for wheat flour in most sauces and gravies, but keep in mind when converting your grandmother's creamed spinach recipe to use half the amount of cornstarch as wheat flour, and cook for about half the amount of time, as cornstarch will thicken a liquid almost immediately, which in turn will thin if overheated or cooked too long. Several of the following recipes eschew cornstarch and rely on gluten-free cream cheese, sour cream, or mayonnaise to create fabulous gluten-free sauces.

If you really have a yen for noodles, don't forget about rice noodles—the flat variety in particular makes an excellent substitute for egg noodles in most recipes, namely Asian-Style Mushroom "Stroganoff" Noodles, a favorite of mine.

Brussels Sprouts with Cream Cheese and Toasted Almonds

egg-free|low-carb

MAKES 4 TO 6 SERVINGS

Dress up fresh Brussels sprouts for the holidays with this quick and easy recipe.

1 pound fresh Brussels sprouts, trimmed, cut in half

¼ cup gluten-free Neufchâtel cream cheese, cut into small pieces

Salt and freshly ground black pepper, to taste

Freshly grated nutmeg, to taste

¼ cup slivered almonds, toasted (see Cook's Tip, page 118)

In a medium stockpot, cook the Brussels sprouts in boiling salted water until tender, about 5 minutes. Drain, return to the pot, add the cream cheese, salt, pepper, and nutmeg, stirring well to thoroughly combine. Transfer to a warmed serving dish and sprinkle with the almonds. Serve at once.

PER SERVING

Calories 109 | Protein 6g | Total Fat 6g |
Sat. Fat 2g | Cholesterol 5mg | Carbohydrate 12g |
Dietary Fiber 5g | Sodium 57mg

Apple-Kasha Stuffing

vegan

MAKES 8 SERVINGS

This tasty side dish is also a wonderful filling for baked portobello mushrooms.

1 cup kasha

¼ cup canola oil

2 medium apples (about 6 ounces each), preferably 1 tart, such as Granny Smith, and 1 sweet, such as McIntosh, peeled, cored, and chopped

1 cup chopped onion

1 cup chopped celery

2 cups gluten-free low-sodium vegetable broth

½ teaspoon ground sage

Salt and freshly ground black pepper, to taste

Preheat the oven to 350F (175C). Lightly oil an 8-inch-square baking dish and set aside.

Heat a medium skillet with a lid over medium-high heat; add the kasha and cook, stirring constantly, until fragrant and toasted, 2 to 3 minutes. Transfer the kasha to a bowl and set aside. Reduce the heat to medium and add the oil. Add the apples, onion, and celery; cook, stirring, until softened, about 5 minutes. Add the broth, sage, salt, and pepper; bring to a boil over high heat. Carefully stir in the reserved kasha. Reduce the heat to medium-low and simmer, covered, until the kasha is tender and the liquid is absorbed, 7 to 10 minutes. Remove from the heat and let stand, covered, for 3 minutes. Uncover and fluff with a fork.

Transfer the kasha mixture to the prepared baking dish. (At this point, the mixture can be cooled to room temperature and refrigerated, covered, for up to 24 hours before continuing with the recipe.) Bake, covered, for 30 minutes (or 45 minutes if refrigerated). Serve hot.

PER SERVING

Calories 177 | Protein 6g | Total Fat 8g |
Sat. Fat 1g | Cholesterol 0mg | Carbohydrate 24g |
Dietary Fiber 4g | Sodium 145mg

Creamy Parmesan Broccoli with Pine Nuts

lacto-ovo|low-carb

MAKES 6 SERVINGS

This is a great way to spruce up frozen broccoli for company. The nuts can be omitted, if desired.

16-ounces frozen broccoli florets, cooked according to package directions, well drained and cooled

Salt and freshly ground black pepper, to taste

¾ cup gluten-free freshly grated Parmesan cheese

4 scallions (white and green parts), chopped

½ cup gluten-free light sour cream

¼ cup gluten-free light mayonnaise

2 tablespoons skim milk

¼ cup pine nuts or chopped walnuts, toasted (see Cook's Tip, page 118)

✂ Preheat the oven to 350F (175C). Lightly grease a 12×8-inch baking dish. Arrange the broccoli along the bottom of the prepared dish. Season with salt and pepper and sprinkle with ¼ cup of the Parmesan cheese; toss well to coat.

In a medium bowl, mix the remaining ½ cup cheese, the scallions, sour cream, mayonnaise, milk, salt, and pepper until well combined; spoon evenly over the broccoli. Bake, uncovered, until lightly browned and bubbly, 18 to 20 minutes. Sprinkle with the pine nuts and serve at once.

PER SERVING

Calories 150 | Protein 10g | Total Fat 10g |
Sat. Fat 3g | Cholesterol 15mg | Carbohydrate 9g |
Dietary Fiber 3g | Sodium 307mg

Roasted Cajun-Style Corn

vegan

MAKES 4 SERVINGS

Cajun spice or seasoning can be found in the spice aisle of most major supermarkets. For a Jamaican-style dish, use jerk seasoning, or for a Mexican-style variation, use chili powder, instead.

4 ears corn

2 tablespoons canola oil

Salt and freshly ground black pepper, to taste

1 teaspoon fresh lemon juice

½ teaspoon Cajun spice, or to taste

¼ teaspoon lemon-pepper seasoning

Preheat the oven to broil.

Using a sharp knife, remove the kernels from each ear of corn. Transfer the kernels to an ungreased baking sheet and, using your fingers to evenly coat each kernel, toss with 1 tablespoon of the oil. Season the corn with salt and pepper and toss with a spatula to combine. Broil about 6 inches from the heating element until lightly browned, stirring a few times and watching carefully not to burn, 7 to 8 minutes. Set aside to cool slightly.

Transfer the corn to a medium bowl and add the remaining oil, the lemon juice, Cajun spice, and lemon-pepper seasoning; toss well to combine. Serve warm or at room temperature.

PER SERVING

Calories 182 | Protein 5g | Total Fat 9g |
Sat. Fat 1g | Cholesterol 0mg | Carbohydrate 27g |
Dietary Fiber 4g | Sodium 69mg

Corn Bread Dressing

lacto-ovo

MAKES 8 TO 10 SERVING

This tasty stuffing is made in two stages, which makes it a good dish for easy entertaining.

2 cups cornmeal

1 tablespoon gluten-free baking powder

1¼ teaspoons salt

1 egg

1 cup skim milk

¼ cup (½ stick) butter, melted and cooled

2 tablespoons canola oil

1 small onion (about 4 ounces), finely chopped

2 stalks celery, finely chopped

1 clove garlic, finely chopped

1 teaspoon dried thyme leaves

½ teaspoon ground sage

1½ cups gluten-free low-sodium vegetable broth

¼ cup gluten-free dried cranberries

¼ cup pecan pieces

¼ teaspoon freshly ground black pepper

Preheat the oven to 425F (220C). Lightly oil an 8-inch-square baking pan and set aside.

In a large bowl, mix together the cornmeal, baking powder, and ¼ teaspoon of the salt until well combined. In a medium bowl, whisk together the egg, milk, and butter until well blended; add to the dry ingredients, stirring well until there are no more lumps. Pour into the prepared pan and bake for 15 to 20 minutes, or until a knife inserted in the center comes out clean.

Transfer to a wire rack and let cool in the pan to room temperature. Cut the corn bread into ½-inch cubes and transfer to a baking sheet. Let dry out at room temperature about 12 hours. (At this point, the cubes can be stored in an airtight container for up to 2 days before proceeding.)

Preheat the oven to 350F (175C). Lightly oil a 2½-quart baking dish and set aside.

In a large nonstick skillet, heat 1 tablespoon of the oil over medium heat. Add the onion, celery, garlic, and dried thyme. Cook, stirring, until vegetables are softened but not browned, 3 to 5 minutes. Remove from the heat and add the reserved corn bread, the remaining 1 teaspoon salt, and remaining ingredients, tossing gently yet thoroughly to combine. Transfer to the prepared baking dish and bake, covered, for 25 minutes. Remove the cover and bake for about 10 minutes, or until the top is lightly browned. Serve warm.

PER SERVING

Calories 270 | Protein 8g | Total Fat 13g |
Sat. Fat 4g | Cholesterol 42mg | Carbohydrate 32g |
Dietary Fiber 4g | Sodium 658mg

Szechwan-Style Green Beans
vegan|low-carb
MAKES 4 SERVINGS

Serve these fragrant and spicy green beans over rice and add some chopped peanuts for a satisfying meal. Szechwan pepper is a mildly hot, reddish-brown pepper found in Asian markets as well as the spice aisle of most major supermarkets. It can be omitted, if desired, but increase the amount of Chinese chili paste to ½ tablespoon.

1 tablespoon peanut oil

1 tablespoon toasted (dark) sesame oil

¼ teaspoon ground Szechwan pepper

¾ pound fresh green beans, trimmed

2 cloves garlic, finely chopped

1 teaspoon finely chopped fresh ginger, or ¼ teaspoon dried ground ginger

⅓ cup reduced-sodium tamari sauce

1 teaspoon Chinese chili paste

In a wok or large nonstick skillet, heat the oils over medium-high heat. Add the Szechwan pepper and cook, stirring constantly, for 15 seconds. Add the beans and cook, tossing and stirring constantly, until just beginning to soften, about 3 minutes. Add the garlic and fresh ginger (if using), and cook, tossing and stirring constantly, until beans are just tender, about 3 minutes. Add the tamari sauce, chili paste, and ground ginger (if using), and let come to a boil; cook for 30 seconds, tossing and stirring constantly. Remove from heat and serve warm.

Asian-Style Mushroom "Stroganoff" Noodles

egg-free

MAKES 6 SERVINGS

Rice noodles stand in nicely for the broad egg noodles served with traditional stroganoff. Make sure you use the flat versus thin (vermicelli-style) rice noodles, both of which are available in Asian markets, specialty stores, and some well-stocked supermarkets.

8 ounces flat-style rice noodles, broken in half

1 tablespoon peanut oil

8 ounces sliced cultivated white mushrooms

2 cloves garlic, finely chopped

¾ cup gluten-free low-sodium vegetable broth

½ tablespoon onion powder

½ teaspoon salt

Freshly ground black pepper, to taste

¾ cup gluten-free light sour cream

½ tablespoon toasted (dark) sesame oil

½ tablespoon tamari sauce

In a large stockpot, soak the noodles according to package directions until almost al dente. (Or see Cook's Tip, page 69, for soaking methods.) Drain well and rinse under cold-running water for 30 seconds. Drain well and set aside.

Meanwhile, in a large nonstick skillet, heat the peanut oil over medium heat. Add the mushrooms and garlic and cook, stirring, until the mushrooms have released most of their liquid, about 5 minutes. Stir in ½ cup of the broth, the onion powder, salt, and pepper; bring to a boil over medium-high heat. Reduce the heat to medium-low and add the rice noodles; cook, stirring and turning often, until the noodles have absorbed most of the liquid and are soft yet firm to the bite, about 3 minutes. Add the sour cream, remaining broth, sesame oil, and tamari sauce; cook, stirring, until well combined and heated through, about 3 minutes. Serve at once.

Mexican Rice

vegan

MAKES 6 TO 8 SERVINGS

To turn this popular side dish into a complete meal for four, add 1 (15-ounce) can rinsed and drained pinto or kidney beans along with the stewed tomatoes.

2 tablespoons extra-virgin olive oil

1 large onion (about 8 ounces), chopped

1 medium green bell pepper (about 6 ounces), chopped

1 cup long-grain white rice

2 large cloves garlic, finely chopped

1 (28-ounce) can stewed tomatoes, juices included

1¾ cups water

1 teaspoon gluten-free chili powder

1 teaspoon ground cumin

½ teaspoon salt

⅛ teaspoon cayenne pepper, or to taste (optional)

Freshly ground black pepper, to taste

In a large deep-sided nonstick skillet with a lid, heat the oil over medium heat. Add the onion and bell pepper and cook, stirring, until softened but not browned, about 3 minutes. Add the rice and garlic and cook, stirring constantly, for 2 minutes. Add the remaining ingredients and bring to a brisk simmer over medium-high heat, breaking up the tomatoes with a large wooden spoon.

Reduce the heat to between low and medium-low, cover, and simmer until the rice is tender and most of the liquid has been absorbed, about 20 to 25 minutes. If the rice is tender but the mixture seems too soupy, cook, uncovered, stirring often, until desired consistency is achieved. Serve warm.

PER SERVING

Calories 212 | Protein 4g | Total Fat 5g | Sat. Fat 1g | Cholesterol 0mg | Carbohydrate 39g | Dietary Fiber 3g | Sodium 525mg

Pineapple Fried Rice

vegan

MAKES 4 SERVINGS

This is a quick, easy, and delicious side dish to make from a leftover pint of Chinese takeout rice. Unsweetened canned pineapple can replace the fresh, if desired.

1 tablespoon peanut oil

4 scallions (white and green parts), thinly sliced

2 cloves garlic, finely chopped

1 teaspoon finely chopped fresh ginger

2½ teaspoons ground turmeric

2 cups cooked white rice (see Cook's Tip, page 145)

¾ cup chopped fresh pineapple

½ cup frozen mixed peas and carrots, cooked according to package directions, well drained

Salt and freshly ground black pepper, to taste

In a large nonstick skillet, heat the oil over medium heat. Add the scallions and cook, stirring, until softened, about 3 minutes. Add the garlic and ginger and cook, stirring, for 1 minute. Add the turmeric and cook, stirring constantly, for 30 seconds. Add the rice and cook, stirring, until thoroughly coated with the turmeric mixture. Add the pineapple, mixed vegetables, salt, and pepper; cook, stirring, until heated through. Serve warm.

PER SERVING

Calories 193 | Protein 4g | Total Fat 4g |
Sat. Fat 1g | Cholesterol 0mg | Carbohydrate 36g |
Dietary Fiber 2g | Sodium 17mg

Polenta-Mushroom Stuffing

vegan|low-carb

MAKES 5 TO 6 SERVINGS

Bland on its own, polenta is coarse-ground yellow cornmeal with a cooked texture similar to porridge. Paired with mushrooms, it makes a memorable stuffing to serve for the holidays or any time a special side dish is in order.

1¾ cups gluten-free low-sodium vegetable broth
½ cup polenta or coarse-ground yellow cornmeal
2 tablespoons canola oil

1 pound cultivated white mushrooms, sliced
1 medium onion (about 6 ounces), chopped
½ teaspoon poultry seasoning or dried thyme
  leaves
Salt and freshly ground black pepper, to taste

Preheat the oven to 375F (190C). Lightly oil an 8-inch-square baking pan and set aside.

In a medium stockpot, bring the broth to a boil over high heat. Slowly add the polenta, stirring constantly with a long-handled wooden spoon. Reduce the heat to low and cook, covered, stirring occasionally, until the polenta is tender, 12 to 15 minutes.

Meanwhile, heat the oil in a large nonstick skillet over medium heat. Add the mushrooms and onion and cook, stirring occasionally, until the onion is translucent and the mushrooms have released all their liquid, about 15 minutes. Remove from the heat and add the poultry seasoning, salt, and pepper. Add the polenta, breaking up with a wooden spoon and tossing well to combine. Transfer to prepared pan and bake, covered, 30 minutes. Serve warm.

PER SERVING

Calories 159 | Protein 8g | Total Fat 6g |
Sat. Fat 1g | Cholesterol 0mg | Carbohydrate 20g |
Dietary Fiber 5g | Sodium 186mg

Spice-Crusted Portobello Mushrooms with Lemon-Raita Sauce

egg-free|low-carb

MAKES 4 SERVINGS

This is a refreshing first course or side dish to serve with any Indian-style meal.

> 1 tablespoon coriander seed, crushed
>
> 1 tablespoon fennel seed, crushed
>
> 1 tablespoon cumin seed, crushed
>
> ½ teaspoon salt
>
> ¼ teaspoon ground cardamom
>
> Freshly ground black pepper, to taste
>
> 4 portobello mushroom caps (about 2 ounces each)
>
> 4 teaspoons extra-virgin olive oil
>
> Lemon-Raita Sauce (recipe opposite)

Combine the coriander, fennel, cumin, salt, cardamom, and pepper in a small bowl. Brush each mushroom cap on all sides with 1 teaspoon of the oil. Rub each mushroom cap on all sides with equal amounts of the spice mixture, letting any excess fall. Set aside.

Heat a nonstick grill pan over medium-high heat. Place the mushrooms, gill sides down, in pan and grill for 3 minutes. Turn over and grill until bottoms are nicely browned, 3 to 4 minutes, rotating each mushroom a half turn after 2 minutes. Transfer to serving plates and top with equal amounts of the sauce (about 5 tablespoons). Serve at once.

PER SERVING

Calories 111 | Protein 5g | Total Fat 7g | Sat. Fat 1g | Cholesterol 3mg | Carbohydrate 10g | Dietary Fiber 1g | Sodium 489mg

LEMON-RAITA SAUCE

egg-free|low-carb

MAKES ABOUT 1¼ CUPS

Use this sauce as a dip or relish for any variety of fresh vegetables.

> 4 ounces English (seedless) cucumber (about ½ medium), unpeeled, finely chopped
>
> 1 cup gluten-free plain low-fat yogurt
>
> 1 tablespoon finely chopped onion
>
> 1 large clove garlic, finely chopped
>
> ½ teaspoon lemon-pepper seasoning
>
> ¼ teaspoon salt, or to taste

Place the cucumber on several layers of paper towels and top with more layers of paper towels. Press and pat well to remove any excess water. Transfer the cucumber to a medium bowl and add the remaining ingredients; stir well to thoroughly combine. Serve at room temperature, or cover and refrigerate for up to 24 hours and serve chilled.

PER SERVING (¼ CUP)

Calories 34 | Protein 3g | Total Fat 1g | Sat. Fat 1g | Cholesterol 3mg | Carbohydrate 4g | Dietary Fiber 0g | Sodium 173mg

Mini Potato Soufflés

lacto-ovo

MAKES 4 SERVINGS

The recipe for these elegant soufflés easily doubles to serve eight for a larger dinner party. Feta or 4 additional tablespoons of cream cheese with chives can replace the goat cheese, if desired.

1 ½ **pounds boiling potatoes, peeled and cut into halves or quarters, depending on size**

6 **tablespoons (1 ½ ounces) gluten-free crumbled goat cheese, at room temperature**

2 **tablespoons gluten-free light cream cheese with chives, at room temperature**

⅓ **cup skim milk**

2 **tablespoons butter**

½ **teaspoon salt**

Freshly ground black pepper, to taste

1 **egg**

Sweet paprika

Preheat the oven to 350F (175C). Lightly grease 4 (4-ounce) ramekins and set aside.

Place the potatoes in a large saucepan or medium stockpot with salted water to cover. Bring to a boil over high heat; reduce the heat to medium-high and cook until tender, about 15 minutes, depending on size. Drain and return to the pan.

Meanwhile, in a small bowl, mash together the goat cheese and cream cheese until well combined. Set aside.

Add the milk, butter, salt, and pepper to the hot potatoes; mash until very smooth. Add the egg, mashing until thoroughly blended.

Fill each of the ramekins halfway with the potato mixture. Using the back of a tablespoon, make an indentation in the center, pushing the potato up along the sides of the ramekin. Fill the indentation with equal portions (about 1 ½ tablespoons) of the goat cheese mixture. Mound equal amounts of the remaining potato mixture on top of each ramekin. Sprinkle the tops lightly with paprika.

Place the ramekins on a baking sheet and bake in the center of the oven for 20 to 25 minutes, or until lightly browned. Serve hot.

PER SERVING

Calories 247 | Protein 9g | Total Fat 13g |
Sat. Fat 8g | Cholesterol 86mg | Carbohydrate 25g |
Dietary Fiber 2g | Sodium 434mg

Potato Kugel

dairy-free

MAKES 8 TO 12 SIDE-DISH OR 6 MAIN-DISH SERVINGS

This traditional Jewish potato casserole always makes a great side dish to feed a crowd.

5 tablespoons canola oil

1 large onion (about 8 ounces), chopped

3 eggs

2 tablespoons potato starch flour

1 teaspoon salt, or to taste

Freshly ground black pepper, to taste

3 pounds russet potatoes, peeled and finely
    grated, squeezed dry between paper towels

Gluten-free ketchup, sour cream, and/or
    applesauce, for topping (optional)

❧ Preheat the oven to 425F (220C). Lightly oil an 11 × 7-inch baking dish and set aside.

In a medium skillet (preferably nonstick), heat 2 tablespoons of the oil over medium heat. Add the onion and cook, stirring occasionally, until lightly browned and fragrant, 5 to 7 minutes. Remove from the heat and let cool for about 5 minutes.

In a large bowl, whisk together the eggs, remaining oil, potato starch flour, salt, and pepper until smooth. Add the onion and oil mixture and stir until well combined. Add the potatoes, tossing well to combine. Transfer to the prepared baking dish and bake for 45 minutes, or until the top is nicely browned. Serve hot with the optional toppings passed separately (if using).

PER SERVING

Calories 225 | Protein 6g | Total Fat 11g |
Sat. Fat 1g | Cholesterol 80mg | Carbohydrate 28g |
Dietary Fiber 3g | Sodium 300mg

Sautéed Herbed Potatoes

vegan

MAKES 6 SERVINGS

While you can make these delicious potatoes any time of the year using dried herbs, there's nothing quite like the flavor of fresh herbs, especially those picked straight from the garden. If you don't have garlic-flavored olive oil, use regular extra-virgin olive oil and use garlic salt in lieu of the coarse variety.

3 pounds russet (baking) potatoes, peeled, and
    cut into 1-inch cubes

3 tablespoons garlic-flavored olive oil

1½ tablespoons whole fresh tarragon, rosemary,
    thyme and/or oregano leaves, chopped, or a
    mixture of 1 teaspoon dried herbs

Salt, preferably the coarse variety, and freshly
    ground black pepper, to taste

❧ Place the potatoes in a large saucepan or medium stockpot with salted water to cover; bring to a boil over high heat. Reduce the heat slightly and cook for 5 minutes. Drain and let stand until dry, about 5 minutes.

In a large nonstick skillet, heat the oil over

medium-high heat until hot but not smoking. Add the potatoes and cook, stirring occasionally, until browned on all sides, about 8 minutes. Add the herbs, salt, and pepper, tossing well to combine. Reduce the heat to medium-low and cook, turning occasionally, until tender, about 5 minutes. Serve warm.

PER SERVING

Calories 195 | Protein 4g | Total Fat 7g |
Sat. Fat 1g | Cholesterol 0mg | Carbohydrate 31g |
Dietary Fiber 3g | Sodium 10mg

Spinach-Basil Rice Timbales

egg-free|low-carb

MAKES 6 SIDE-DISH OR 2 TO 3 MAIN-DISH SERVINGS

For carefree entertaining, these tasty timbales can be kept in the muffin pan in a warm oven for up to one hour before inverting onto a platter and serving. If using as a main course, serve on top of your favorite pasta sauce.

2 cups hot cooked white rice (see Cook's Tip, opposite)

½ cup finely chopped fresh spinach

3 ounces gluten-free light cream cheese with chives and onion, in 4 pieces, softened

2 tablespoons gluten-free freshly grated Parmesan cheese

2 tablespoons finely chopped fresh basil

½ teaspoon salt, or to taste

Freshly ground black pepper, to taste

Preheat the oven to 350F (175C). Lightly oil a 6-cup muffin pan.

In a large bowl, mix together all ingredients until thoroughly combined. Spoon the rice mixture into the muffin cups, packing it lightly. Bake for about 10 minutes, or until heated through. Invert onto a platter and serve at once.

PER SERVING

Calories 121 | Protein 4g | Total Fat 3g |
Sat. Fat 2g | Cholesterol 9mg | Carbohydrate 19g |
Dietary Fiber 0g | Sodium 116mg

Cook's Tip

One-third cup of uncooked regular long-grain white rice, basmati rice, or jasmine rice will yield about 1 cup cooked. One-quarter cup of uncooked brown rice will yield about 1 cup cooked. To make 2 cups cooked long-grain white rice, combine ⅔ cup white rice and 1⅓ cups salted water in a medium saucepan; bring to a boil over high heat. Reduce the heat to low, cover, and simmer until all the water has been absorbed, 17 to 20 minutes. Fluff with a fork and serve. To make 2 cups cooked brown rice, combine ½ cup brown rice and 1 cup plus 2 tablespoons salted water in a medium saucepan. Cook as directed for white rice, increasing cooking time to 35 to 40 minutes.

Easy Ratatouille

vegan|low-carb

MAKES 6 TO 8 SERVINGS

This popular French Provençal side dish easily becomes a hearty main course for four if served over rice or polenta. Parboiling the eggplant in liberally salted water eliminates the time-consuming need for salting and draining the eggplant before cooking.

4 large tomatoes (about 8 ounces each)

1 eggplant (about 1 pound), unpeeled, cut into 1-inch cubes

¼ cup extra-virgin olive oil

2 medium onions (about 6 ounces each), chopped

2 medium green bell peppers (about 6 ounces each), cut into thin strips

2 medium zucchini (about 6 ounces each), sliced lengthwise in half, then cut into 1-inch-thick pieces

2 large cloves garlic, finely chopped

1 tablespoon finely chopped fresh parsley

½ teaspoon dried oregano

2 tablespoons chopped fresh basil

Bring a large pot of water to a boil over high heat; add the tomatoes and boil for 20 seconds. Remove the tomatoes from the pot (do not turn off the heat) and transfer to a colander. Rinse under cold running water; peel away the skins. Coarsely chop and reserve all accumulated juices.

Meanwhile, liberally salt the boiling water (use about 2 tablespoons salt) and add the eggplant; return to a boil. Reduce the heat to medium and cook until the eggplant is just tender, about 5 minutes, stirring occasionally. Drain.

In a large deep-sided nonstick skillet with a lid, heat the oil over medium heat. Add the onions and cook, stirring, until softened, about 3 minutes. Add the bell peppers, zucchini, and garlic and cook, stirring, for 2 minutes. Add the eggplant, tomatoes and accumulated juices, parsley, and oregano; bring to a simmer over medium-high heat. Reduce the heat, cover, and simmer gently until the vegetables are tender, 30 to 45 minutes. Stir in the basil and serve warm or at room temperature.

PER SERVING

Calories 168 | Protein 4g | Total Fat 10g | Sat. Fat 1g | Cholesterol 0mg | Carbohydrate 20g | Dietary Fiber 6g | Sodium 19mg

Creamed Spinach Casserole

egg-free|low-carb

MAKES 4 SERVINGS

If you don't have cream cheese with chives, use the plain variety and add 1 to 2 tablespoons chopped fresh chives when you combine the ingredients.

1 (10-ounce) box frozen chopped spinach, cooked according to package directions, well drained

3 ounces gluten-free light cream cheese with chives, softened

2 tablespoons gluten-free light sour cream

2 tablespoons skim milk

½ teaspoon garlic salt

Freshly ground black pepper, to taste

Preheat the oven to 350F (175C). Lightly grease an 8-inch-square baking dish.

In a medium bowl, mix together all the ingredients until well combined. Transfer to the prepared baking dish and bake for 20 to 30 minutes, or until lightly browned. Serve warm.

PER SERVING

Calories 78 | Protein 5g | Total Fat 5g |
Sat. Fat 3g | Cholesterol 17mg | Carbohydrate 4g |
Dietary Fiber 2g | Sodium 399mg

Summer Squash Casserole

lacto-ovo|low-carb

MAKES 6 SERVINGS

This is a light and lovely side dish casserole, ideal for summer entertaining.

1 pound zucchini squash, preferably a mixture of green and yellow, sliced crosswise into ½-inch-thick rounds

¼ cup gluten-free light mayonnaise

1 egg, lightly beaten

1 cup gluten-free shredded reduced-fat cheddar cheese

1 teaspoon onion powder

Salt and freshly ground black pepper, to taste

Preheat the oven to 350F (175C). Lightly grease a 13 × 9-inch baking dish and set aside.

In a large stockpot filled with boiling salted water, boil the zucchini until just tender, about 2 minutes. Drain and rinse under cold running water to cool slightly. Drain well.

Meanwhile, in a large bowl, mix together the mayonnaise, egg, half of the cheese, the onion powder, salt, and pepper; add the zucchini, tossing gently to combine. Transfer to the prepared baking dish and sprinkle evenly with the remaining cheese. Bake for about 25 minutes, or until lightly browned and bubbly. Serve at once.

PER SERVING

Calories 80 | Protein 7g | Total Fat 4g |
Sat. Fat 1g | Cholesterol 43mg | Carbohydrate 5g |
Dietary Fiber 1g | Sodium 178mg

Sweet Potato Pancakes

dairy-free

MAKES 4 SERVINGS

Rich in vitamins A and C, these savory Hanukah treats are delicious anytime of the year, all on their own, or served with sour cream, ketchup, or applesauce.

> 2 medium sweet potatoes (about 6 ounces each), peeled and grated
> 2 tablespoons rice flour
> 1 teaspoon onion powder
> ½ teaspoon garlic powder
> ½ teaspoon salt
> Freshly ground black pepper, to taste
> 2 eggs, lightly beaten
> 2 tablespoons canola oil

In a large mixing bowl, toss together the sweet potatoes, rice flour, onion powder, garlic powder, salt, and pepper until well combined. Add the eggs and toss well to combine.

In a large nonstick skillet with a lid, heat half the oil over medium heat. Working with about half the batter, drop the sweet potato mixture by heaping tablespoonfuls into the skillet. Cook, covered, until lightly browned, about 5 minutes per side. Repeat with remaining oil and batter. Serve at once.

PER SERVING

Calories 208 | Protein 5g | Total Fat 10g |
Sat. Fat 1g | Cholesterol 106mg | Carbohydrate 26g |
Dietary Fiber 3g | Sodium 309mg

Broiled Parsley Tomatoes

egg-free|low-carb

MAKES 4 SERVINGS

For a distinctively Italian flavor, add ¼ teaspoon dried oregano to the parsley butter, if desired.

> 2 tablespoons butter, softened
> 2 teaspoons finely chopped fresh parsley
> ¼ teaspoon garlic salt
> Freshly ground black pepper, to taste
> 4 large plum tomatoes (about 3 ounces each), halved lengthwise

Preheat the oven to broil. Lightly oil a baking sheet.

In a small bowl, mash together the butter, parsley, garlic salt, and pepper. With a knife, make deep cuts in the cut surface of each tomato. Place the tomatoes, cut sides up, on prepared baking sheet. Spread evenly with the parsley butter (about 1 teaspoon per half).

Broil 4 to 6 inches from heating element until lightly browned, 3 to 4 minutes. Serve at once.

PER SERVING

Calories 67 | Protein 1g | Total Fat 6g |
Sat. Fat 4g | Cholesterol 15mg | Carbohydrate 4g |
Dietary Fiber 1g | Sodium 193mg

Stuffed Vine-Ripened Tomatoes with Basil, Pine Nuts, and Garlic

vegan|low-carb

MAKES 4 SERVINGS

These are the quintessential no-cook summer side dish. They can also be served as a first course over mixed greens.

- 1 cup finely chopped fresh basil (about 3 cups loosely packed leaves)
- ¼ cup pine nuts
- 1 tablespoon extra-virgin olive oil, plus additional to taste
- 2 to 3 large cloves garlic, finely chopped
- Freshly ground black pepper, to taste
- 4 medium tomatoes, about 6 ounces each

In a small bowl, mix together the basil, pine nuts, the 1 tablespoon oil, garlic, and pepper until combined. Set aside.

Cut a thin slice from the top of each tomato and discard. Gently squeeze out the seeds from each tomato. Using a small sharp knife or a melon baller, scoop out the pulp and reserve, discarding any white core. Chop the pulp and add to the basil mixture, tossing well to combine.

Spoon equal portions of the basil mixture into each tomato. Serve at room temperature, or cover and refrigerate for a minimum of 3 hours, or overnight, and serve chilled.

PER SERVING

Calories 147 | Protein 7g | Total Fat 10g |
Sat. Fat 1g | Cholesterol 0mg | Carbohydrate 14g |
Dietary Fiber 7g | Sodium 19mg

Stuffed Tomatoes with Herbed Tzatziki

lacto-ovo|low-carb

MAKES 4 FIRST-COURSE OR SIDE-DISH SERVINGS

This herbed variation of the classic Greek mixture of cucumber and yogurt makes a great dip for raw vegetables, as well.

- 4 (4- to 5-ounce) tomatoes
- ½ cup gluten-free plain low-fat yogurt
- 2 tablespoons gluten-free light mayonnaise
- 1 (6-ounce) cucumber, peeled, seeded, and finely chopped
- ½ teaspoon fresh lemon juice, plus additional, as necessary
- ¼ cup finely chopped red onion
- ½ tablespoon finely chopped fresh flat-leaf parsley
- ½ tablespoon finely chopped fresh mint
- ½ tablespoon finely chopped fresh dill
- ¼ teaspoon salt, or to taste
- Freshly ground black pepper, to taste
- 4 cups mixed greens
- Extra-virgin olive oil, as needed

Cut a thin slice from the top of each tomato. Scoop out the inside of each tomato with a melon baller or small spoon. Discard the tops and pulp. Lightly salt the insides and turn upside down on paper towels to drain for about 15 minutes.

In a medium bowl, mix together the yogurt and mayonnaise. Add the cucumber, the ½ teaspoon lemon juice, onion, parsley, mint, dill, salt, and pepper; stir well to thoroughly blend. Carefully fill the tomato shells with the cucumber-yogurt mixture. Cover and refrigerate for a minimum of 2 hours, or overnight.

To serve, divide the greens equally among 4 serving plates. Drizzle the greens with desired amounts of oil and lemon juice. Top with a stuffed tomato and serve at once, with additional oil and lemon juice passed separately, if desired.

PER SERVING

Calories 78 | Protein 4g | Total Fat 2g |
Sat. Fat 1g | Cholesterol 4mg | Carbohydrate 12g |
Dietary Fiber 3g | Sodium 84mg

Vegetables Primavera

vegan|low-carb

MAKES 6 SERVINGS

This is a simple yet special way to serve fresh vegetables. Use this recipe as a model to dress up your favorites.

3 tablespoons gluten-free low-sodium vegetable broth

2 tablespoons extra-virgin olive oil

1 tablespoon gluten-free Dijon mustard

2 teaspoons white wine vinegar

Salt and freshly ground black pepper, to taste

1½ cups sliced fresh zucchini, preferably a mixture of green and yellow

1 cup baby carrots

1 cup chopped red bell pepper

3 cups broccoli florets

2 tablespoons finely chopped fresh parsley or basil

In a small bowl, whisk together 1 tablespoon of the broth, 1 tablespoon of the olive oil, the mustard, vinegar, salt, and pepper. Set aside.

In a large nonstick skillet with a lid, heat the remaining oil over medium heat. Add the zucchini, carrots, and bell pepper; cook, stirring, until softened, about 5 minutes. Add the broccoli and remaining broth; cover and cook until the broccoli is crisp-tender, 3 minutes. Add the mustard mixture and cook, stirring, until just heated through. Serve warm, sprinkled with the parsley.

PER SERVING

Calories 78 | Protein 2g | Total Fat 5g |
Sat. Fat 1g | Cholesterol 0mg | Carbohydrate 8g |
Dietary Fiber 3g | Sodium 69mg

Braised Fall Vegetables

vegan|low-carb

MAKES 8 SERVINGS

This is an ideal low-carb choice to serve a crowd around the holidays.

- **2 tablespoons canola oil**
- **1/2 medium head cabbage (about 1 pound), cut into 8 wedges**
- **4 medium carrots (about 1 pound), quartered lengthwise, then halved crosswise, or 1 (16-ounce) bag baby carrots, left whole**
- **2 cups cauliflower florets**
- **1 large red onion (about 8 ounces), cut into 8 wedges**
- **1 cup gluten-free low-sodium vegetable broth, reduced over high heat to 1/4 cup**
- **2 tablespoons cider vinegar**
- **1 teaspoon sugar**
- **1 teaspoon dried thyme**
- **1/2 teaspoon salt**
- **1/4 teaspoon freshly ground black pepper**

❦In a large nonstick skillet with a lid, heat the oil over medium heat. Add the cabbage and carrots; cook, covered, for 5 minutes, stirring once or twice with a wooden spoon. Gently stir in the cauliflower, onion, broth, vinegar, sugar, thyme, salt, and pepper; bring to a boil over medium-high heat. Reduce the heat, cover, and simmer gently, stirring a few times, until the vegetables are crisp-tender, 7 to 10 minutes. Serve warm.

PER SERVING

Calories 98 | Protein 4g | Total Fat 4g |
Sat. Fat 0g | Cholesterol 0mg | Carbohydrate 14g |
Dietary Fiber 4g | Sodium 371mg

Wild Rice with Mushrooms

vegan|low-carb

MAKES 6 SERVINGS

Lower in carbs than the standard variety, wild rice is expensive but well worth the splurge every now and again for special occasions and dinner parties. Paired with succulent mushrooms, it's simply delicious!

- **3 cups water, plus additional as necessary**
- **3/4 cup wild rice, rinsed well with cold water, drained**
- **1/2 teaspoon salt, plus additional to taste**
- **2 tablespoons extra-virgin olive oil**
- **2 cloves garlic, finely chopped**
- **1/2 teaspoon dried thyme leaves**
- **16 ounces cultivated white mushrooms, sliced**
- **1/2 teaspoon onion powder**
- **2 tablespoons chopped pimiento or chopped roasted red bell peppers (optional)**
- **Freshly ground black pepper, to taste**

❦In a medium saucepan, bring the water, rice, and salt to a boil over high heat. Reduce the heat to medium and simmer briskly, uncovered, until rice is just tender, 40 to 45 minutes, stirring a few times and adding water after about 30 minutes, if necessary, to prevent the rice from sticking to the bottom of the pan. Drain in a sieve and return to the pan. Cover and let stand until the rice is fairly dry, 5 minutes, stirring once or twice. Set aside until needed.

Meanwhile, in a large nonstick skillet, heat the oil over medium heat. Add the garlic and thyme and cook, stirring, for 30 seconds. Add the mushrooms and cook, stirring often, until the mushrooms have released most of their liquid, about 5 minutes. Add the onion powder and stir well until dissolved. Add the reserved rice and pimiento (if using); cook, stirring, until the rice has absorbed most of the liquid, about 3 minutes. Season with pepper and additional salt, if necessary. Serve at once.

PER SERVING

Calories 133 | Protein 5g | Total Fat 5g |
Sat. Fat 1g | Cholesterol 0mg | Carbohydrate 19 |
Dietary Fiber 2g | Sodium 6mg

Broiled Zucchini with Rosemary and Chive Butter

egg-free|low-carb

MAKES 6 SERVINGS

Any herb—basil, oregano, parsley, mint, or thyme—can replace the rosemary, if desired.

3 tablespoons butter, softened

2 tablespoons finely chopped chives or the green parts of scallions

1 tablespoon finely chopped fresh rosemary, or 1 teaspoon dried rosemary

1 teaspoon fresh lemon juice

½ teaspoon lemon-pepper seasoning

½ teaspoon coarse salt

¼ teaspoon freshly ground black pepper

4 medium zucchini (about 6 ounces each), trimmed, cut crosswise into ½-inch-thick rounds

Preheat the oven to broil. Lightly grease a large baking sheet.

In a small bowl, mash together all ingredients except the zucchini until well combined; set aside.

Place the zucchini on the prepared baking sheet and broil 4 to 6 inches from the heating element until lightly browned, about 3 minutes per side. Remove from the oven and, while still hot, spread evenly with the rosemary-chive butter. Serve at once.

PER SERVING

Calories 68 | Protein 2g | Total Fat 6g |
Sat. Fat 4g | Cholesterol 15mg | Carbohydrate 4g |
Dietary Fiber 2g | Sodium 246mg

South-of-the-Border Zucchini Pancakes

dairy-free|low-carb

MAKES 6 SERVINGS

These tasty low-carb pancakes are a wonderful accompaniment to any Mexican-style meal.

4 medium zucchini (about 6 ounces each), grated
or finely chopped

1 teaspoon salt

2 eggs, lightly beaten

½ cup cornmeal

½ teaspoon dried oregano

¼ teaspoon ground cumin

Freshly ground black pepper

2 tablespoons extra-virgin olive oil

Salsa, gluten-free shredded cheddar cheese,
and/or sour cream, for topping (optional)

❧In a large bowl, combine the zucchini and half of the salt. Transfer to a colander and let stand for 15 minutes. Press with the back of a large spoon to squeeze out the moisture. Transfer to several layers of paper towels and squeeze to rid of excess moisture. Return to the bowl and add the eggs, cornmeal, remaining salt, oregano, cumin, and pepper, tossing until thoroughly combined.

In a large nonstick skillet, heat half of the oil over medium-high heat. Working with about half the batter, drop the zucchini mixture by the heaping tablespoons into the skillet and cook until golden, about 3 minutes per side. Repeat

with remaining oil and batter. Serve warm, with the toppings (if using).

PER SERVING

Calories 123 | Protein 4g | Total Fat 7g |
Sat. Fat 1g | Cholesterol 71mg | Carbohydrate 13g |
Dietary Fiber 2g | Sodium 380mg

Zucchini-Cheese Crisps

egg-free|low-carb

MAKES 4 TO 6 SERVINGS

This tasty side dish is a lower-carb alternative to French fries.

⅓ cup gluten-free cornflake crumbs (see second
Cook's Tip, page 181)

2 tablespoons gluten-free grated Parmesan cheese

½ teaspoon garlic salt

¼ teaspoon freshly ground black pepper

2 medium zucchini (about 8 ounces each),
unpeeled, cut lengthwise in half, then cut
lengthwise into thin strips (about the width of
French fries)

¼ cup canola oil

❧Preheat the oven to 375F (190C).

Combine the crumbs, cheese, garlic salt, and pepper in a large self-sealing plastic bag. Place the zucchini on an ungreased baking sheet and toss with the oil. Transfer to the plastic bag and shake to coat evenly with the crumb mixture. Return the zucchini to the baking sheet. Spread in a single layer, redistributing the cornflake crumb mixture with your fingertips as necessary. Bake in the upper third of the oven for 10 to 15 minutes, or until lightly golden. Serve at once.

PER SERVING

Calories 178 | Protein 3g | Total Fat 15g | Sat. Fat 2g | Cholesterol 2mg | Carbohydrate 10g | Dietary Fiber 2g | Sodium 396mg

Brunch
and Egg Dishes

Eggs and egg dishes are not only nutritious and economical, but usually quick and easy to prepare. Their versatility is legion: they can be scrambled, fried, poached, hard-cooked, baked, or cooked in omelets, frittatas, tortillas, stratas, and soufflés. Though brunch favorites, they can be served at any meal in the day. For vegetarians on a gluten-free diet, they are an excellent means of adding extra protein (6 grams per egg), particularly when partnered with cheese. While eggs contain relatively high amounts of cholesterol (about 213 milligrams per egg), they are relatively low in saturated fat (2 grams per egg). Furthermore, egg yolks are an abundant dietary source of lutein, essential for good eye health. Other traditional brunch dishes—pancakes, waffles, French toast, crepes, and muffins—require a bit of tweaking to become gluten-free, but your efforts will be well rewarded after one bite of any of the following recipes.

Asparagus and Provolone Cheese Strata

lacto-ovo

MAKES 6 SERVINGS

This is an easy yet elegant brunch casserole that can be prepared the night before for stress-free entertaining. To ensure that the filling doesn't become overly runny, pat the cooked asparagus dry with paper towels before assembling.

½ pound fresh medium-thick asparagus, trimmed

4 eggs

1½ cups skim milk

1 cup half-and-half

1 tablespoon chopped fresh chives

1 teaspoon chopped fresh thyme, or ¼ teaspoon dried

1 teaspoon onion powder

½ teaspoon salt

¼ teaspoon freshly ground black pepper

8 ounces gluten-free sandwich bread (6 to 8 slices), crusts removed, each slice cut into quarters

6 ounces sliced provolone cheese, preferably the smoked variety

½ cup gluten-free freshly grated Parmesan cheese

Lightly grease an 11×7-inch baking dish. In a large stockpot filled with boiling salted water, boil the asparagus until tender, about 5 minutes, depending on thickness. Drain and rinse under cold running water. Drain well. Trim off the tips and cut the stalks lengthwise in half. Cut into 1-inch lengths. Pat dry between paper towels.

In a large bowl, whisk together the eggs, milk, half-and-half, chives, thyme, onion powder, salt, and pepper. Cover the bottom of the prepared dish with half of the bread. Cover the bread with half of the provolone, all the asparagus, remaining bread, and ending with the remaining provolone cheese. Pour the egg mixture over all. Cover and refrigerate for a minimum of 3 hours, or overnight.

Preheat the oven to 325F (165C).

Place the strata in the center of the oven and bake, uncovered, for 30 minutes, or until the top is beginning to brown and the center is almost set. Sprinkle evenly with the Parmesan cheese and transfer to the lower rack. Bake for 10 to 15 minutes, or until a knife inserted in the center comes out clean. Remove from the oven and let stand for a minimum of 10 minutes before cutting into wedges and serving.

PER SERVING

Calories 358 | Protein 21g | Total Fat 19g | Sat. Fat 10g | Cholesterol 182mg | Carbohydrate 26g | Dietary Fiber 1g | Sodium 833mg

Shirred Eggs with Asparagus and Browned Butter

lacto-ovo|low-carb

MAKES 6 SERVINGS

Fragrant browned butter with a squeeze of fresh lemon juice is a quick and easy stand-in for Hollandaise sauce. While shirring, or baking, may not be the fastest method of preparing eggs, it is by far the easiest. During the fifteen minutes or so that your eggs are baking, you have time to prepare the other components of this virtually instant yet elegant brunch.

12 eggs

Salt, preferably the coarse variety, and freshly ground black pepper, to taste

2 pounds medium asparagus

6 tablespoons unsalted butter

1½ tablespoons fresh lemon juice (the juice from half a medium lemon)

Gluten-free freshly grated Parmesan cheese (optional)

Preheat the oven to 350F (175C). Lightly oil a 12-cup muffin pan. Carefully break an egg into each muffin cup. Season the eggs with salt and pepper. Bake in the center of oven to desired doneness, about 15 minutes for medium-set yolks.

Meanwhile, bring a large pot of salted water to a boil over high heat. Prepare an ice-water bath and set aside. Add the asparagus to the water and cook until crisp-tender, 4 to 5 minutes, depending on thickness. Drain and immediately transfer to the ice-water bath. Let stand for 5 minutes to cool. Drain well.

In a large skillet, heat the butter over medium heat, swirling the skillet occasionally until the butter turns a deep brown. Immediately add the asparagus and toss until thoroughly coated and heated through. Remove from the heat and add the lemon juice, salt, and pepper, tossing well to combine.

To serve, loosen the eggs in the muffin cups with the tip of a sharp knife. Divide asparagus and browned butter sauce evenly among 6 heated serving plates. Top each serving with 2 eggs. Sprinkle the eggs with the cheese (if using). Serve at once.

PER SERVING

Calories 269 | Protein 15g | Total Fat 22g | Sat. Fat 10g | Cholesterol 456mg | Carbohydrate 5g | Dietary Fiber 2g | Sodium 243mg

Cook's Tip

If you want to make half of the recipe and don't have a 6-cup muffin pan, fill the empty cups halfway with water to promote even cooking. Individual 6-ounce custard molds may also be used.

Brie Quiche

lacto-ovo|low-carb

MAKES 6 SERVINGS

I like to serve this scrumptious quiche with a garnish of grapes.

1 tablespoon canola oil

1 bunch scallions (white and green parts), thinly sliced

8 ounces brie cheese, cut into small cubes (with rind)

1 prebaked Savory Pastry Crust (see Cook's Tip, page 175, variation with egg wash)

3 eggs

½ cup skim milk

½ cup gluten-free light sour cream

Salt and freshly ground black pepper, to taste

✀ Preheat the oven to 350F (175C).

In a medium nonstick skillet, heat the oil over medium heat. Add the scallions and cook, stirring, until softened, 3 to 5 minutes. Remove from the heat and let cool slightly.

Arrange the brie on the bottom of the baked pastry. In a medium bowl, whisk together the eggs, milk, sour cream, salt, and pepper until thoroughly blended. Stir in the scallions. Pour the egg mixture over the brie. Bake in the center of the oven for 35 to 40 minutes, or until set and lightly browned. Let stand for 10 minutes before cutting into wedges and serving. Serve at once.

PER SERVING

Calories 369 | Protein 14g | Total Fat 26g | Sat. Fat 14g | Cholesterol 173mg | Carbohydrate 20g | Dietary Fiber 1g | Sodium 480mg

Baked French Toast

lacto-ovo

MAKES 4 SERVINGS

If at all possible, after soaking both sides of the bread in the egg mixture, cover the baking dish and refrigerate for a few hours or overnight for maximum absorption, turning a few times.

3 eggs

1 cup skim milk

2 tablespoons sugar

1 teaspoon gluten-free pure vanilla extract

½ teaspoon ground cinnamon

¼ teaspoon salt

8 slices gluten-free sandwich bread

2 tablespoons butter

Pure maple syrup or confectioners' sugar, to serve

✀ Preheat the oven to 450F (230C).

In a large bowl, whisk together the eggs, milk, sugar, vanilla, cinnamon, and salt. Transfer to a 13×9-inch baking dish and place the bread in the mixture, overlapping as necessary.

Let stand for 10 minutes, then turn the bread over and let stand for an additional 10 minutes.

Smear the butter on a standard-size baking sheet with sides. Place the baking sheet in the oven for 1 minute, or until hot. Working quickly, arrange the bread on the hot baking sheet. Bake in the upper third of the oven for 5 minutes, or until the tops are golden and puffy. Turn over and bake for 3 to 4 minutes, or until the tops are golden and puffy. Serve at once, with maple syrup passed separately.

PER SERVING

Calories 307 | Protein 12g | Total Fat 12g | Sat. Fat 5g | Cholesterol 176mg | Carbohydrate 38g | Dietary Fiber 1g | Sodium 575mg

Buckwheat Pancakes

lacto-ovo

MAKES 4 SERVINGS (8 TO 10 PANCAKES)

These wholesome pancakes are delicious as well as nutritious. Serve with pure maple syrup, if possible.

1 cup buckwheat flour

2 tablespoons light brown sugar

1 teaspoon gluten-free baking powder

½ teaspoon baking soda

½ teaspoon salt

¼ teaspoon ground cinnamon

⅛ teaspoon ground nutmeg

1 egg, lightly beaten

1 cup nonfat buttermilk

1 tablespoon canola oil

In a large bowl, mix together the dry ingredients until well combined. In a small bowl, whisk together the liquid ingredients until well blended; stir into the dry mixture just until moistened.

Heat a large nonstick skillet over medium heat. Working in batches, pour the batter by ¼ cupfuls onto the skillet and cook until bubbles form on top of the pancakes, 2 to 3 minutes; turn and cook until the second side is light golden brown, about 2 minutes. Serve at once.

PER SERVING (¼ RECIPE)

Calories 176 | Protein 5g | Total Fat 6g | Sat. Fat 1g | Cholesterol 53mg | Carbohydrate 28g | Dietary Fiber 4g | Sodium 536mg

Buttermilk Pancakes

lacto-ovo

MAKES 4 SERVINGS (12 TO 14 SMALL PANCAKES)

Though maple syrup is the traditional accompaniment, try spreading these buttermilk pancakes with strawberry cream cheese, rolling them up, and dusting them with confectioners' sugar for your next brunch sensation.

¾ cup nonfat buttermilk

1 egg

1 tablespoon canola oil

½ cup tapioca flour

¼ cup cornmeal

1 teaspoon gluten-free baking powder

Pinch salt

Pure maple syrup, to serve

❦ In a medium bowl, whisk together the buttermilk, egg, and oil until smooth and well blended. In a small bowl, sift together the tapioca flour, cornmeal, baking powder, and salt; stir into the buttermilk mixture just until the ingredients are moistened (mixture will be slightly lumpy).

Heat a large nonstick skillet over medium heat. Working in batches, drop the batter by heaping tablespoons into the skillet and cook until light golden brown, 2 to 3 minutes per side. Serve at once, with maple syrup.

PER SERVING

Calories 177 | Protein 3g | Total Fat 5g | Sat. Fat 1g | Cholesterol 53mg | Carbohydrate 31g | Dietary Fiber 2g | Sodium 141mg

Buttermilk Waffles

lacto-ovo

MAKES ABOUT 5 BELGIAN-STYLE WAFFLES

These are excellent topped with strawberries and whipped cream, or ice cream.

1 cup white rice flour

½ cup potato starch flour

¼ cup tapioca flour

2 teaspoons gluten-free baking powder

1 tablespoon sugar

½ teaspoon salt

1½ cups nonfat buttermilk

¼ cup canola oil

2 eggs, beaten

❦ Heat a nonstick waffle maker according to manufacturer's instructions.

In a large bowl, mix together the dry ingredients until thoroughly combined. Add the liquid ingredients, whisking until smooth and well blended. Pour into waffle maker and cook in batches according to manufacturer's instructions (usually 4 to 5 minutes per waffle). Serve at once.

Granola

vegan

MAKES 10 SERVINGS

This is delicious served with plain yogurt and sliced bananas, or by itself as a healthy snack.

- ¾ cup hazelnuts
- ½ cup slivered almonds
- ½ cup walnut pieces
- ⅓ cup sunflower seeds
- 2 cups rice bran
- ⅓ cup packed light brown sugar
- ⅓ cup pumpkin seeds
- ½ cup gluten-free raisins
- ⅓ cup sweetened shredded coconut

Preheat the oven to 350F (175C). Spread the hazelnuts on an ungreased light-colored baking sheet and toast in the center of the oven until lightly golden and fragrant, 7 to 10 minutes, stirring once. Immediately remove from the baking sheet and set aside to cool slightly. Rub in a damp kitchen towel to remove most of their skins.

Place the almonds, walnuts, and sunflower seeds on the cooled baking sheet; bake for 3 to 4 minutes, or until slightly toasted, stirring once. Immediately remove from the baking sheet and set aside to cool slightly.

Transfer the nuts and sunflower seeds to a large bowl and add the remaining ingredients; toss well to thoroughly combine. Store at room temperature in an airtight container for up to 1 week.

Goat Cheese and Apple Omelet

lacto-ovo|low-carb

MAKES 2 SERVINGS

Don't pass on this unusual omelet—the combination of goat cheese and apples is a delightful taste sensation.

- ⅓ cup finely chopped unpeeled Granny Smith apple (about 2 ounces)
- 2 ounces gluten-free crumbled goat cheese
- 3 eggs
- 1 teaspoon water
- Salt and freshly ground black pepper, to taste
- 1 tablespoon butter

In a small bowl, combine the apple and goat cheese; set aside. In another small bowl, whisk together the eggs, water, salt, and pepper until just blended; set aside.

Heat an omelet pan or 8-inch nonstick skillet over medium-high heat until a drop of water sizzles on its surface. Add the butter and swirl to coat pan. Quickly add egg mixture. Swirl pan with one hand while stirring eggs in a circular motion with a fork (tines of fork should be parallel to but not touching bottom of pan). When the eggs begin to set, quickly push cooked egg toward center of pan, allowing uncooked egg to run underneath. Arrange the apple-cheese mixture over one half of the surface. Fold plain half over filled half. Remove from the heat, cover, and let stand for 1 minute. Slide onto a serving plate, divide in half, and serve at once.

PER SERVING

Calories 303 | Protein 18g | Total Fat 23g | Sat. Fat 13g | Cholesterol 364mg | Carbohydrate 5g | Dietary Fiber 1g | Sodium 251mg

Piperade
dairy-free|low-carb

MAKES 4 SERVINGS

From the Spanish Basque country, this classic open-faced omelet is always popular. For a milder rendition, omit the jalapeño chili, if desired.

2 tablespoons extra-virgin olive oil

1 large onion (about 8 ounces), cut lengthwise in half, then thinly sliced crosswise

1 large green bell pepper (about 8 ounces), chopped

½ small jalapeño chili, seeded and finely chopped

2 medium tomatoes (about 6 ounces each), chopped

1 large clove garlic, finely chopped

1 teaspoon dried oregano

½ teaspoon dried thyme

Salt and freshly ground black pepper, to taste

8 eggs, lightly beaten

In a large nonstick skillet with a lid, heat the oil over medium heat. Add the onion, bell pepper, and chili and cook, stirring, until softened, 3 to 5 minutes. Add the tomatoes, garlic, oregano, thyme, salt, and black pepper and bring to a simmer over medium-high heat. Reduce the heat and simmer gently, uncovered, until the mixture is reduced and thickened, about 20 minutes, stirring occasionally.

Increase the heat to medium-high and pour in the eggs. Cook, stirring quickly and constantly, until the mixture is creamy and beginning to set, 2 to 3 minutes. Cover and return to low heat; cook until set but still creamy, about 5 minutes, stirring once or twice. Serve immediately.

PER SERVING

Calories 264 | Protein 15g | Total Fat 17g | Sat. Fat 4g | Cholesterol 425mg | Carbohydrate 14g | Dietary Fiber 3g | Sodium 136mg

Crustless Pizza Quiche

lacto-ovo|low-carb

MAKES 6 SERVINGS

Feel free to add any of your favorite toppings to this scrumptious pizza-style quiche.

4 ounces gluten-free Neufchâtel cream cheese, softened

4 eggs

¼ cup skim milk

½ teaspoon dried oregano, plus additional, as desired

¼ teaspoon garlic powder

Salt and freshly ground black pepper, to taste

2 cups gluten-free shredded part-skim mozzarella cheese

1 cup gluten-free freshly grated Parmesan cheese

½ cup gluten-free prepared pizza sauce

¼ cup chopped onion (optional)

¼ cup chopped green bell pepper (optional)

Preheat the oven to 350F (175C). Lightly grease an 8½- or 9-inch pie plate.

In a medium bowl, with an electric mixer on medium speed, beat together the cream cheese and eggs until smooth. On low speed, beat in the milk, oregano, garlic powder, salt, and pepper. Spread 1 cup of the mozzarella cheese in the bottom of the prepared pie plate, then top evenly with the Parmesan cheese. Slowly pour the egg mixture over the cheeses. Bake in the center of the oven for about 40 minutes, or until puffed and browned, and a knife inserted in the center comes out clean. Remove from the oven (do not turn off heat).

Spread the pizza sauce evenly over the top of the set egg mixture, then sprinkle evenly with the remaining mozzarella cheese, onion, and/ or bell pepper (if using), and additional oregano, if desired. Return to the oven and bake for 8 to 10 minutes, or until the cheese is melted and just beginning to brown. Let stand for 10 minutes before cutting into wedges and serving warm.

PER SERVING

Calories 284 | Protein 23g | Total Fat 19g | Sat. Fat 11g | Cholesterol 187mg | Carbohydrate 6g | Dietary Fiber 0g | Sodium 702mg

Potato Cheese Puff
with Poached Eggs

lacto-ovo

MAKES 6 SERVINGS

This is an excellent company brunch dish, as the potatoes can be cooked and assembled in the casserole twenty-four hours ahead of baking.

3 pounds russet potatoes, peeled, cut into chunks

¼ cup skim milk

1 cup gluten-free light sour cream or gluten-free plain low-fat yogurt

1 cup gluten-free low-fat cottage cheese

1 cup gluten-free shredded reduced-fat cheddar cheese

2 tablespoons finely chopped fresh chives or the green parts of scallions

Salt and freshly ground black pepper, to taste

2 tablespoons butter, melted

6 eggs

Preheat the oven to 350F (175C). Lightly grease a 13×9-inch baking dish and set aside.

In a medium stockpot, place the potatoes in enough salted water to cover by a few inches. Bring to a boil over high heat. Reduce the heat to medium-high, and cook until the potatoes are very tender, about 25 minutes. Drain well in a colander.

Transfer the potatoes to a large bowl (or return to stockpot) and add the milk; mash until smooth. Add the sour cream, cottage cheese, cheddar cheese, chives, salt, and pepper; mix well to thoroughly combine. Spread evenly in the prepared baking dish and brush with the melted butter. Make 6 indentations (large enough to comfortably hold a cracked egg) in the top. (At this point, the dish can be cooled to room temperature and refrigerated, covered, for up to 24 hours before continuing with the recipe.)

Bake for 35 to 40 minutes, or until slightly puffed and just beginning to brown. Remove from the oven. Working with 1 egg at a time, crack each egg into a small container or cup and carefully slide into each indentation. Sprinkle each egg lightly with salt and pepper. Return to the oven and bake for 15 to 20 minutes, or until the eggs are medium-set. Let stand for 5 minutes before cutting into wedges and serving.

PER SERVING

Calories 320 | Protein 20g | Total Fat 12g | Sat. Fat 5g | Cholesterol 232mg | Carbohydrate 34g | Dietary Fiber 3g | Sodium 395mg

Oven-Baked Breakfast Potatoes

vegan

MAKES 4 TO 6 SERVINGS

Though optional, cumin seed lends this easy potato dish a Southwestern flavor that complements many of the book's Mexican-style entrées.

2 tablespoons canola oil

1 cup chopped onion

½ cup chopped green bell pepper

2 (15-ounce) cans sliced potatoes, rinsed and well drained

1 teaspoon cumin seed (optional)

Salt and freshly ground black pepper, to taste

Preheat the oven to 350F (175C). Lightly oil a baking sheet with sides and set aside.

In a large skillet, heat the oil over medium heat. Add the onion and bell pepper and cook, stirring occasionally, until softened and beginning to brown, about 5 minutes. Add the potatoes, cumin seed (if using), salt, and pepper; toss carefully until well combined. Transfer the potato mixture to the prepared baking sheet and spread out in a single layer. Bake for 15 minutes. Using a spatula, turn over and bake for 15 to 20 minutes, or until the potatoes are lightly browned. Serve warm.

PER SERVING

Calories 164 | Protein 4g | Total Fat 7g |
Sat. Fat 1g | Cholesterol 0mg | Carbohydrate 23g |
Dietary Fiber 4g | Sodium 641mg

Mashed Potato–Crusted Broccoli and Cheese Quiche

lacto-ovo

MAKES 4 SERVINGS

Use the mashed potato crust as a base for any of your gluten-free quiche fillings. This is a good choice to serve company for brunch as the crust can be assembled a day ahead of baking.

1¼ pounds boiling potatoes, peeled, halved, or quartered, depending on size

3 eggs

¾ cup plus 2 to 3 tablespoons skim, 2 percent, and/or whole milk

Salt and freshly ground black pepper, to taste

1 tablespoon butter or canola oil

1 teaspoon onion powder

1 cup gluten-free shredded reduced-fat cheddar cheese

¾ cup frozen broccoli florets or pieces, slightly undercooked according to package directions, drained

Preheat the oven to 350F (175C). Lightly oil a 9-inch pie plate and set aside.

Place the potatoes in a large saucepan or medium stockpot with salted water to cover; bring to a boil over high heat. Reduce the heat slightly and cook until the potatoes are tender, about 20 minutes, depending on size. Drain well.

Meanwhile, whisk together the eggs and ¾

cup milk until well blended. Season with salt and pepper and set aside.

Transfer the potatoes to a bowl and mash briefly with a potato masher or a fork. Add the 2 tablespoons milk, butter, and onion powder and mash until the mixture is not quite smooth, adding additional milk for a softer consistency, if desired. Season with salt and pepper. Transfer to the prepared pie plate and mold into a crust with your fingers, building up the sides. (At this point, the crust can be covered and refrigerated for up to 24 hours before continuing with the recipe.) Bake for 15 minutes in the center of the oven.

Remove the crust from the oven. Sprinkle the shredded cheese along the bottom of the crust, then top with the broccoli. Pour the egg mixture over all. Bake for about 45 minutes, or until set. Let stand for 10 minutes before cutting into wedges and serving warm.

PER SERVING

Calories 247 | Protein 17g | Total Fat 9g | Sat. Fat 4g | Cholesterol 174mg | Carbohydrate 26g | Dietary Fiber 3g | Sodium 289mg

Rice Flour Crepes with Strawberry Preserves

lacto-ovo

MAKES 8 CREPES

Fill these crepes with any of your favorite fruit preserves, as well as Nutella chocolate-hazelnut spread or lemon curd. While you can use all regular white rice flour in the recipe, the resulting crepes will not be as tender.

½ **cup white rice flour**

½ **cup sweet rice flour (see Cook's Tip, opposite)**

1 **cup skim milk**

2 **eggs**

1 **tablespoon canola oil**

2 **teaspoons sugar**

¼ **teaspoon gluten-free vanilla extract**

¼ **teaspoon salt**

8 **teaspoons butter or gluten-free margarine**

¾ **to 1 cup strawberry preserves**

Confectioners' sugar

Whipped cream (optional)

In a medium mixing bowl, beat together the flours, milk, eggs, oil, sugar, vanilla, and salt until smooth. Heat a large nonstick skillet over medium heat. Add 1 teaspoon of the butter, swirling to evenly coat. Using a ¼-cup measure, pour the batter into the skillet, turning to thinly and evenly distribute the batter into a circle about 8 inches in diameter. Cook until very lightly browned, about 30 seconds per side.

Transfer to a plate and cover with foil to keep warm while preparing the remaining crepes.

To serve, spread each crepe with 1½ to 2 tablespoons of the preserves; roll up, and sprinkle with confectioners' sugar. Serve at once, garnished with whipped cream (if using).

PER SERVING

Calories 235 | Protein 4g | Total Fat 8g | Sat. Fat 4g | Cholesterol 67mg | Carbohydrate 38g | Dietary Fiber 1g | Sodium 148mg

VARIATIONS: *To make* Savory Crepes with Herbed Cream Cheese: *Omit the sugar, vanilla extract, and optional whipped cream from the recipe. Replace the strawberry preserves with a gluten-free herbed cream cheese spread, cream cheese with chives, or cream cheese with garden vegetables, and the confectioners' sugar with freshly shredded Parmesan cheese (if desired). Proceed as otherwise directed.*

To make Savory Crepes with Asparagus: *Prepare the crepes as directed for Savory Crepes with Herbed Cream Cheese, filling with lightly steamed or blanched asparagus spears before rolling up.*

Cook's Tip

Sweet rice flour, derived from glutinous, or sticky, rice, helps tenderize the somewhat gritty texture of regular white rice flour in certain recipes. It is available in Asian markets and specialty stores, such as Trader Joe's.

Ricotta Cheese Pancakes

lacto-ovo|low-carb

MAKES 5 TO 6 SERVINGS (ABOUT 16 SMALL PANCAKES)

These high-protein, calcium-rich pancakes are delicious topped with strawberry preserves or orange marmalade.

4 eggs, lightly beaten
2 cups gluten-free reduced-fat ricotta cheese
½ cup rice flour
¼ cup potato starch flour
½ teaspoon gluten-free baking powder
2 tablespoons canola oil

Place the eggs, cheese, rice flour, potato starch flour, baking powder, and canola oil in a large mixing bowl. Using an electric mixer, beat until the batter is smooth and well blended.

Heat a large nonstick skillet over medium heat. Pour approximately ¼ cup of the batter into the skillet and cook until light golden brown, 2 to 3 minutes per side. Serve at once.

PER SERVING (PER PANCAKE)

Calories 94 | Protein 7g | Total Fat 4g | Sat. Fat 1g | Cholesterol 66mg | Carbohydrate 8g | Dietary Fiber 0g | Sodium 172mg

Crustless Roasted Red Pepper and Cheddar Quiche

lacto-ovo|low-carb

MAKES 4 TO 6 SERVINGS

You will never miss the crust in this savory low-carb quiche. Vegan cheese substitutes are not recommended here, as they don't melt well. Also, some brands may contain damaging glutens.

1 (12-ounce) jar roasted red bell peppers, drained well and patted dry with paper towels, cut into bite-size pieces

2 cups gluten-free shredded reduced-fat cheddar cheese

4 eggs, lightly beaten

½ cup skim milk

2 tablespoons chopped fresh parsley

Salt and freshly ground black pepper, to taste

8 grape or cherry tomatoes, halved

Preheat the oven to 375F (190C). Lightly oil an 8½- or 9-inch pie plate.

Arrange the peppers in the bottom of the prepared pie plate. Top with all but 2 tablespoons of the shredded cheese.

In a medium bowl, whisk together the eggs, milk, parsley, salt, and black pepper. Slowly pour over the bell peppers and cheese. Top evenly with the tomatoes.

Bake in the center of the oven for 30 minutes, or until lightly browned and a knife inserted in the center comes out clean, sprinkling with the remaining cheese the last few minutes of cooking. Let cool for 10 minutes before cutting into wedges and serving. Serve warm.

PER SERVING

Calories 214 | Protein 22g | Total Fat 9g | Sat. Fat 4g | Cholesterol 225mg | Carbohydrate 10g | Dietary Fiber 2g | Sodium 430mg

Southwestern-Style Cheese and Egg Bake

lacto-ovo|low-carb

MAKES 6 SERVINGS

I like to serve this with the optional salsa and Oven-Baked Breakfast Potatoes (page 164) prepared with the optional cumin seed to create a delicious Mexican-style brunch.

8 ounces gluten-free shredded reduced-fat Monterey Jack cheese

1 (4-ounce) can chopped mild green chilies, drained

8 ounces gluten-free shredded reduced-fat cheddar cheese

4 eggs

½ cup half-and-half

½ cup gluten-free light sour cream

Salt and freshly ground black pepper, to taste

Salsa, to serve (optional)

Preheat the oven to 350F (175C). Lightly grease an 8-inch-square baking dish.

Spread the Monterey Jack cheese evenly along the bottom of the prepared pie dish. Distribute the chilies evenly over the cheese, then sprinkle evenly with the cheddar cheese.

In a medium bowl, whisk together the eggs, half-and-half, sour cream, salt, and pepper; slowly pour over the cheese and chili mixture. Bake for 35 to 45 minutes, or until puffed and browned and a knife inserted in the center comes out clean. Let stand for 10 minutes before cutting into wedges and serving warm, with the salsa passed separately (if using).

PER SERVING

Calories 247 | Protein 25g | Total Fat 13g | Sat. Fat 6g | Cholesterol 172mg | Carbohydrate 5g | Dietary Fiber 0g | Sodium 490mg

---

Crustless Spinach Quiche

lacto-ovo|low-carb

MAKES 4 TO 6 SERVINGS

Create your own favorite crustless quiches and pies using this recipe as a model—frozen chopped broccoli and cheddar cheese is an especially delicious combo.

1¼ cups skim milk

3 eggs

1½ tablespoons potato starch flour

1 teaspoon onion powder

½ teaspoon salt

Freshly ground black pepper, to taste

2 cups (8 ounces) gluten-free shredded reduced-fat Swiss, cheddar, or Monterey Jack cheese

1 (10-ounce) package frozen chopped spinach, cooked according to package directions, well drained

Preheat the oven to 350F (175C). Lightly grease an 8½- or 9-inch pie plate and set aside.

In a medium bowl, beat together the milk, eggs, flour, onion powder, salt, and pepper until thoroughly blended. Arrange the cheese in the bottom of the prepared pie plate. Top evenly with the spinach. Slowly pour the egg mixture over the top. Bake for about 40 minutes, or until puffed and browned, and a knife inserted in the center comes out clean. Let stand for 10 minutes before cutting into wedges and serving warm.

PER SERVING

Calories 221 | Protein 24g | Total Fat 8g | Sat. Fat 4g | Cholesterol 173mg | Carbohydrate 13g | Dietary Fiber 2g | Sodium 620mg

Zucchini-Mushroom Frittata

lacto-ovo│low-carb

MAKES 4 SERVINGS

Use this recipe as a model for other frittata fillings as well.

 1 tablespoon extra-virgin olive oil

 ¼ cup finely chopped onion

 2 small zucchini (about 3 ounces each), unpeeled, coarsely chopped

 1 cup sliced cultivated white mushrooms

 4 eggs, lightly beaten

 ½ teaspoon salt

 Freshly ground black pepper, to taste

 ¼ cup gluten-free freshly grated Parmesan cheese

 Preheat the oven to broil.

In a large nonstick ovenproof skillet, heat the oil over medium heat. Add the onion and cook, stirring, until softened, about 3 minutes. Add the zucchini and mushrooms and cook, stirring, until the mushrooms begin to release their liquid, 4 to 5 minutes. Add the eggs, salt, and pepper, stirring quickly to combine. Reduce the heat to low and cook, without stirring, until the eggs begin to set, about 5 minutes. Remove from the heat and sprinkle with the Parmesan cheese.

Place the skillet in the oven 8 to 10 inches from the heating element. Broil until the cheese is melted and the eggs are lightly browned, about 5 minutes. Remove the skillet from the oven and let stand for 5 minutes before cutting into wedges and serving.

PER SERVING

Calories 147 │ Protein 11g │ Total Fat 11g │ Sat. Fat 3g │ Cholesterol 217mg │ Carbohydrate 4g │ Dietary Fiber 1g │ Sodium 449mg

Desserts

Desserts are everybody's favorite part of the meal. Years ago, before the dawn of the gluten-free market, desserts for those with wheat allergies and celiac disease more often than not came down to a piece of fruit. Of course, fresh fruit is still the number one choice, especially for cooks in a hurry searching for a safe, simple, and virtually instant gluten-free dessert option that is healthful as well. When you want something more than fruit but almost as easy, ice cream with a homemade fruit or chocolate topping is always a crowd-pleaser—just be certain the ice cream (or topping) you purchase is free of any of the hidden glutens listed in the Introduction (see pages 4–6). Baking, of course, is another story—but with more time and a bit of effort, gluten-free cakes, pies, and cookies can be served up that will please everyone at the dinner table—even your gluten-eating guests will come back for seconds. And remember, practice makes perfect—the pie crust you roll out the first time will be easier the second time and, after the third time, will be part of the repertoire you'll need to create your own delicious pies and pastries.

Apple Crisp

MAKES 6 SERVINGS

This old-fashioned dessert is delicious with a scoop of vanilla ice cream. Sliced peaches or fresh berries (use about 4 cups) can replace the apples, if desired.

- 4 medium apples (about 6 ounces each), preferably Red or Golden Delicious, unpeeled, cored, and thinly sliced
- 2 tablespoons fresh lemon juice
- ½ cup plus 2 tablespoons sugar
- ½ cup brown rice flour
- 1 teaspoon ground cinnamon
- ½ teaspoon salt
- ¼ cup vegetable shortening or butter, softened

Preheat the oven to 400F (205C). Lightly oil an 8-inch-square baking dish.

In a large bowl, toss the apples with the lemon juice and the 2 tablespoons sugar. Transfer to the prepared dish.

In a medium bowl, combine the ½ cup sugar, flour, cinnamon, and salt. With a fork or your fingers, work the shortening into the dry ingredients until the mixture resembles coarse meal. Sprinkle the topping evenly over the apples. Cover tightly and bake for 25 minutes. Uncover and bake for 5 to 10 minutes, or until the top is golden. Serve warm or at room temperature. Or cover and refrigerate the completely cooled apple crisp for up to 2 days and serve chilled, return to room temperature, or reheat in a warm (300F, 150C) oven.

PER SERVING

Calories 269 | Protein 1g | Total Fat 9g | Sat. Fat 4g | Cholesterol 0mg | Carbohydrate 48g | Dietary Fiber 3g | Sodium 179mg

Baked Cinnamon-Raisin Apples with Walnuts

vegan

MAKES 4 SERVINGS

These fragrant baked apples are delicious with a dollop of whipped cream.

- 1 cup gluten-free raisins
- ¼ cup walnut pieces
- ½ teaspoon gluten-free pure vanilla extract
- ¼ teaspoon ground cinnamon
- 4 medium tart baking apples (about 6 ounces each), preferably Granny Smith, cored with bases intact
- 4 teaspoons sugar
- ½ cup water

Preheat the oven to 375F (190C).

In a small bowl, mix together the raisins, walnuts, vanilla, and cinnamon until well combined. Fill the center of each apple with equal amount of the raisin mixture. Transfer the apples to a baking dish just large enough to accommodate them in a single layer. Sprinkle the apples evenly with the sugar. Add the water to the dish and cover loosely with foil. Bake for 30 minutes. Uncover and bake for 10 to 15 minutes, or until fork tender. Serve warm.

PER SERVING

Calories 251 | Protein 4g | Total Fat 5g |
Sat. Fat 0g | Cholesterol 0mg | Carbohydrate 54g |
Dietary Fiber 5g | Sodium 8mg

French-Style Glazed Apple Tart

lacto-ovo

MAKES 8 SERVINGS

Inspired by the custard-filled, apricot-glazed apple tarts popular throughout northern France, this dessert is divine with a dollop of whipped cream.

1 Gluten-Free Sweet Pastry Crust (recipe
  opposite)
1 egg white lightly beaten with 1 tablespoon
  water to make an egg wash
8 tablespoons apricot jam
1 teaspoon water
1 cup half-and-half
1 egg
1 egg yolk

2 tablespoons sugar
½ teaspoon gluten-free pure vanilla extract
2 medium Golden Delicious apples (about 6
  ounces each), peeled, cored, and very thinly
  sliced

Preheat the oven to 350F (175C).

Prick the prepared pastry crust along the bottom and sides with a fork. Bake in the center of the oven for 10 to 12 minutes, or until very lightly browned. Remove from the oven. Using a pastry brush, brush the bottom and sides with the egg wash. Return to the oven and bake for 3 to 4 minutes, or until the egg wash is set. Let cool.

Meanwhile, in a small saucepan, heat the jam and water over medium-low heat until the jam is melted, stirring occasionally. Brush a thin film of the jam mixture (about 2 tablespoons) evenly along the bottom of the pie shell. Let the pie shell cool. Keep remaining jam mixture warm.

In a medium bowl, whisk together the half-and-half, egg, egg yolk, sugar, and vanilla until well blended. Set aside.

Working from the edge, pack the apples in slanted overlapping concentric circles in the prepared pie shell. Pour the egg mixture evenly over the apples. Bake in the center of the oven for 30 to 35 minutes, or until the custard is set. Remove the tart from the oven and let cool for 5 minutes.

Brush the remaining jam mixture evenly over the warm apple tart. Transfer to a rack and let cool for about 30 minutes. Serve warm, at room temperature, or chilled. The completely cooled pie can be stored, covered, in the refrigerator for up to 2 days.

PER SERVING

Calories 262 | Protein 4g | Total Fat 13g |
Sat. Fat 7g | Cholesterol 85mg | Carbohydrate 35g |
Dietary Fiber 1g | Sodium 181mg

GLUTEN-FREE SWEET PASTRY CRUST

egg-free

MAKES 1 (9-INCH) PIE CRUST

This light and flaky pastry crust is the perfect foundation for fruit and custard pies. Instead of rolling out the disk of dough between waxed paper, you can always press it into the pie plate with your fingers.

- ¾ **cup white rice flour**
- 1 **teaspoon sugar**
- ½ **teaspoon xanthan gum**
- ¼ **teaspoon salt**
- ⅓ **cup butter, in about 5 pieces**
- 2 **tablespoons cold water, plus additional if necessary**

In a food processor fitted with the knife blade, pulse the dry ingredients until thoroughly combined. Add the butter and pulse until the mixture resembles coarse meal. Add the water a little at a time, pulsing until a ball forms.

Form dough into a disk with your hands. Roll out the dough between 2 sheets of waxed paper or aluminum foil. The dough should be about 1½ inches larger in diameter than the pie plate. Peel one sheet of waxed paper away from the dough. Place the pie crust in an ungreased 9-inch pie plate. Remove the top sheet of waxed paper. Trim excess dough and crimp edges to form a decorative border. Proceed as directed in recipe.

PER SERVING (⅛ OF RECIPE)

Calories 124 | Protein 1g | Total Fat 8g |
Sat. Fat 5g | Cholesterol 20mg | Carbohydrate 13g |
Dietary Fiber 0g | Sodium 144mg

Cook's Tip

If a recipe requires a prebaked pie shell, preheat the oven to 350F (175C). Prick the bottom and sides of the dough with a fork and bake in the center of the oven for 10 to 12 minutes, or until very lightly browned. To safeguard against a soggy crust, seal with an egg wash as directed in the above recipe, if desired. Cool before filling.

VARIATION: *To make* Savory Pastry Crust: *Omit the sugar and proceed as otherwise directed in recipe.*

To make Herbed Pastry Crust: *Omit the sugar and add ½ tablespoon mixed dried herbs (such as thyme, rosemary, oregano) to the dry mixture before pulsing.*

No-Cook Apple Pie

vegan

MAKES 8 SERVINGS

This raw apple pie is scrumptious topped with vanilla ice cream or whipped cream. For best results, serve within twenty-four hours of preparing. Raisins can replace the dates in the walnut crust, if desired.

2 cups walnuts

½ cup chopped pitted dates

5 medium apples (5 to 6 ounces each), preferably Golden or Red Delicious, peeled, cored, and quartered

½ cup gluten-free raisins

¼ cup light corn syrup

2 tablespoons fresh lemon juice

1 teaspoon ground cinnamon

½ teaspoon ground nutmeg

Lightly grease a 9-inch pie plate and set aside.

Place the walnuts and dates in a food processor fitted with the knife blade; process until a smooth paste is formed. Using your fingers, press into prepared pie plate.

Place the apples in the food processor; pulse until coarsely chopped, working in batches, if necessary, so as not to overprocess. Transfer to a large bowl and add the raisins, corn syrup, lemon juice, cinnamon, and nutmeg; stir well to thoroughly combine. Spoon the filling into the pie plate, packing the top with the back of the spoon. Cover with plastic wrap and refrigerate for a minimum of 3 hours, or up to 1 day, and serve chilled.

PER SERVING

Calories 327 | Protein 8g | Total Fat 18g | Sat. Fat 1g | Cholesterol 0mg | Carbohydrate 40g | Dietary Fiber 5g | Sodium 9mg

Arrowroot Cake

lacto-ovo

MAKES 8 SERVINGS

This puddinglike cake is one of my favorites. Often used as a thickener for sauces, arrowroot powder is also a key ingredient in various gluten-free cookies and cakes. It is available in health food stores, some supermarkets, and many Caribbean markets.

½ cup butter, softened

¾ cup sugar

2 eggs, separated

1 cup arrowroot powder

¾ teaspoon baking soda

¾ teaspoon cream of tartar

3 tablespoons milk

1 teaspoon ground cinnamon

Whipped cream (optional)

Preheat the oven to 325F (165 C). Lightly oil an 8-inch-square baking pan.

In a large bowl, using an electric beater, beat the butter and sugar until creamy. Beat in the egg yolks. Add the arrowroot, baking soda, cream of tartar, egg whites, milk, and cinnamon and beat until combined. Transfer to the prepared pan. Bake in the center of the oven for about 40 minutes (check after about 20 minutes and cover loosely with foil if cake is browning too quickly), or until the edges are set and pulling away from the sides of the pan, and a toothpick inserted in the center comes out almost clean (most of the middle of the cake will be slightly soft). Cool in the pan on a rack for about 30 minutes before cutting into wedges and serving warm, with whipped cream (if using).

PER SERVING

Calories 254 | Protein 2g | Total Fat 13g |
Sat. Fat 8g | Cholesterol 85mg | Carbohydrate 34g |
Dietary Fiber 1g | Sodium 253mg

Indonesian-Style Warm Bananas in Cinnamon-Coconut Milk

vegan

MAKES 4 TO 6 SERVINGS

This simple yet delicious dessert can be enjoyed any time of the year.

4 large ripe yet firm bananas

1½ cups light coconut milk

3 tablespoons sugar

¼ teaspoon plus ⅛ teaspoon ground cinnamon, plus additional as necessary

Peel the bananas and slice into bite-size pieces. In a medium saucepan, bring the coconut milk, sugar, and cinnamon to a gentle boil over medium-high heat, stirring until the ingredients are incorporated. Add the bananas and let mixture return to a boil. Reduce the heat and simmer gently, stirring occasionally, until the bananas are tender but not mushy, 2 to 3 minutes. Serve hot, with an additional sprinkling of cinnamon, if desired.

PER SERVING

Calories 232 | Protein 4g | Total Fat 8g |
Sat. Fat 7g | Cholesterol 0mg | Carbohydrate 41g |
Dietary Fiber 3g | Sodium 37mg

Fresh Berry Gratin

egg-free

MAKES 6 SERVINGS

This is the quintessential summertime dessert, ideal for carefree entertaining.

4 cups fresh blueberries, raspberries, strawberries, and/or blackberries

¼ cup plus 1 tablespoon granulated sugar

1 cup gluten-free light sour cream

1 tablespoon light brown sugar

Fresh mint, for garnish (optional)

✣ Preheat the oven to broil. Lightly grease an 8- or 9-inch gratin or pie dish.

Arrange the berries in a single layer in the prepared gratin. Sprinkle evenly with 1 tablespoon of the granulated sugar. Spread evenly with the sour cream, leaving about 1 inch of exposed berries around the edge. Sprinkle evenly with the remaining granulated sugar, then sprinkle evenly with the brown sugar.

Broil 4 to 6 inches from the heating element until lightly browned and bubbly, 2 to 3 minutes, turning the gratin often to promote even browning and taking care not to burn it. Serve warm, garnished with the mint (if using).

PER SERVING

Calories 106 | Protein 1g | Total Fat 1g |
Sat. Fat 0g | Cholesterol 3mg | Carbohydrate 24g |
Dietary Fiber 3g | Sodium 12mg

Summer Berries on a Cloud

dairy-free

MAKES 8 SERVINGS

This is a light and lovely summertime dessert you can make well in advance of expected guests. If using strawberries, halve or quarter if large. If using gluten-free ice cream or frozen yogurt as a topping, let it soften for a few minutes at room temperature for easier scooping.

3 tablespoons fresh orange juice

1 tablespoon fresh lemon juice

1 tablespoon sugar

3 cups fresh raspberries, blackberries, blueberries, and/or strawberries

1 Meringue Shell (recipe below)

Gluten-free vanilla ice cream, frozen yogurt, or whipped cream (optional)

✣ In a medium stainless steel or glass bowl, combine the orange juice, lemon juice, and sugar, stirring to dissolve the sugar. Add the fruit and toss gently to combine. If not serving immediately, cover and refrigerate for up to 24 hours, tossing occasionally.

With a slotted spoon, transfer the berries to the cooled meringue shell. Pour the remaining juices into a small pitcher. If desired, arrange 8 scoops of ice cream or frozen yogurt toward the rim of the filled shell, or top with whipped cream; serve immediately, passing the reserved juices separately. Alternatively, cut into 8 pieces and pass the toppings (if using) and reserved juices separately.

PER SERVING

Calories 112 | Protein 2g | Total Fat 0g |
Sat. Fat 0g | Cholesterol 0mg | Carbohydrate 27g |
Dietary Fiber 2g | Sodium 21mg

MERINGUE SHELL

dairy-free|low-carb

MAKES 1 (9-INCH) PIE SHELL

Use this meringue shell as a base for various fruit and ice cream fillings.

3 egg whites, at room temperature

¼ **teaspoon cream of tartar**

½ **teaspoon gluten-free vanilla extract**

¾ **cup sugar**

Preheat the oven to 250F (120C). Line a baking sheet with parchment paper and set aside.

In a medium stainless steel mixing bowl, beat the egg whites with an electric mixer on low speed until foamy. Add the cream of tartar and gradually increase the speed to high. When the egg whites begin to form soft peaks, add the vanilla extract and half of the sugar (6 tablespoons), 2 tablespoons at a time. Continue beating until very stiff, shiny peaks are formed, about 10 more minutes (do not underbeat). With a rubber spatula, gently fold in the remaining sugar, 2 tablespoons at a time.

With a rubber spatula, spread the meringue mixture on the prepared baking sheet into a 9-inch circle, pushing it up around the circumference to form a deep-sided free-form pie shell. Bake in the center of the oven for 1 hour. Reduce the heat to 200F (95C) and bake for 1 hour. The meringue shell should be firm on the outside and slightly colored.

Place the meringue shell with parchment on a rack and cool to room temperature. Carefully peel away the parchment and transfer the meringue shell to a serving platter. (At this point, the meringue shell may be set aside at room temperature for a few hours before serving or wrapped securely in plastic wrap and refrigerated up to 3 days. The meringue shell may also be stored in the freezer for several weeks.)

PER ⅛ OF RECIPE

Calories 80 | Protein 1g | Total Fat 0g |
Sat. Fat 0g | Cholesterol 0mg | Carbohydrate 19g |
Dietary Fiber 0g | Sodium 21mg

Blueberry Cheesecake

lacto-ovo

MAKES 8 SERVINGS

This scrumptious cheesecake is also delicious made with fresh raspberries. Mascarpone, a sweet Italian dessert cheese, can be found in Italian and gourmet markets, as well as many well-stocked supermarkets.

1 cup gluten-free nonfat ricotta cheese

⅔ cup mascarpone cheese

⅓ cup gluten-free light sour cream

2 eggs

⅔ cup sugar

1 tablespoon cornstarch mixed with 1 tablespoon water

2 tablespoons fresh lemon juice

1¼ cups fresh blueberries

Cornflake Pie Crust (recipe opposite)

Preheat the oven to 300F (150C).

In a large bowl, using an electric mixer on medium speed, beat together the ricotta cheese, mascarpone cheese, sour cream, eggs, sugar, cornstarch mixture, and lemon juice until smooth. Stir in 1 cup of the blueberries. Pour into the pie crust and arrange the remaining blueberries over the top.

Bake in the center of the oven for about 50 minutes, or until the sides of the cheesecake are set but the center is slightly wobbly. Turn off the heat and transfer the cake to the bottom oven rack. Close the oven door and leave for 30 minutes or until the center is set. Remove from the oven and let cool in the pan to room temperature. Cover and refrigerate for a minimum of 8 hours, or up to 2 days. Serve chilled.

PER SERVING

Calories 362 | Protein 11g | Total Fat 21g | Sat. Fat 5g | Cholesterol 87mg | Carbohydrate 35g | Dietary Fiber 2g | Sodium 218mg

CORNFLAKE PIE CRUST

egg-free

MAKES 1 (9-INCH) DEEP-DISH PIE CRUST

An excellent gluten-free substitute for a graham cracker crust, this simple yet delicious crust is perfect for cheesecake, cream pies, and custard tarts.

1 cup blanched almonds

1 cup gluten-free cornflake crumbs (see second Cook's Tip opposite)

2 tablespoons light brown sugar

¼ cup unsalted butter, melted

Process the almonds in a food processor fitted with a knife blade until finely ground. (Do not overprocess, as the almonds may turn into a paste.) Transfer to a medium bowl and add the cornflake crumbs and sugar, tossing well to combine. Add the butter and mix well. Using your fingers, pinch to thoroughly blend. Press into the bottom and sides of a 9-inch deep-dish pie pan. Chill for 1 hour (or up to 2 days) before filling and baking as directed in recipe.

Cook's Tips

For no-bake fillings, chill crust as directed, and then bake at 350F (175C) for 10 minutes. Cool and fill.

Gluten-free cornflake crumbs are located next to the bread crumbs in most well-stocked supermarkets. If prepared from scratch, make sure the cornflakes used are free of damaging glutens, namely barley malt.

Brownies

lacto-ovo|low-carb

MAKES 16 BROWNIES

These yummy, fudgelike brownies freeze well, so why not make an extra batch?

2 ounces semisweet chocolate

½ cup butter (1 stick), softened

1 cup superfine sugar

2 eggs, lightly beaten

½ teaspoon gluten-free pure vanilla extract

¾ cup (3 ounces) ground almonds

½ teaspoon gluten-free baking powder

Pinch salt

1 cup (4 ounces) chopped walnuts

Preheat the oven to 350F (175F). Line an 8-inch-square baking pan with parchment or waxed paper.

Place the chocolate in the top of a double boiler over barely simmering water; cook, stirring, until melted and smooth. Set aside to cool slightly.

In a large bowl, beat the butter and sugar with an electric mixer until light and fluffy. Beat in the eggs, chocolate, vanilla, almonds, baking powder, and salt on low speed. Stir in the walnuts. Spread the mixture in the prepared pan and bake for about 30 minutes, or until a toothpick inserted in the center comes out almost clean. (After about 20 minutes, if brownies seem to be browning too quickly, cover loosely with foil until done.)

Let cool in the pan on a wire rack to room temperature. Cut into 16 squares. Completely cooled brownies can be placed in an airtight container and stored for up to 2 days at room temperature, in the refrigerator for up to 1 week, or in the freezer for up to 1 month.

Cardamom Sponge Cake
with **Strawberry Coulis**
dairy-free

MAKES 8 TO 10 SERVINGS

Potato starch flour is a perfect substitute for wheat flour in this delicious sponge cake. If cardamom is not available, substitute with additional grated dried lemon peel.

> **6 eggs, separated, plus 1 egg, unseparated**
> **Pinch salt**
> **1½ cups superfine sugar**
> **1½ tablespoons fresh lemon juice**
> **1 teaspoon grated dried lemon peel**
> **½ teaspoon ground cardamom**
> **¾ cup potato starch flour, sifted**
> **Strawberry Coulis (recipe opposite)**

Preheat the oven to 350F (175C). In a large mixing bowl, using an electric mixer on medium speed, beat the egg whites with the salt until stiff but not dry. Set aside.

In another large mixing bowl, beat the egg yolks and egg on medium speed until frothy. Gradually add the sugar, lemon juice, lemon peel, and cardamom, beating until thoroughly blended. Gradually add the potato starch flour, stirring until thoroughly blended. Using a rubber spatula, gently yet thoroughly fold in the egg whites. Pour into an ungreased 10-inch tube or Bundt pan. Bake on the lower rack of the oven for 35 to 45 minutes, or until the cake springs back when touched gently with your fingertips. Invert the pan onto a cooling rack and cool thoroughly before removing the pan. Serve at room temperature with the Strawberry Coulis.

PER SERVING (WITHOUT STRAWBERRY COULIS)

Calories 271 | Protein 7g | Total Fat 5g |
Sat. Fat 1g | Cholesterol 186mg |
Total Carbohydrate 52g | Dietary Fiber 1g |
Sodium 61mg

Cook's Tip

Potato starch flour (often referred to as potato starch) is a considerably lighter flour than potato flour, which also has a more pronounced potato flavor. Substituting one for the other in recipes, particularly those requiring baking, is not recommended.

STRAWBERRY COULIS
vegan|low-carb

MAKES ABOUT 2¼ CUPS

Spoon this versatile sauce over countless cakes, gluten-free ice cream, and frozen yogurt. Raspberries can easily replace the strawberries, if desired.

> **3 cups fresh strawberries, hulled**
> **3 to 4 tablespoons confectioners' sugar**
> **2 to 3 teaspoons fresh lemon juice**

Combine all the ingredients in a food processor fitted with the knife blade, or in a blender. Process until smooth and pureed. Serve chilled or at room temperature.

PER SERVING (ABOUT ¼ CUP)

Calories 24 | Protein 0g | Total Fat 0g | Sat. Fat 0g | Cholesterol 0mg | Carbohydrate 6g | Dietary Fiber 1g | Sodium 1mg

Cherry-Cranberry Tarts

vegan|low-carb

MAKES 4 SERVINGS

These tasty crustless tarts are ideal to serve when you want something light to conclude a filling meal. Thawed frozen or canned cherries, well drained, can be used in lieu of the fresh variety. If tart cherries are preferred, omit the lemon juice.

> 1½ **cups pitted sweet cherries, about half cut in half**
> 6 **tablespoons dried sweetened cranberries**
> 2½ **tablespoons sugar**
> 1½ **teaspoons fresh lemon juice**
> 1½ **teaspoons cornstarch**
> **Whipped cream (optional)**

Preheat the oven to 400F (205C). Lightly oil 4 (4-ounce) ramekins and set aside. In a small bowl, combine all the ingredients, except the whipped cream (if using). Divide evenly among the prepared ramekins. Bake in the center of the oven for about 20 minutes, or until the fruit is bubbly. Serve warm or at room temperature, accompanied by the whipped cream (if using).

PER SERVING

Calories 80 | Protein 1g | Total Fat 1g | Sat. Fat 0g | Cholesterol 0mg | Carbohydrate 20g | Dietary Fiber 1g | Sodium 0mg

Chocolate Chip Cookies

lacto-ovo|low-carb

MAKES ABOUT 48 COOKIES

These delicate, crispy cookies keep for several days stored in an airtight container. They are also delicious crumbled over gluten-free ice cream, frozen yogurt, or baked fruit.

> 1 **cup packed light brown sugar**
> 1 **teaspoon gluten-free baking powder**
> ½ **cup salted butter, softened**
> 2 **eggs**
> 2 **teaspoons gluten-free pure vanilla extract**
> 1 **cup potato starch flour (see Cook's Tip, opposite)**
> ½ **cup white rice flour**
> ½ **cup semisweet chocolate chips**

In a large bowl, beat the sugar, baking powder, and butter with an electric mixer until creamy. Add the eggs and vanilla and beat on low speed for 1½ minutes. Add the potato starch flour and rice flour; beat on low speed for 1 minute. Stir in the chips until evenly distributed. Cover and refrigerate for 1 hour, or overnight.

Preheat the oven to 375F (190C). Lightly grease a baking sheet and set aside.

Drop the chilled dough by rounded teaspoons on prepared baking sheet, leaving about 3 inches between each cookie. Bake for about 8 minutes, or until lightly browned. Immediately remove from the baking sheet and transfer to a wire rack to cool. Repeat with remaining dough, cleaning and greasing baking sheet after each use.

PER SERVING (PER COOKIE)

Calories 68 | Protein 1g | Total Fat 3g | Sat. Fat 2g | Cholesterol 14mg | Carbohydrate 10g | Dietary Fiber 0g | Sodium 33mg

Cook's Tips

Chilling the dough for 1 hour prevents drop cookies from spreading too much.

If a chocolate pie crust is called for in a recipe, allow about half the cookies to dry out overnight, then grind in a food processor or blender (you will need about 2 cups fine cookie crumbs). Transfer the cookie crumbs to a small bowl and stir in ½ cup melted butter or gluten-free margarine. Press the mixture into a 9-inch pie plate and proceed as directed in the recipe.

Chocolate Chip Meringue Cookies

lacto-ovo|low-carb

MAKES ABOUT 30 MERINGUES

Crispy on the outside, soft on the inside, these melt-in-your-mouth meringues are delightful with a cup of coffee.

3 egg whites, at room temperature
⅛ teaspoon cream of tartar
½ teaspoon gluten-free vanilla extract
⅔ cup sugar
½ cup semisweet chocolate chips
Unsweetened cocoa powder, for dusting (optional)

Preheat the oven to 275F (135C). Line 2 standard-size baking sheets with parchment paper and set aside.

In a large stainless steel mixing bowl, beat the egg whites with an electric mixer on low speed until foamy. Add the cream of tartar and increase the speed to high. When the egg whites begin to form soft peaks, add the vanilla and the sugar, 1 tablespoon at a time. Beat on high speed until stiff but not dry peaks form. Using a rubber spatula, gently fold in the chocolate chips.

Drop the mixture by teaspoonfuls, 1 inch apart, onto prepared baking sheets. Bake for 25 to 30 minutes, or until crisp and very lightly colored, switching the placement of the baking sheets halfway through cooking time.

Remove parchment paper with meringues and transfer to a wire rack to cool to room temperature. Carefully peel away the meringues from the parchment paper and transfer to a covered plastic container, separating layers with waxed paper as necessary (meringues will be sticky). Hold at room temperature for about 24 hours, or until slightly hardened, or up to 3 days. Dust with cocoa powder before serving (if using).

PER SERVING (¹⁄₃₀ OF RECIPE)

Calories 37 | Protein 1g | Total Fat 1g |

Sat. Fat 1g | Cholesterol 0mg | Carbohydrate 7g |

Dietary Fiber 0g | Sodium 6mg

Chocolate Pots de Crème

lacto-ovo

MAKES 4 SERVINGS

This easy yet elegant French custard dessert is always nice to serve for special occasions.

1 cup whole milk or half-and-half

²⁄₃ cup semisweet chocolate chips

2 eggs

3 tablespoons sugar

Whipped cream (optional)

Unsweetened cocoa powder, for dusting (optional)

Preheat oven to 350F (175C).

In a medium heavy-bottomed saucepan, heat the milk and chocolate over low heat until chocolate is melted and mixture is smooth, stirring constantly. Let cool slightly.

In a small bowl, whisk together the eggs and sugar until thoroughly blended. Gradually add to the chocolate mixture, whisking constantly. Pour into 4 ungreased 6-ounce custard cups (or 5 or 6 pots de crème cups).

Place the cups in a baking pan in the center of the oven. Pour boiling water into the pan to within ½ inch of the tops of the cups. Bake for about 20 minutes, or until set. Let cool in the water bath for about 10 minutes. Remove the cups from the water bath and let cool to room temperature. Cover and refrigerate for a minimum of 3 hours, or up to 1 day. Serve chilled, with whipped cream dusted with cocoa powder (if using).

PER SERVING

Calories 289 | Protein 7g | Total Fat 16g |

Sat. Fat 9g | Cholesterol 115mg | Carbohydrate 36g |

Dietary Fiber 2g | Sodium 66mg

Chocolate Ricotta Pie

lacto-ovo

MAKES 8 SERVINGS

Really a crustless cheesecake, this delicious dessert should be served within twenty-four hours of baking for best results.

> 1 (15-ounce) container gluten-free low-fat ricotta cheese
>
> 1 cup sugar
>
> 3 eggs
>
> 1½ teaspoons gluten-free pure vanilla extract
>
> ¼ teaspoon gluten-free almond extract
>
> ½ teaspoon grated dried orange peel
>
> ⅛ teaspoon ground cinnamon
>
> ¾ cup mini chocolate chips
>
> 1 cup gluten-free light sour cream

Preheat the oven to 350F (175C). Lightly grease an 8½- or 9-inch pie dish and set aside.

In a large bowl, combine the ricotta cheese and ¾ cup of the sugar. Add the eggs, one at a time, beating well with an electric mixer after each addition. Add the extracts, orange peel, and cinnamon and mix briefly. Stir in all the chocolate chips except for about 2 tablespoons. Slowly pour into the prepared pie dish, gently swirling through the batter to evenly distribute the chocolate chips. Bake in the center of the oven for about 45 minutes, or until browned and a toothpick inserted in the center comes out clean. Transfer to a rack and let cool completely.

To make the topping, combine the sour cream and remaining ¼ cup sugar in a small saucepan. Cook over medium-low heat, stirring constantly, until the mixture is the consistency of thick cream, 3 to 4 minutes. Slowly pour the topping over the pie so that the entire surface is covered to within ¼ inch of the edge. Let cool completely before sprinkling with the reserved chocolate chips. Cover and refrigerate for a minimum of 3 hours, or up to 1 day. Cut into wedges and serve chilled.

PER SERVING

Calories 293 | Protein 12g | Total Fat 10g | Sat. Fat 6g | Cholesterol 103mg | Carbohydrate 42g | Dietary Fiber 1g | Sodium 280mg

Easy Refrigerator Chocolate Fudge

egg-free

MAKES 16 PIECES

This incredibly easy recipe tastes remarkably like candy-shop fudge.

> 1 pound (3 cups) semisweet chocolate chips
>
> 4 tablespoons (½ stick) butter
>
> 1 (14-ounce) can sweetened condensed milk
>
> ½ cup chopped walnuts (optional)

Butter an 8-inch-square baking dish and line with waxed paper.

In the top of a double boiler over barely simmering water, melt the chocolate chips and butter, stirring often. Remove from the heat and add the remaining ingredients, stirring well to thoroughly blend. Pour into prepared baking dish and let cool for about 10 minutes. Transfer to the refrigerator and chill until firm, about 3 hours. Cut into squares and serve chilled. The fudge can be stored, covered, in the refrigerator for several days.

PER SERVING (1 PIECE)

Calories 241 | Protein 3g | Total Fat 13g |
Sat. Fat 8g | Cholesterol 16mg | Carbohydrate 32g |
Dietary Fiber 0g | Sodium 64mg

In a large bowl, mix all the ingredients until thoroughly blended. Drop by rounded teaspoonfuls, 2 inches apart, on prepared baking sheets. Press down lightly with the back of the spoon to even the thickness. Working with 1 baking sheet at a time, bake in the center of the oven for about 10 minutes, or until light golden.

Cool for 5 minutes on the baking sheet; peel the macaroons off the parchment paper and transfer to a wire rack to cool to room temperature. Store in a covered plastic container for a few days at room temperature.

PER SERVING (1/36 OF RECIPE)

Calories 57 | Protein 1g | Total Fat 3g |
Sat. Fat 2g | Cholesterol 3mg | Carbohydrate 8g |
Dietary Fiber 0g | Sodium 30mg

Easy Coconut Macaroons

egg-free|low-carb

MAKES ABOUT 3 DOZEN MACAROONS

Baking macaroons doesn't get much easier than this simple yet delicious recipe.

3 cups sweetened shredded coconut

1 cup sweetened condensed milk

1½ teaspoons gluten-free pure vanilla extract

½ teaspoon gluten-free almond extract

Pinch salt

Preheat the oven to 350F (175C). Line 2 baking sheets with parchment paper.

Hawaiian Coconut Cake

lacto-ovo|low-carb

MAKES 24 SERVINGS

Known as butter mochi, this chewy coconut cake gets its distinctive gelatinous texture from sweet rice flour, which is derived from glutinous, or sticky, rice. I purchase my sweet rice flour from Trader Joe's.

3 cups sweet rice flour

2½ cups sugar

2 teaspoons gluten-free baking powder

¼ teaspoon salt

2 (14-ounce) cans unsweetened coconut milk (not light)

5 eggs

¼ cup (½ stick) unsalted butter, melted and cooled

1 teaspoon gluten-free pure vanilla extract

❧ Preheat the oven to 350F (175C).

In a very large bowl, using a wire whisk, mix together the rice flour, sugar, baking powder, and salt. In a large bowl, whisk together the coconut milk, eggs, butter, and vanilla. Gradually add the coconut milk mixture to the flour mixture, whisking until batter is thoroughly combined.

Pour the batter into an ungreased 13×9-inch baking pan, smoothing the top. Bake in the center of the oven for about 1½ hours, or until the top is golden, the cake begins to pull away from the sides of the pan, and the center is firm. (After about 50 minutes, if cake seems to be browning too quickly, cover loosely with foil until done.) Cool the cake in the pan on a rack for about 2 hours. Cut completely cooled cake into 24 squares and serve at room temperature. Or cover and refrigerate for up to 3 days, and serve chilled.

PER SERVING

Calories 183 | Protein 3g | Total Fat 11g | Sat. Fat 9g | Cholesterol 50mg | Carbohydrate 18g | Dietary Fiber 1g | Sodium 71mg

Spanish Caramel Flan

lacto-ovo

MAKES 8 SERVINGS

This classic Spanish custard is a terrific company dessert, as it can be prepared a day ahead of unmolding and serving.

½ cup plus 6 tablespoons sugar

4 eggs, lightly beaten

2 egg yolks

1¼ cups half-and-half

1¼ cups whole milk

1½ teaspoons gluten-free pure vanilla extract

¼ teaspoon salt

❧ Preheat the oven to 325F (165C).

In an 8½- or 9-inch-round flameproof baking dish, heat the ½ cup of sugar over medium-high heat, shaking the pan frequently (but not stirring) until the sugar begins to liquefy, 2 to 3 minutes. Reduce the heat to low and cook, stirring occasionally, until the sugar is golden brown, 4 to 5 minutes, taking care not to burn it (some small lumps are okay). Remove from the heat and set aside.

In a medium bowl, whisk together the eggs, egg yolks, half-and-half, milk, the 6 tablespoons sugar, vanilla, and salt until well blended. Pour into the caramel-coated baking dish. Place the filled baking dish into a larger baking dish and place in the center of the oven. Carefully pour hot water into the larger dish to a depth of 1 inch. Cover the filled baking dish loosely with foil and bake for 45 minutes. Uncover and bake for 15 minutes, or until the top is lightly browned and a knife inserted in the center comes out clean. (When you shake the flan dish, the custard should jiggle like a gelatin dessert.)

Allow the flan to cool to room temperature in the water bath. Remove from the water bath, cover, and refrigerate for a minimum of 6 hours, or up to 1 day. To unmold, loosen the sides of the flan with the tip of a thin sharp knife. (When you move the dish from side to side, the flan should slip freely from the edges.) Place a flat serving platter with a raised rim on top of the mold. Holding the platter and mold together tightly, flip them over. The flan should slip easily onto the platter, along with most of the caramel sauce. Use a spoon to remove more caramel and spoon it around the custard. (The bottom of the pan will have a hard layer of caramel still on it.)

To serve, cut the flan into wedges, spooning the caramel sauce over each slice. Serve chilled.

PER SERVING

Calories 212 | Protein 6g | Total Fat 9g | Sat. Fat 5g | Cholesterol 179mg | Carbohydrate 26g | Dietary Fiber 0g | Sodium 134mg

Cook's Tip

If you don't have an 8½- or 9-inch flameproof round baking dish, caramelize the ½ cup of sugar in a heavy medium saucepan and immediately pour into an ungreased 8½- or 9-inch round baking dish, swirling the dish until the caramel coats as much of the bottom as possible. The caramel will harden almost immediately but will melt again later as the flan bakes.

Grapes in Sour Cream Sauce
egg-free
MAKES 4 SERVINGS

This quick and easy dessert dresses up ordinary grapes in fine style.

- **½ cup gluten-free light sour cream**
- **2 tablespoons plus 4 teaspoons light brown sugar**
- **3 cups stemmed seedless white grapes**

In a small saucepan, combine the sour cream and the 2 tablespoons sugar. Cook, stirring constantly, over medium-low heat until the mixture is the consistency of thick cream, 3 to 4 minutes. Transfer to a medium bowl and add the grapes; toss well to thoroughly coat. Cover and refrigerate for a minimum of 3 hours or overnight.

To serve, divide the grape mixture equally among 4 dessert bowls and sprinkle each with 1 teaspoon of the remaining sugar. Serve chilled.

PER SERVING

Calories 127 | Protein 2g | Total Fat 1g |
Sat. Fat 0g | Cholesterol 2mg | Carbohydrate 31g |
Dietary Fiber 2g | Sodium 23mg

Neapolitan Strawberry Sundaes

lacto-ovo

MAKES 4 SERVINGS

You can make these Italian sundaes as simple or as fancy as you please, depending on the number of optional ingredients used—in any instance, they will taste scrumptious.

> 1 cup sliced fresh strawberries
>
> 1 tablespoon sugar
>
> Chocolate-Hazelnut Sauce (recipe opposite)
>
> 1 pint (2 cups) gluten-free Neapolitan
>   ice cream
>
> Whipped cream (optional)
>
> Hazelnuts, toasted (optional; see Cook's Tip,
>   page 118)

> Chocolate sprinkles (optional)
>
> 4 drained maraschino cherries with stems
>   (optional)

In a small bowl, toss together the strawberries and sugar until combined. Cover and refrigerate for a minimum of 2 hours, or overnight.

Spoon ¼ cup of the sauce into each of 4 bowls. Top each with ½ cup of the ice cream. Spoon equal portions of strawberries and accumulated juices over the top. Top with the garnishes in the order suggested (if using). Serve at once.

PER SERVING

Calories 407 | Protein 14g | Total Fat 29g |
Sat. Fat 8g | Cholesterol 15mg | Carbohydrate 30g |
Dietary Fiber 4g | Sodium 264mg

CHOCOLATE-HAZELNUT SAUCE

egg-free|low-carb

MAKES 1 CUP

Nutella is a rich and creamy gluten-free chocolate-hazelnut spread highly popular in Europe, particularly in Italy, where it is often thinned with water, milk, or cream, then spooned over ice cream or used as a dip for fresh or dried fruit. It can be located in most major supermarkets near the peanut butter.

> ¾ cup Nutella chocolate-hazelnut spread
>
> 4 tablespoons water

In a small bowl, whisk together the Nutella and water until smooth.

PER SERVING (PER TABLESPOON)

Calories 71 | Protein 3g | Total Fat 6g |

Sat. Fat 1g | Cholesterol 0mg | Carbohydrate 3g |

Dietary Fiber 1g | Sodium 58mg

room temperature, in the refrigerator for up to 1 week, or in the freezer for up to 1 month.

PER SERVING

Calories 170 | Protein 6g | Total Fat 11g |

Sat. Fat 2g | Cholesterol 24mg | Carbohydrate 15g |

Dietary Fiber 1g | Sodium 77mg

VARIATION: *To make* Peanut Butter–Chocolate Chip Cookies: *Use half the amount of chopped peanuts and replace with semisweet chocolate chips.*

Peanut Butter Cookies

dairy-free|low-carb

MAKES ABOUT 3 DOZEN COOKIES

Chopped walnuts can replace the peanuts, if desired. For a lower-fat cookie, omit the nuts altogether—while less crunchy, the cookies will still be delicious.

- **2 cups creamy peanut butter**
- **2 cups sugar**
- **4 eggs, lightly beaten**
- **1½ cups unsalted chopped peanuts**

Preheat the oven to 350F (175C). Lightly grease a large baking sheet.

In a large bowl, mix together the peanut butter, sugar, and eggs until well combined. Add the peanuts, stirring well to combine. Spoon the dough by heaping tablespoons onto the prepared sheet, allowing about 2 inches between each cookie. Bake for 10 to 12 minutes, or until lightly browned.

Let cool for 5 minutes on the baking sheet before removing and placing on a wire rack to cool completely. Cooled cookies can be placed in an airtight container and stored for up to 2 days at

Nirvana Bars

egg-free|low-carb

MAKES 20 BARS

These heavenly bars freeze well. Almonds or walnuts can replace the pecans, if desired. Gluten-free corn-flake crumbs can be used in lieu of the crushed corn-flakes (see the second Cook's Tip, page 181).

- **½ cup salted butter**
- **1½ cups crushed gluten-free cornflakes**
- **1 (14-ounce) can sweetened condensed milk**
- **1 cup plus 2 tablespoons semisweet chocolate chips**
- **1 cup sweetened shredded coconut**
- **1 cup chopped pecans**

Preheat the oven to 350F (175 C).

Place the butter in a 13×9-inch baking pan

and set it in the oven until the butter is melted. Tilt the pan to coat the bottom evenly.

Sprinkle the cornflakes in the pan and toss to coat with the butter; spread evenly along the bottom. Pour the condensed milk evenly over the cornflakes. Sprinkle evenly with 1 cup of the chocolate chips, then the coconut, then the pecans. Using the back of a spatula, press the mixture firmly into the pan. Sprinkle with the remaining chocolate chips, then press gently in with your fingers.

Bake 20 to 25 minutes, until set and slightly golden.

Cool in the pan on a wire rack. Cut into 20 bars and serve at room temperature. Alternatively, cover and refrigerate up to 1 week and serve chilled or return to room temperature, or freeze for up to 1 month.

PER SERVING (PER BAR)

Calories 205 | Protein 3g | Total Fat 14g |
Sat. Fat 7g | Cholesterol 19mg | Carbohydrate 20g |
Dietary Fiber 1g | Sodium 103mg

Piña Colada Fruit Dip

egg-free|low-carb

MAKES 4 TO 6 SERVINGS

Serve this versatile dip year-round using seasonal fresh fruits—strawberries, melon, and pineapple are perfect dippers in the spring and summer, while grapes, orange segments, and bananas are ideal choices in the fall and winter.

1 (6-ounce) container gluten-free low-fat piña
    colada yogurt
¼ cup gluten-free whipped cream cheese
2 tablespoons confectioners' sugar
¼ teaspoon gluten-free lemon extract
Fresh whole strawberries or bite-size pieces of
    fresh melon, pineapple, bananas, or other
    fresh fruits

In a small bowl, whisk together all ingredients, except the fruit, until well blended. Cover and refrigerate for a minimum of 1 hour, or up to 2 days, and served chilled, accompanied by the fruit.

PER SERVING (ABOUT ¼ CUP DIP ONLY)

Calories 106 | Protein 3g | Total Fat 5g |
Sat. Fat 3g | Cholesterol 17mg | Carbohydrate 12g |
Dietary Fiber 0g | Sodium 65mg

Polenta Chocolate-Currant Cake

vegan

MAKES 8 SERVINGS

Raisins or any dried fruit can replace the currants, if desired.

3 cups water
1 cup polenta or coarse-ground yellow cornmeal
½ teaspoon gluten-free baking powder
3½ ounces bittersweet chocolate, in small pieces
½ cup gluten-free zante currants or raisins
¼ cup sugar
Confectioners' sugar (optional)

❧ Lightly oil a 9-inch springform pan and set aside.

In a medium stockpot, bring the water to a boil over high heat. Slowly add the polenta and baking powder, stirring constantly with a long-handled wooden spoon. Reduce the heat to low and stir in the chocolate, currants, and sugar; cook, covered, for about 15 minutes, or until the polenta is tender, stirring occasionally. Remove from the heat and let stand, covered, for 5 minutes. Immediately transfer to prepared pan, spreading the top evenly with a spatula or the back of a wooden spoon. Let cool to room temperature.

Remove the sides of the pan. Sprinkle with the confectioners' sugar (if using), and serve. Or cover and refrigerate up to 3 days before serving chilled or returning to room temperature.

PER SERVING

Calories 187 | Protein 3g | Total Fat 7g | Sat. Fat 4g | Cholesterol 0mg | Carbohydrate 32g | Dietary Fiber 5g | Sodium 25mg

Pumpkin Ice Cream Pie

lacto-ovo

MAKES 8 SERVINGS

Always a crowd-pleaser, this is an excellent gluten-free substitute for traditional pumpkin pie around the fall and winter holidays.

2 cups walnuts, ground (about 1½ cups pieces)
¼ cup butter or margarine, melted
3 tablespoons granulated sugar
4 cups gluten-free light vanilla ice cream, softened
1 cup canned pumpkin puree
½ cup packed light brown sugar
1½ teaspoons pumpkin pie spice

❧ Lightly oil a 9-inch aluminum pie or cake pan.

In a medium bowl, combine the walnuts, butter, and granulated sugar until thoroughly combined. Press the mixture firmly into the prepared pan. Place in the freezer and chill until firm, about 30 minutes.

In a large bowl, mix together the remaining ingredients until well blended. Pour into the crust. Place in the freezer and freeze until firm, about 3 hours, or up to 1 week (cover with plastic wrap after the mixture has frozen). Serve frozen, cut into wedges.

PER SERVING

Calories 394 | Protein 9g | Total Fat 23g |
Sat. Fat 7g | Cholesterol 41mg | Carbohydrate 40g |
Dietary Fiber 2g | Sodium 105mg

Raspberry Sorbet–Meringue Cake

dairy-free

MAKES 8 SERVINGS

Wow your guests with this refreshing dessert for that next special occasion or festive gathering. Any flavor sorbet can replace the raspberry, if desired.

½ **cup confectioners' sugar, plus additional for serving**

1 **tablespoon cornstarch**

4 **egg whites**

½ **cup superfine sugar**

1 **(12-ounce) package unsweetened frozen raspberries (3 cups), thawed**

4 **tablespoons granulated sugar**

1 **quart (4 cups) raspberry sorbet, softened**

Preheat the oven to 275F (135C). Line 2 baking sheets with parchment or waxed paper.

Trace 3 (8-inch) circles, 2 on 1 sheet, 1 on the other sheet.

In a small bowl, sift together the ½ cup confectioners' sugar and cornstarch; set aside. In a large bowl, beat the egg whites with an electric mixer until soft peaks form. Slowly beat in the superfine sugar and beat until stiff but not dry peaks form. With a rubber spatula, gently fold in the confectioners' sugar–cornstarch mixture.

Divide the egg white mixture evenly among the circles on the baking sheets; using a spatula or back of a spoon, spread evenly out to the edges. Bake for 1 hour, or until firm and very lightly browned, switching the placement of the baking sheets in the oven halfway through the cooking time. Turn off the oven and allow the meringues to cool in the oven. Carefully peel the paper away from the meringues. (At this point, the meringues can be refrigerated in airtight containers for up to 2 weeks.)

In a food processor fitted with the knife blade, or in a blender, puree the raspberries until smooth. Strain through a sieve into a small bowl to remove the seeds. Stir in the granulated sugar.

To assemble the cake: Trim the meringues to fit a 9-inch springform pan. Place 1 meringue in the bottom of the pan (save the best one for the top). Spread half of the sorbet over the top. Top with another meringue and spread with the remaining sorbet. Top with the last meringue. Double wrap in plastic and freeze for a minimum of 2 hours or up to 1 week.

To serve the cake: If the cake is frozen solid, let thaw slightly in the refrigerator for 30 minutes to 1 hour before serving. Run a knife around the pan to loosen the cake. Release the sides of the pan and transfer the cake to a serving platter. Sprinkle with confectioners' sugar. Cut into wedges and serve at once, with the raspberry sauce.

PER SERVING

Calories 292 | Protein 3g | Total Fat 2g |
Sat. Fat 1g | Cholesterol 50mg | Carbohydrate 68g |
Dietary Fiber 2g | Sodium 58mg

Baked Coconut-Basmati Rice Pudding

lacto-ovo

MAKES 8 SERVINGS

This Indian-inspired rice pudding is a special conclusion to any meal. Regular long-grain white rice can replace the basmati variety, if desired. For a dairy-free dish, replace the cream and whole milk with full-fat coconut milk.

1 cup light coconut milk

½ cup heavy cream

½ cup whole milk

2 cups cooked basmati rice (see Cook's Tip, page 145)

½ cup gluten-free golden raisins

2 eggs, lightly beaten

½ cup sugar

½ teaspoon ground cardamom

1 teaspoon gluten-free pure vanilla extract

½ cup chopped unsalted pistachio nuts

Unsweetened shredded coconut (optional)

Preheat the oven to 350F (175C).

In a medium bowl, combine the coconut milk, cream, milk, rice, raisins, eggs, sugar, cardamom, and vanilla. Transfer to an ungreased 1½-quart baking dish and place in a slightly larger pan. Place in the center of the oven; fill the larger pan with hot water to come halfway up the sides of the baking dish. Bake, uncovered, for about 1½ hours, or until the mixture is creamy and most of the liquids are absorbed, stirring occasionally after 30 minutes. Stir in the pistachios and serve warm or at room temperature, garnished with the coconut (if using). Or cover and refrigerate for up to 3 days and serve chilled.

PER SERVING

Calories 292 | Protein 7g | Total Fat 13g |
Sat. Fat 6g | Cholesterol 76mg | Carbohydrate 39g |
Dietary Fiber 2g | Sodium 45mg

Fruited Arborio Rice Pudding Cake

lacto-ovo

MAKES 12 SERVINGS

This moist cake is delicious with a dollop of whipped cream. While you can use regular long-grain white rice instead of the arborio rice, the cake will be slightly harder if served chilled. To make six servings, halve the recipe and bake in an 8-inch springform pan for about twenty-five minutes.

4 eggs, beaten

2 medium-size ripe bananas, mashed

²⁄₃ cup packed light brown sugar

1 teaspoon grated dried orange peel

1 teaspoon ground cinnamon

½ teaspoon gluten-free pure vanilla
  extract

¼ teaspoon gluten-free pure almond
  extract

¼ teaspoon ground nutmeg

3 cups cooked arborio rice, at room temperature
  (see Cook's Tip, opposite)

2 cups gluten-free low-fat cottage cheese

2 medium apples (about 6 ounces each), peeled
  and finely chopped

1 cup gluten-free golden raisins

1 cup gluten-free dark raisins

½ cup gluten-free chopped dried pineapple

½ cup blanched almonds, roughly chopped
  (optional)

Whipped cream (optional)

Preheat the oven to 400F (205C). Lightly grease a 10-inch springform pan.

In an extra-large bowl, whisk together the eggs, bananas, sugar, orange peel, cinnamon, extracts, and nutmeg. Add the remaining ingredients, except the optional whipped cream, stirring well to thoroughly combine. Transfer to the prepared pan and bake for 30 minutes, or until a knife inserted in the center comes out clean.

Let cool completely in the pan before removing the sides. Cut into wedges and serve at room temperature, with whipped cream (if using). Or the cooled cake can be covered and refrigerated for up to 3 days and served chilled or return to room temperature.

PER SERVING

Calories 296 | Protein 9g | Total Fat 3g |
Sat. Fat 1g | Cholesterol 72mg | Carbohydrate 62g |
Dietary Fiber 3g | Sodium 184mg

Cook's Tip

For an easy method of cooking arborio or other rice, cook pasta style in a large stockpot of salted water until al dente, 12 to 15 minutes for white rice, 20 to 25 minutes for brown rice. Drain in a colander (do not rinse) and use as directed in recipe.

Orange-Marinated Strawberries

vegan|low-carb

MAKES 4 SERVINGS

These strawberries also make a delicious topping for gluten-free vanilla ice cream or frozen yogurt.

4 thin strips orange zest

¾ cup fresh orange juice

2½ tablespoons orange marmalade

½ tablespoon fresh lemon juice

1 pint (2 cups) fresh strawberries

In a small saucepan filled with boiling water, boil the orange zest for 1 minute. Drain and finely chop.

In a medium stainless steel or glass bowl, stir together the orange juice, marmalade, lemon juice, and orange zest. Add the strawberries and toss gently yet thoroughly to combine. Let stand at room temperature for 20 minutes. Toss again and serve at room temperature. Or cover and refrigerate for a minimum of 2 hours or overnight and serve chilled.

PER SERVING

Calories 76 | Protein 1g | Total Fat 0g | Sat. Fat 0g | Cholesterol 0mg | Carbohydrate 19g | Dietary Fiber 3g | Sodium 8mg

Sweet Potato Pudding

lacto-ovo

MAKES 8 SERVINGS

Perfume your home with the warm scents of cinnamon and nutmeg as this wholesome cold-weather pudding bakes in the oven.

3 eggs

1¼ cups skim milk

½ cup light corn syrup

½ cup packed light brown sugar

2 tablespoons canola oil

1 teaspoon ground cinnamon

¼ teaspoon ground nutmeg

¼ teaspoon salt

2 pounds sweet potatoes, peeled and finely grated

Whipped cream, gluten-free vanilla ice cream, or frozen yogurt (optional)

Preheat the oven to 325F (165C). Lightly oil an 8-inch-square baking dish and set aside.

In a large bowl, beat the eggs. Add the milk, corn syrup, brown sugar, oil, cinnamon, nutmeg, and salt; whisk until thoroughly blended. Stir in the sweet potatoes. Transfer to the prepared baking dish and bake in the center of the oven for 1 hour and 15 minutes, or until a knife inserted between the center and edge comes out clean.

Serve warm or at room temperature. Or cover and refrigerate completely cooled pudding for up to 3 days and serve chilled, with the whipped cream or ice cream (if using).

PER SERVING

Calories 301 | Protein 6g | Total Fat 6g |
Sat. Fat 1g | Cholesterol 80mg | Carbohydrate 59g |
Dietary Fiber 3g | Sodium 144mg

Metric Conversion Charts

Comparison to Metric Measure

When You Know	Symbol	Multiply By	To Find	Symbol
teaspoons	tsp	5.0	milliliters	ml
tablespoons	tbsp	15.0	milliliters	ml
fluid ounces	fl. oz.	30.0	milliliters	ml
cups	c	0.24	liters	l
pints	pt.	0.47	liters	l
quarts	qt.	0.95	liters	l
ounces	oz.	28.0	grams	g
pounds	lb.	0.45	kilograms	kg
Fahrenheit	F	$\frac{5}{9}$ (after subtracting 32)	Celsius	C

Fahrenheit to Celsius

F	C
200–205	95
220–225	105
245–250	120
275	135
300–305	150
325–330	165
345–350	175
370–375	190
400–405	205
425–430	220
445–450	230
470–475	245
500	260

Liquid Measure to Liters

¼ cup	=	0.06 liters
½ cup	=	0.12 liters
¾ cup	=	0.18 liters
1 cup	=	0.24 liters
1¼ cups	=	0.30 liters
1½ cups	=	0.36 liters
2 cups	=	0.48 liters
2½ cups	=	0.60 liters
3 cups	=	0.72 liters
3½ cups	=	0.84 liters
4 cups	=	0.96 liters
4½ cups	=	1.08 liters
5 cups	=	1.20 liters
5½ cups	=	1.32 liters

Liquid Measure to Milliliters

¼ teaspoon	=	1.25 milliliters
½ teaspoon	=	2.50 milliliters
¾ teaspoon	=	3.75 milliliters
1 teaspoon	=	5.00 milliliters
1¼ teaspoons	=	6.25 milliliters
1½ teaspoons	=	7.50 milliliters
1¾ teaspoons	=	8.75 milliliters
2 teaspoons	=	10.0 milliliters
1 tablespoon	=	15.0 milliliters
2 tablespoons	=	30.0 milliliters

Index

Page numbers in **bold** indicate tables.